11⁹⁵

THE PIT
AND THE TRAP

LEYB ROCHMAN

THE PIT
AND THE TRAP

A CHRONICLE OF SURVIVAL

Introduction by Aharon Appelfeld

HOLOCAUST LIBRARY
NEW YORK

The Assistance of *Zachor: Holocaust Resource Center* and its Chairman, Mr. Irvin Frank of Tulsa, Oklahoma, in making this publication possible is gratefully acknowledged. *Zachor* arranged for the translation and editing of this neglected classic. Translation from the Yiddish by Moshe Kohn, edited by Sheila Friedling.

Cover Design by Michael Meyerowitz
Printed in the United States of America

LEYB ROCHMAN (1918–1978)

Terror, and pit, and trap
Upon you who dwell on earth!
He who flees at the report of terror
Shall fall into the pit;
And he who climbs out of the pit
Shall be caught in the trap.

Isaiah 24:17-18

INTRODUCTION

Leyb Rochman was twenty-one years old when the war broke out. At that time he was already totally at home in Jewish culture and was writing professionally in Yiddish. On the face of it, his prewar life was no different from that of his contemporaries: he came from a typical orthodox family in a Polish market town and went on to pursue his religious studies in the neighboring big city. He lost his father at a very young age and found a surrogate home in the court of the Porisover Rebbe. In the 1920s and 30s Hasidism had long since fallen from its peak. Nonetheless, young Rochman was able to bask in the splendor that emanated from behind the shadows, to absorb the truths that broke through the tawdriness.

We met in Jerusalem in the early fifties. I, too, was a survivor, fourteen years his junior. By Israeli standards, I was something of an old-timer. I was studying at the university and even tried my hand at writing. In truth, my life was torn, clouded over, rootless. Everything I did was really an attempt to run from myself. The years of my youth lost in the Great Destruction sought a redemption they could not find.

It was my good fortune to spend long and fruitful years in Rochman's domain. He led me from place to place, like an older brother. First poetry, then prose. And in the same course— Midrash, Kabbalah and Hasidism. We kept at it for years—once a week and sometimes every day. With my own puny resources, with the scraps of knowledge I had managed to accumulate, I would never have arrived at all these hidden dimensions. Leyb Rochman was one of the very last who embodied all of Jewish culture. Under a single roof he housed the modern Yiddish poets Mani Leyb and Moyshe Leyb Halpern with the nineteenth-century hasidic classics—not as oppositions, but on a single continuum.

T. S. Eliot once wrote that the collective memory of a tribe is revealed through its individual writer, and the more all-encompassing his memory, the greater his worth as a writer. In our generation, Jewish memory has not only been severely depleted but also fragmented, and not only into its sacred and secular domains. Each piece has been further splintered into languages and subjects. Today one can only speak of Jewish memory as of a distant ideal.

Leyb Rochman is one of the very few writers in whom the entire ordeal of his generation found its Jewish expression.

What are the attributes of Rochman's writing? I would go so far as to say that his is a religious impulse that was transmuted in an irreligious age and therefore sought its outlet in aesthetic forms. I do not say this lightly. His writings, beginning with his first book, *The Pit and the Trap*, require not simply an act of concentrated reading, but of communion with the text. Rochman, a first-rate storyteller with a marvelous sense of humor, renounced all frivolities when it came to his writing. He required absolute seriousness with no frills attached.

During his lifetime, Leyb Rochman wrote three books: *And In Your Blood Shall You Live*, translated as *The Pit and the Trap* (1949), *With Blind Steps Over the Earth* (1968), and a collection of short fiction, *The Deluge* (1978), published shortly before he died. The first book was written mostly in Switzerland, after the war, on his sickbed. It is one of the most subdued, unsentimental documents ever written about the Holocaust.

Organized in the form of a diary, *The Pit and the Trap* is much like the stories of many other Holocaust survivors. Yet Rochman's book is altogether different. A group of Jews seeks refuge in the villages from the ubiquitous terror. The murderers are everywhere: those who chase down their victims with the blood lust of the hunt and those who collaborate behind the scenes; those who close their doors with full deliberation and those who block their ears to the cries of the hunted. A death warrant has gone out on all the Jews and with this warrant all mercy seems to have gone dead. All the gates are made of iron. Only the forests offer protection—at times.

It is a story of survivors that repeats with untold variations a single, bitter truth, that during the Holocaust, total darkness reigned in the world. The Jew reached his point of utter degradation: an insect to be stomped out. Rochman's story has a different twist, however. An old whore who lives at the fringes of society offers refuge to the hunted. There is nothing particularly kind or gracious about her, and certainly there's no love lost on the Jews. But something inside her, the bitterness that accumulated over the years, her loneliness, the money they bribe her with—all this together has its effect and she offers them a hideout in her cottage. It's clear she's putting her life in danger. If she's caught, her fate will be that of the Jews, yet something within her, no clearly-defined motive, compels her to help them.

The essence of the book, in my opinion, lies in the unwilling dialogue between the old woman who offers protection and the young people who are condemned to death. The bond is one of love and hate, self-interest and self-reproach. Those who seek protection must constantly be on their guard, to plead, cry, accuse and promise the impossible. The one who offers protection replies: Who are these people? What do I need them for? They're nothing but Jews, the children of Death. I'm risking my neck for their sake. Hence the wonder of it all, that she continues to hold onto them, to do what the morally upright and God-fearing individual did not do. Her weaknesses, which are the core of her humanity, are the spark of hope in the utter darkness.

Is there a new message in all of this? Perhaps. The lesser evil, at any rate, makes its appearance in this book in an altogether novel way: in the character of Aunty. She is no citizen of sterling credentials; her past record leaves much to be desired; in her youth she squandered her favors far and wide, but even in her old age she has lapses of generosity. The womenfolk of the village don't sing her praises for nought. For the Jews hidden in her cottage, she alone bears the image of God.

Then there's Auntie's brother, Felek. A crook by profession. Who would expect him, of all people, to uphold the sixth commandment at the risk of his own life! Yet, there they are, the least likely angels of mercy in fact or fiction.

The literature of the Holocaust is extremely diversified. One sometimes feels that there's a hidden competition: who can tell the more horrible tale. No wonder that the ears and eyes balk at hearing and reading any more. It is difficult to absorb a terror that knows no bounds. In this respect Rochman's book is different. Though it stays scrupulously close to the facts, complete with accurate names and dates, it is a book of hope. Not of facile hope or of saccharine optimism but of a tempered faith in humankind.

AHARON APPELFELD

Mevaseret Tsiyon, Israel

To the Sacred Memory of My Unforgettable Ones:

My mother, Rivke Blume (Rivkele), and my beloved sister, Miriam Rokhel—who perished on Elul 8 or 9, 5702 (1942) in Minsk Mazowiecki or Treblinka; my beloved sisters Dina and Esther—who perished in Elul (?) 5702 in Radom or Treblinka; my older brother, Yankev Yosef Meir—who was incinerated in Birkenau in autumn 1942; my mother-in-law, Chava, and my brother-in-law, Shmuel Yosef—perished on Elul 9, 5702 in Treblinka; my sister-in-law, Chaya Gitl—murdered on Elul 12, 5702 in the Kopernik camp; my brother-in-law, Chaim Menachem—killed on Tevet 1, 5703 when he jumped from the train traveling to Treblinka, killed either by the jump or by the peasants who caught him; my beloved uncles and aunts: Velvl, Moyshe Boruch, Yankev Chaim and Avrom, and Feygele, Zlatke, Toybe, Feygele; my cousins: Motl, Hendele, Rivke, Yosl, David, Motl, Tsirele, Hershl, Tosl, Teltse, Gnendl, Nekhometshe, Miriam, Rivkele, Moyshele, Chaiml, my brother's daughter, Zisl, and her husband, Menachem, and all my relatives, comrades, and friends—who starved to death in the Warsaw Ghetto, or were shot to death, tortured to death, choked to death, gassed to death, burned to death, or otherwise hideously removed from this world; and the whole community of men, women and children of my home city, Minsk-Mazowiecki, who perished in Treblinka—

MAY GOD AVENGE THEIR BLOOD!

Today is Wednesday, February 17, 1943. Exactly twelve weeks have passed since we went into hiding here at Felek's. Twelve weeks are eighty-four days and, if my arithmetic is correct, 2,016 hours. That's my count. All of us are constantly reckoning the time. We count even the individual minutes and seconds.

Felek hid us as soon as we arrived here. That night we put up a false wall, and we are inside it. This partition (with a little opening at the bottom through which food is passed to us) is very close to the real wall, and our hideaway is extremely narrow and long. Sitting is impossible, and we stand shoulder to shoulder facing the partition. It's also impossible to turn around. We stand still, shoulders drawn and hands at our side, like a row of soldiers at attention. It's dark in there and we can barely see each other. There's no place for daylight to filter through. This fact particularly upset me. So I obstinately set out to find at least some small crack. I scoured every inch of the partition and finally found a tiny speck of light high above it. Full of excitement, I told the others of my discovery. We all studied that speck of brightness and decided that it really was a message from the sun. I was happy, because my mission had been successful, and because it brought us some relief; it means that we aren't completely alone: at least the sun is thinking of us a little.

As I said, we stand closely pressed on all sides. We often rest our heads on the partition. As our foreheads rub the ceiling boards, all sorts of memories come to mind. There's plenty to think about. In whispers we share our memories. Sometimes a discussion flares up. Once someone observed that we were facing east. How symbolic. We're the first to get the rays of the sun each morning; we're facing Eretz Yisrael (the Land of Israel). In Eretz Yisrael lies our future, if, with God's help, we survive. What's more, east means the Eastern Front. Things are going well there now. The Russians are coming closer. They're only 1,800 kilometers away. If they arrive, the death sentence hanging over us will be canceled.

We've started making plans. We were discussing Eretz Yisrael, and getting excited. Ephraim maintains that a new Jewish nation will flourish in Eretz Yisrael. We must struggle with all our might to survive so that the Jewish seed can be transplanted in Eretz Yisrael. Later, the thought depressed me; the root has been pulled out, and who knows whether the branch, even if it gets to Eretz Yisrael, will ever take hold and grow again. I expressed my doubts. Eventually we calmed down. Although we came to no conclusions, we did agree that we had a mission. We were encouraged a bit.

After all our discussions, we were quiet for a few hours. Silence is pleasant in the dark: it's easier to think. Each of the five of us is immersed in his own thoughts. Thinking about Eretz Yisrael, I see that girl who worked with us in the camp for a few weeks. Rivke Steynbok was her name. She had a pale face, black hair, and deep eyes that were even blacker. I don't know whether she always looked that way or only from the time she was taken out of a hiding place to be shot (that time, she was saved by some miracle). Once she told me that as she was being led to her execution, the thought suddenly flashed her mind that she would never see Eretz Yisrael. Her intuition didn't deceive her: after we went into hiding here, we heard that she was burned alive in the Kopernik camp together with three hundred other Jews. I don't know what went on in her mind then, but now I keep seeing her: cheeks paler than ever and the look in her eyes even more penetrating. My own depressing thoughts probably cause me to look like that too. No matter how dull the brain, the heart's still pounding. How I want to see Eretz Yisrael! But it no longer depends on us alone. As long as we aren't discovered, there's still hope. But if they find us, it'll be. . . . It will be much worse for us than for that girl. She has us to remember her. Who will think of us?

Often, after much thought, I consider our hideaway. It seems to be solidly built: the boards are square against each other. The outside of the partition, that is, the side facing the inside of the house, is papered to match the other walls of the house. No, there's no way of telling from the other side that it's a false wall. But we have to reduce our voices to the lowest possible whisper, because the partition is very thin. Just our luck that the Feleks re-

ceive a constant stream of visitors, all of whom, as though to spite us, sit right alongside the partition. Once, a peasant woman dropped in for a short visit. "Can't stay long," she apologized, "but who can pass up a few minutes with good friends." This, at 9:00 a.m. as she sat herself down right beside the wall. At 2 p.m., we thought we couldn't hold out any longer. To stand completely still for five hours is more than a human being was meant to bear. And if that weren't enough, you can't stop itching and you grit your teeth. You resist the urge until you think you have it conquered. The itch is gone. Then suddenly it appears somewhere else. For the first few hours we believed the woman each time she said, "Well, I have to be going." Then we lost all hope. Finally, at 2 p.m., Mrs. Szudak (that's her name) stood up. Our hearts began to beat louder. But no sooner did she finish taking her leave with "Jesus Christ be praised forever," than a "Hello!" rang out. It was a nine-year-old peasant girl. She too chose to stand directly next to our wall. It wouldn't have mattered, except that Esther, who had a cold, suddenly let out a loud cough. She couldn't hold back any longer. I gave her a hard pinch in her side. Ephraim, hearing her cough, thought that the girl had left and began sneezing away. I thought I would go out of my mind. But the whole thing tickled my sister-in-law Zippora, and she burst out laughing. I was sure that it was all up with us, that all our efforts had been wasted. But miraculously, the little girl is a bit deaf and she didn't hear a thing. At any rate, that's what Felek, our host, told us from the other side of the wall. Zippora, overjoyed that her laughter hadn't caused us any harm, began to weep. I pinched her and said:
"Tzipporele, we mustn't laugh and we mustn't cry!"

Yes, we must beware of everybody, even of children, Just let some child get a whiff of you behind the wall and the secret is out, and within a few days the whole area will be talking: "Another five Jews found and shot." An innocent child could indirectly be our murderer. Harmlessly, the child could tell its mother, who would tell it to a crony of hers, who would pass the news along. Don't blame us. We suspect everyone. And with good reasons: Once, with a full house of visitors, Felek's cat suddenly recalled having seen some food being passed to us through the little door at the bottom of the partition. She must have been hungry, and, with a cat's memory, she forgot that conversation with us is forbidden in the presence of strangers. Instead, planting herself right in front of our little door, she started scratching at it and meowing.

I shudder to think of the moment when, after the cat had been scratching and meowing away for a while, one of the guests, a young peasant asked: "What does that cat want inside the wall?"

Our clever host Felek had a ready reply: "I guess she smells mice."

* * *

How many acquaintances does a person have? It's a difficult question to answer. It depends on the person. I, aged twenty-five, had tens of thousands of acquaintances until a few months ago. Of course, there are varying degrees of acquaintanceship. There are comrades, colleagues, friends—intimate friends and casual ones—immediate family and relatives—close relatives and distant ones; there are nodding acquaintances, people whom you've met just once, and people you've seen a number of times: people whom you know only by sight and those you know by sound; people you know as neighbors. And there are one's enemies—they're also acquaintances: you know them.

Acquaintances fill up your entire life. You live for them and create for them. You do good for them and steal for them. You boast to them and are shamed by them. They're the ones that keep you from wrongdoing.

God, all five of us are like one person—without acquaintances and relatives. Like a child. No, a child has parents, sisters and brothers, family, while we, thank God, have only ourselves. Except for a handful of relatives overseas. Who knows whether they're still alive? There's a war on.

All our acquaintances belong to the past: parents, family, relatives, everybody you know! Maybe some acquaintance of yours is stuck away in a hole somewhere just as you are here, and he doesn't know that you're alive just as you don't know that he is either.

But that's not true. There are Felek; his wife; Felek's sister, "Auntie." These are new acquaintances; you didn't know them before. None of your old acquaintances—no one—is alive.

We have plenty of new ones: Stassko Guczak and his brother, Jozef; Jaszko Odrobinszczak; Mrs. Rechniakow; Szudek and his wife and Marishka; the "expellee" whose home the Germans had taken over, sending him to find quarters somewhere else; "Kapusta," the "Cabbage Head"; "Halleluja" and "Logidzak"; Cereniak; practically the whole village and also people from other villages who call on our hosts—including even the village headman. Fortunately, we know them but they don't know us. That is, we've never seen them, either, and we're terrified of being seen by them, but we know them by sound, from their frequent visits to our hosts on the other side of the wall. We can tell them apart by their voices, even when they're hoarse. We know them and their families, their speech patterns and personalities, their good and bad features, and even those deeds known to no one but themselves. We know everything. Frequently they pour their hearts out to Felek on the other side of the wall, certain that no one else is listening. Once Szudek confided in Felek about a little theft he planned, and went on to tell him about many others that he had already committed. We could hear the smile in Felek's voice as he said to him: "Hold your tongue, Szudek! They say that walls have ears."

"Don't be silly," Szudek said, continuing his confession.

Almost every evening Mariszka, Felek's cousin, drops in and sits with Auntie on the bed of our partition. She pours out her heart about her successes and failures in love, about how she lost her virginity, and even about her menstrual cycles. In the dark, behind the wall, Esther and Zippora blush with embarrassment, because of us, the three men. On the other side, Auntie laughs and Mariszka, thinking that she's laughing at her, gets up in a huff saying, "Good night!" We're pleased, because it's a sign that nobody knows about us. We keep wondering though, what all those people would think if they knew that behind the wall, people were listening to their confessions. They'd probably feel bad, even though we don't really count as people. We're just part of the wall.

All those tales and true confessions on the other side of the wall put Felek in a good mood. He likes the comedy of it all. Every night, after the guests have left, he has himself a good, long laugh. We're pleased by his good mood, and we try to cheer him along.

Once, at about ten o'clock at night, after Mariszka had left, all the lights in the house were turned off. I came out of our hideaway, went over to the window, and peered outside from behind the curtain. I wanted to make certain that Mariszka didn't suspect anything, that she didn't stop outside, sometimes by the wall of the house, to listen for suspicious sounds.

I peered out. I could make out human shadows. I looked around. Suddenly, just to one side of the window, I saw Mariszka standing and listening. Trembling all over, I crawled over to Felek and Auntie and told them. They came to the window and saw for themselves.

Felek and Auntie shuddered. For a few moments we all just stood there. Mariszka kept on standing there with one ear against the side of the window frame. Felek wanted to go outside to ask her what she was doing. Quaking with fear, I restrained him.

Suddenly, I saw Mariszka dash away from the window over to the wall of Felek's stable, bend down, drag something out, tuck it into her large scarf, wrap it up, and run off.

I told Felek, but he couldn't see anything; Auntie started laughing. "Peat," she said. "She's stolen some peat for fuel. She's helped herself to some peat through a broken board in the stable wall and run off with it."

Felek keeps his peat directly beside the wall. Mariszka had stood beside our window simply to check whether anyone was watching her.

We calmed down. But Felek was stunned. He was mortified about our seeing his thieving relative steal from him. He mumbled something with embarrassment.

But Felek has reason to smile too. Now he understands why Mariszka brings peat along on her evening visits. She steals that peat from her sister, with whom she's living, and brings it here supposedly as a gift. Sitting with the Feleks around the little stove, she stokes the flames with chunks of peat. Then, on her way home, she steals peat from Felek to bring to her sister.

Felek smiles sheepishly.

Not every day behind the wall is gray or monotonous. Some of them are quite colorful, especially the Sundays and holidays when the house is full of peasant men and women coming to visit.

The second day of the Christmas period was a good day for us, right from the start. At eight o'clock—our hosts are still yawning—the front door opens: "Jesus Christ be praised forever!" It's tall Jaszko Odrobinszczak. When he canes his daughter, her cries can be heard throughout the village. We can hear him stretching. It seems he isn't fully awake. Even his laugh sounds tired.

"Jaszko's in a jolly mood today," Auntie remarks.

He laughs more heartily. "Why not laugh?" he says, "when there's going to be a little profit with the help of Lord Jesus."

Without waiting to be asked, he says: "Haven't heard, eh? Posters. Anybody turning in a Jew to the German police gets ten pounds of sugar, plenty of cash, and lots of other goods too. Let me just lay my hands on a Jew bastard or two and I'm all set for life. Ha, ha, ha! You'll see."

"Bull!" exclaims Auntie. "And where are you going to get yourself a Jew? There aren't any left."

"'Seek and ye shall find,'" he says. "Lord Jesus will help."

Esther and Zippora are shaking. I feel it. They're trembling all over, and I'm afraid they'll cause the wall to shake, so I start pinching them. But I quickly relax as Auntie tells Jaszko that she too would love to lay her hands on some "big fish" of a Jew; her weak heart could stand some sugar for a pickup.

Now I had to smile: Our Auntie never loses her wits. But we can feel her heart skipping some beats along with ours.

Then old Cereniak enters. He knows it all. He knows for a fact that after you drink heavily sugared tea, you're full for hours. He knows for a fact that the Jews used to eat with silver spoons. He knows for a fact that all the Jews are condemned to die because they don't believe in Lord Jesus. He knows for a fact that not a Jew will remain alive, even though he knows there are still a few hiding out with Christians.

Some squeaky-voiced peasant woman asks him how Jews can be hidden. He stands up, puts a hand on our partition, and says: "Here's a wall. You make another wall, and Jews can stay inside. Or there's the cellar."

"Halleluja," who came in a few minutes earlier, pipes up to say that Cereniak is an old fool and should stop talking nonsense. There are no Jews left. Only a few days ago the last 300 Jews were burned alive in the Kopernik school in Minsk.

Hearing this news, Cereniak perks up: he knows exactly how a person is burned alive and he'd like to describe it to everyone.

But Halleluja wants to finish his story. It seems that the German police aren't really such bad guys. With his own eyes he saw the building with the Jews burning inside. The flames were everywhere. The Germans were shooting into the building from all sides, and those who jumped from the building were killed in the yard by machine-gun fire. A lot of Poles were standing some distance away watching it all. Somebody pointed to a young Jew woman about to jump from a second-story window. The bullets riddled her like a sieve. She remained draped over the window sill where the flames burned half of her body, and the other half dropped into the yard. Oh, he nearly forgot the main point, about the Germans.

"All of us, about a hundred Poles, are standing there, watching and thinking. Suddenly, a German comes running up to us, a police guard, his gun pointing. We start running away. He laughs and says: 'Come, Poles, the Jews are rich. Help yourselves to their wealth.' At first we thought he was joking. But then another German came over and called us. Now we saw that it wasn't a joke at all."

Everybody in the room "Oohed" and "Ahed," but Halleluja wouldn't let himself be interrupted. The Jews were well-dressed. So all the people there helped themselves to something. One took a pair of boots or shoes; somebody else took a coat, or a pair of pants, or long winter underwear. He wasn't able to get close quickly enough, so he ended up with only an odd shoe, but a good one, and he'll be able to use the material to repair his boots. The leather's good quality. But the point is that the Germans aren't such bad guys at all; they're even decent. They didn't let anybody grab too much while somebody else didn't get anything. Everyone got something. As we were pulling the clothes off the corpses, there was one German who kept pushing the button on some gadget he was holding, laughing all the while and saying "Thank you" in Polish.

Cereniak couldn't restrain himself. "They photographed it all!" he shouted.

Auntie asked Felek for some water. "Womenfolk are weak. They can't take such stories," Halleluja says.

"I'm just thirsty," Auntie says, trying hard to keep the tremor out of her voice.

"I'm also a womanfolk," the squeaky-voiced woman, Mrs. Stasz, pipes up, "but still, I realize that if there were still a Jew alive, bread would cost a gold mine today, and we'd all be starving to death."

Cereniak explains that the cost of living is actually higher now than when the Jews were still alive, because, as he points out, the Jews smuggled and gave competition, which keeps prices down, but being burned alive, he knows, hurts something awful.

"There was screaming as though the whole town were burning," Halleluja interrupts, but Cereniak ignores him: "You can go on burning alive for an hour and a half, till your gall burst, and then—poof!—it's all over."

* * *

Even during a catastrophe miracles come to pass that everyone can see. This day also had its miracle. The day ended at 5 p.m. Everybody had gone. It was turning dark outside. Felek and his wife went visiting. Only Auntie stayed home. She locked the door, moved the half-curtains to cover the windows, and, letting out a sigh, opened the little door to our hideaway. "Come out of your ghetto for a while," she whispered. "It's dark outside. Nobody's around, and I've locked up everywhere."

No sooner had we taken a few steps into the room then she said: "For Heaven's sake, you'll be your own murderers! Don't stand; bend down. And crawl on the floor. Somebody might come up to the window."

We got down and crawled into the corners of the room. Auntie ran from window to window humming nervously to herself. She quickly tired of this, and sat down on a stool next to one of the windows. Esther and Zippora crawled over to her from their respective corners and laid their heads in her lap. Auntie—it seems that some of our Jewish ways had rubbed off on her—started swaying and continued to hum that melody of hers. Ephraim and Froiman dozed off in their corners. I also felt like snoozing, but some indefinable dread overtook me, and I felt that I had to get back to our hideaway as soon as possible. But

Auntie, who kept glancing outside from under the window curtain, called to me:

"Juzek, why is the sky so red in the west? A pity: they say that it's the Jews burning in Hell because they didn't believe in Lord Jesus."

I crawled over to the window and looked outside: miles and miles of snow, trees draped in white. A high frost, apparently, the trees and fields glistened and the western sky was in flames. I heard a strange murmur outside, but inside it was silent. I don't know how long that went on. I might even have dozed off, only suddenly, Auntie posed me a riddle: "Juzek, what is heaven and what is earth? What's a Jew and what's a Christian? What's that murmur outside? What is life and what is death? I don't understand a thing, Juzek. There's something heavy on my heart. I don't know what it is. Not sadness. Something. I don't know what!"

* * *

It's several months now that my name is Jozef-Juzek. Along with our parents, relatives, friends, and everything else that belonged to us, our Jewish names have gone, too. But that's not a tragedy. We know exactly where our names are buried and, if God grants us life, they will be resurrected. Meanwhile, I'm not Leybl, but Juzek; my wife isn't Esther but Hella; her young sister is Kasza instead of Zippora; my friend Ephraim is Olek, and Froiman's "Christian" name is Staszek instead of Israel Aaron. That's what we're called in Felek's home, because that's what our forged documents say. We all have false papers. Though I have no idea of what use they are to us men. We are circumcised Jews, and our noses and eyes also give us away. Still, we sit in our hole with the documents in our pockets. Esther and Zippora bleached their hair before we came here, and according to Felek and Auntie they can pass for pure Aryans and go anywhere they wish, especially since they have those documents. But they don't want to benefit either from their Aryan appearance or from the documents; they prefer to stay with us. We wouldn't let them go in any case: it's better not to take risks. Yet we need the Polish pseudonyms so that no Jewish names slip into our host's conversation, especially in the proximity of strangers. And the documents will be happily destroyed, God willing, after the war at the wedding of my friend, Ephraim, and my young sister-in-law, Zippora-Kasza.

Talking about it makes me feel good, and also reminds me of another heart-warming incident. A few days ago, Felek knocked at our little door, asked me to come out, and told me to get ready for March 19th, my "name day," St. Jozef's Day. They plan to make a party. Felek, his wife, and Auntie will put on their holiday best, go to church, pray for all of us, and then have a festive meal of bread and eggs. But I'll have to provide the liquor.

Auntie and Mrs. Felek come running out of the kitchen, grab my hand, and shower me with blessings. I feel like a real celebrant. Auntie kisses me, and then makes her wish that we be free by March and that my name once more be Leybl, and no longer Jozef-Juzek.

* * *

Lately, we're humanitarians. In our hideway—or our "ghetto," as Auntie calls it—we're free to establish any social order at all. So absolute freedom prevails: freedom of life, of course, not of speech or movement. We share our lodging with mice, bugs, and a few frighteningly huge spiders. They exploit our tolerance and do whatever they please. The walls are covered with spiderwebs, and the spiders keep spinning away: webs for shelter or for trapping—who knows? Conversation is forbidden in here, so we can't ask.

* * *

I'm already engrossed in my writing, and have visions of thousands of people reading my work. Yet my wretched lines are written by a man with the death sentence stamped on his brow for all to see.

For some time the others urged me to keep a diary or just jot down random notes. In our situation, they said, everything should be recorded. For whom? I haven't the slightest glimmer of hope. Every few days, in all kinds of holes and crevices, shadows of what were once human beings—Jews—are discovered. And every decent Christian and loyal Pole considers it his duty to hand them over to "justice."

In the Latlowicze region, they say, the peasants and townspeople alike tie up their victims with rope and drag them to the police stations. One doesn't have to be a German in order to qualify as an executioner. Patriotic Polish policemen are also permitted to do the job, and so many exploit their opportunities. Some of them do their target practice on little children. Death from a bullet is something of a privilege. In Garwolin, they say, police take their victims to the slaughterhouse. There, a sharp long-bladed axe quickly separates the head from the trunk, and the walls of the slaughterhouse are splattered with human blood. The Warsaw "blue" police are told to save on bullets and labor by dropping little children into sewage manholes.

"Keep a diary!" Froiman advises me to mail what I've written to a Christian acquaintance and ask him to hand it over to Jews after the war. That way I can bequeath to the world, after I'm gone, interesting descriptions, "sensational" material, maybe even literature.

But this kind of writing frightens me. I fear that I'm already desecrating the memory of the forgotten dead; ten years from now or even sooner, practically no one will remember them or this horrible cataclysm. No, Froiman my friend, I'm not sending this to any Christian. If God permits us to live, then my writing will survive. If not, nobody need know of these words, just as nobody will know about me.

* * *

Indeed, a curse has befallen both the living and the dead; especially the dead who are doubly cursed with a horrible death that will go unremembered and unwept. I've been thinking about it ever since the beginning of this catastrophe. Entire families perished at once, parents and children together, without a trace, with no one to mourn them. But even in families where some member managed to stay alive—a child, a sister, a brother—there were only a few tears shed in the first few days, and then, nothing. No more weeping those early dead, just as now there is no one to mourn the latest victims, the slave-laborers. In normal times, a dead loved one was mourned for weeks, months, even years. But not now.

Still, the greatest curse of all seems to be the curse of being alive, the shameless desire to live: we want to live, to seize one more day, and another one. Every hour, it seems, is a prize snatched from the Angel of Death, snatched from Hitler. A kind of revenge upon the enemy. Despite him, another day, another week. We keep reckoning the minutes and hours until we accumulate days. We're gulping doses of time, each dose more poisonous than the previous one.

Old Cereniak has been here again. He came to sell Felek some piping for our little iron stove. He hauled himself off to town, to Kaluszyn, and under the ruins of abandoned Jewish houses he dug up some rusty sections of pipe. He also brought along a tin container. Felek bought it from Cereniak for us to use as a toilet, telling him he needed it as a garbage bin.

Cereniak sat there for hours telling Felek about Kaluszyn. A complete wreck, he said. Not a house left standing. Of its 6,000 people, 90 percent were Jews. Now you hardly see a living soul. The remaining Polish townsfolk and the peasants from the surrounding village are busy dismantling Jewish houses. The Germans sold it all to them for pennies, and now they're diligently tearing down the roofs, the walls, and the foundations looking for the treasures buried by the Jews. Even if they don't find anything, they still received a bargain. The bricks and the woodwork alone are worth a fortune. The farmers drag everything back to their villages and build themselves houses. It only costs them a negligible amount.

"Those bandits don't let any outsider near the place," Cereniak added. It seems that they drove him away before he could dig around in the rubble heaps. All he managed to grab were those few pieces of pipe, the tin container, and two spoons. Now he'll be able to eat with silver spoons, like an aristocrat. But they wouldn't let him take a thing more and chased him away. They paid for it, so it's all theirs, they told him. Even that expellee from Poznan has luck, Cereniak gripes. He goes there every day and always comes back with something to sell, making a decent living. He knows how to do it, stealing into the place and finding valuables.

Cereniak is pleased with his pipes and tin container, and asks Felek if there isn't something else he needs. He'll try to get to Kaluszyn again and find something without getting caught.

* * *

What a festive day! The moment she got up in the morning, Mrs. Felek started fussing around the house—sweeping, dusting, putting flowers everywhere; she spread a white cloth on the table next to our partition, on which she placed a saucer filled with water and, beside that, a brush. The place looked festive, even though it was an ordinary weekday. We couldn't see anything that was going on, but we sensed it through the wall.

Across the partition, Auntie told us that the priest was coming to the village on his Christmas rounds today and would be calling at the Feleks. It wasn't important to us, yet we also started looking forward to his coming. Our intuition told us to expect something.

At eleven o'clock a cart pulled into our yard. The priest walked rapidly into our kitchen. "Jesus Christ be praised!" he said.

"Forever and ever, Amen!" answered the Feleks and invited the priest into the house. He went right over to the table next to our partition. We couldn't see him, but we felt his breath, I think.

The priest got down on his knees, and quickly said aloud: "Lord, protect all the dwellers of this house, all those taking shelter under its roof. Help them, Jesus Christ. Amen!"

When the priest had gone, I left the hideaway and entered the house. I looked around: on our partition hung an icon of the Holy Mother and Child.

Auntie started crying: "Yes, Lord Jesus and the Mother of God are protecting you! Now I know that all of them are lying: it isn't true that Lord Jesus is taking revenge on the Jews. He's protecting you!"

"That's right," I mumbled, "he's protecting his brothers."

Flustered, I went right back into the hideaway. There in the darkness, I felt that God, the one God, was really with us. I remembered the passage in Psalms: "I am with him in his travail."

* * *

In the village, there's a thriving table trade in Jewish possessions. This trade is flourishing upon the ruins of the Jewish towns. People are buying, selling, wheeling and dealing. Every house is packed with goods looted during the liquidation of the Jewish ghettos. No sooner had the Jews been taken out of the ghettos and murdered, than thousands of peasants, even grandmothers and children, swarmed into them. People hauled off everything they could manage in hundreds of heaping cartloads. What they couldn't take immediately they later bought for next to nothing from the Germans, at a "clearance sale" of Jewish "second-hand goods." What's more, a field day was declared on the few Jews who had managed to scatter into the countryside and woods. They were murdered, and their corpses stripped of shoes and clothing.

The village sprang to life. The houses are packed with furniture, pots and pans, clothing and bedding. There isn't enough room for it all. People look for buyers, but it's hard to find customers for everything. So the best furniture is chopped up for firewood. The clothes are made over, and people sleep under three quilts and on top of six pillows and four mattresses. Old grandmothers deck themselves in flowery girlish dresses. Peasant men sport hasidic coats or *kapotes*—ordinary weekday ones and satin Sabbath ones. Little flaxen peasant heads jut out from fancy baby carriages upholstered in silk. Farm girls wear elegant blouses and skirts made out of prayer-shawls; bonnets made of the black velvet hats worn by Hasidim; and fur scarves made out of the hasidic *shtrayml*. Farmers' tables are set with silver Kiddush cups and spiceboxes, and their dressers and buffets decorated with silver Torah plates, Torah pointers and Sabbath candlesticks.

The wind sweeps across the countryside scattering thousands of pages torn from Pentateuchs, the Talmud, commentaries, books of Musar (ethics) and Hasidism, the *Tsena Ur'ena*, chapbooks, classical and modern Jewish literature, scientific and philosophical works. These pages are tightly piled in the peasants' outhouses; then sold in the shops as wastepaper by the pound and kilogram; used for wrapping ham, herring, and the like. The leather bindings are worked over into useful items such as handbags and wallets.

Business is flourishing in the village, and the priest makes his Christmas rounds, going from cottage to cottage, crossing himself as he proclaims: "Lord God, take under Thy shelter all the dwellers of this abode, those sheltering themselves under this roof. Help them, Jesus Christ. Amen!"

February 25, 1943. At 12 noon, we'll be living in this hideaway exactly three months. I'm calculating again. From the 17th to the 25th eight full days have passed, thank God. For you Americans, English, and other foreigners, eight days are simply eight days. Or sometimes eight minutes. You're too busy to count, so you don't know how much time this really is.

Actually, eight days are 192 hours. 192 hours are 11,520 minutes. 11,520 minutes are 691,200 seconds. And do you know how many thoughts, ordinary ones and maddening ones, can torment a person in 691,200 seconds, particularly when one can't sleep at night, and especially since only last night we heard three rifle shots not far from us.

On this day, Wednesday, just three months ago, we made our way here from Minsk. At five in the morning it was still dark outside. The weather was good and frosty (it was November 25th). Silently, so as not to wake the neighbors, we left Auntie's apartment in Minsk: My wife, my sister-in-law and I (our friends got here afterwards), with Auntie leading the way. She had three tasks to perform. First, she had to be our guide; second, to be our guard. Third and most important: Felek didn't know that we were coming to him, and we had no idea whether he would agree to let us in; so Auntie had taken it upon herself to "work on" him. We knew her fairly well and were sure that we could rely on her. Jews were still being employed in factories and workshops, but rumor had it that the "liquidation" would take place any day. So, having nothing to lose, we followed her; we had agreed that should we be caught, God forbid, we wouldn't inform on Auntie.

Esther and Zippora, with bleached hair and the forged documents in their pockets, walked boldly alongside Auntie. I walked behind them in my disguise: knee-high golf trousers tucked into sport boots instead of long pants and ordinary shoes, and newly grown Polish-style whiskers. My face was wrapped in a scarf—ostensibly against the cold weather—and only my eyes and whiskers showed.

I began to feel like a proper Pole, as I walked erectly behind them on the road. Just as it was turning light, two young peasants came toward us. As soon as they saw me they blurted, "Kike!" and continued on their way. But we were disturbed. We immediately left the main road and took to the side paths. We trudged for hours through stretches of bog, marshy woods and snow-covered fields, avoiding the villages and roads. At last, there was Felek's cottage in the distance. Auntie pointed it out to us. A wretched, solitary farmhouse, a little straw hut, it sat like a speck of gray in the snowy wasteland. A few more gray specks: the barn, the stable, some trees. Nearby were woods and a few more houses, and field after field spread out like an endless array of white tablecloths. We dragged our feet through the snow and there was no end to it. With every step we took it seemed that the little farm receded farther into the distance. The white fields stretched on and on.

We didn't get there until just before noon.

There we stood before a small wooden cottage with a straw roof resembling a rotten mushroom. The yard looked like a chicken coop, and it was scattered with chicken droppings. A solitary cow mooed away in the barn. Auntie vanished through a small clay door. We felt lost and cowered behind some moldy wooden walls. It seemed as if a huge eye somewhere were focusing on us and swallowing us up. We looked for a hole to crawl into. After a while, Auntie appeared in the doorway and signaled for us to come in.

* * *

I've been mentioning our host, Felek, quite a bit. We're well settled into this cottage of his. I've already described the interior of the house and our hideaway, but I haven't said a word about Felek himself.

He's tall, lanky, and slightly bow-legged. Standing, he looks as though he's about to topple over. Pockmarked face. Two large dim eyes—one of them totally blind, the other cloudy and crossed, three-quarters blind. Officially, he's an independent farmer. His land provides him with enough to keep his household on bread and potatoes for one quarter of the year. For the other three-quarters, he subsisted—as we have only just learned—on the proceeds of theft. But no, he wasn't a thief; he never stole a thing in his life! He only "helped himself" once in a while. In the middle of the night, when his neighbor was asleep, he picked his lock and "helped himself" to some potatoes or grain. Never, Auntie assures us, did he take more than just enough to eat. The world might consider him an underworld type, though he's devoutly religious and also a patriot of sorts; still, an underworld character. So all the persuasion of pious Christians and passionate Polish patriots couldn't convince him that it was his sacred duty to murder Jews. That underworld heart of his just couldn't understand why it was all right to kill people for no reason. He had one answer for all of them: "All I know is that the Lord said, 'Thou shalt not murder!'"

Try and convince an underworld character—a tough, fearless, earthy man!

Auntie looked around carefully and led us into the small house with the dank, gloomy walls and the earthen kitchen. He was sitting on a low, thick log, opposite his wife—a squat peasant woman with a pock-marked face and beady green eyes, wrapped in a long, blue, tattered apron—thinking. I guess he had just run out of food, so he was thinking.

"Good morning!"

"Good morning!"

Auntie introduced us, and—for the second time, I suppose—quietly explained to him what it was all about. We stood there confused, gazing at the whites of his eyes, trying to read their meaning at this crucial moment. But his eyes sent no signals. So we waited while our advocate, Auntie, worked on our behalf, sometimes talking loudly, winking, or subtly whispering.

Felek broke into a smile, and we felt a little better.

Then he let out a long "No-o-o!" We didn't say a word. We seemed to have lost our tongues.

But a few minutes later he wore an earnest expression when he said: "Well, all right!"

This was after Auntie had quietly told him again that if he agreed, he would no longer need to steal, and would even have enough to buy himself clothing. Or maybe it was the pack of tobacco and the new trousers I gave him which seemed to kindle a tiny flame in his dim eyes.

A dear little flame, which is still burning and shedding light.

* * *

We've already been through a great deal of joy and trouble with him—yes, together with him—because when we suffer, he suffers along with us; and when we have a rare bit of happiness, he rejoices with us. Along with us, that "underworld character" looks forward to the day when we can peacefully emerge from this hole in his house, even though at that time he may have to start "helping himself" again. He awaits that day fervently, this cool-tempered man, who grins when he's told of the posters that are mounted everywhere: "Anyone caught hiding Jews will be executed."

If she weren't so bashful, my wife, Esther, would often shower kisses all over the blind pockmarked face of that underworld character nearly forty years older than she who's constantly struggling with his doubts, and his conscience, with a world gone half-mad, with himself: Who knows whether Lord Jesus won't punish him for hiding infidels?

Only a crusty underworld character such as Felek could stand up to such a struggle.

* * *

Living in this hideout, we've become acquainted with new people, new customs, a totally new way of life. We now know many things that we never knew before: The meaning of different dreams, of various phenomena. We even learned the language of the birds. We now know that after peasants die, they often like to return home at night. Many neighbors have seen them with their own eyes. Mrs. Felek often opens our little door after dark and tells us fantastic tales about the forest, bandits, ghosts, demons, bears, wildcats and sorcery. They're marvelous stories, but rather frightening, and we're too terrified to listen to the climax. Mrs. Felek always assures us that if we were to hear the end, we would all cry; but since it's dark now she doesn't want to frighten us. She often tries to calm us, Mrs. Felek.

Once she told us that God the Father is also a Jew. She told us to look at the icon: there He is, with a long, white, Jewish beard. Though there's one thing she doesn't understand: why does He have a Christian name, Jozef? Oh, yes, indeed, the priest himself told her that Lord Jesus' father's name is Saint Jozef.

Another consoling thought for me: My new name is Jozef, just like God's "father." But what's the good of it? I don't have a white beard. Instead, I have a pair of yellow whiskers that clash with my Jewish eyes, nose, forehead, and black hair.

Either way, Mrs. Felek likes me. Only what a pity I don't believe in Lord Jesus. Many times I feel sorry for her and I swear: "So help me God, I'm a believer!"

After a few weeks behind the wall, we've gotten to recognize all the visitors by their voices. As soon as the door opens and we hear a "Good morning," we know who's there. But a "Good morning" from a new voice frightens us.

Early one morning the door opens. Two new voices: "Good morning. Good morning." One is the voice of a young man; the other, of a boy. We were stunned, but not for the reason you think. These "Good mornings" had a familiar ring to them. Not the voices, but their accent. There was something familiar, something warm about it. I could swear that they were Jews.

They're itinerant beggars, I heard them say. They speak in a fearful undertone. My friends behind the wall turn restless.

Yes, Jews! I hear Auntie encourage them. She gives them some hot soup to eat now and some bread for later.

They don't complain or sigh, though both of them—they are brothers from Radom—have frozen feet, limp a bit, and are ragged and barefooted. Auntie asks them why they are dressed that way.

"There are all sorts of people," the older one replies. "Along the way, some people robbed us of our clothing. Then, someone else gave us these rags."

"Ah-h-h!" says the younger voice. "It's warm in here. It's good to warm up after a cold night in the barn."

A neighbor, lame Florek, has come inside. After a few moments he says: "How old are you?"

The boy answers: "Ten."

"Oh! They're crawling with lice, those bastards! Get out of here, you scurvy, lousy, dirty Jews!"

The two quickly run outside. Auntie chuckles. Florek suggests grabbing a hatchet and killing them.

"It isn't worth it," Felek says. "Lousy wretches—it's not worth soiling your hands with them."

Just then, for the first time in many weeks, coming from outside, behind the wall of our hideaway, we hear Yiddish spoken:

"You see," the older of the two said, "there are all sorts of people. There's that Christian woman. She probably works hard to keep herself going. But she gave us a piece of bread, and another one. Then there's that lame fellow!" The younger boy shivered: "Br-r-r! It's cold after that warm soup. Even colder than before."

The Yiddish words are both warm and sharp.

They left. Almost immediately the door opened. It was Jaszko Odrobinszczak. "Damn it, too late! I'm always late! I'm looking for those two bastards. They spent the night in Szudek's barn. Been looking for them for over an hour. Everywhere I've tried, they've already been and gone. It's damn cold for me to be wandering around this way. Damn! A pair like that are worth ten kilos of sugar, a load of cash, and plenty of commodities."

He's ready to continue his hunt when Szudek comes in and reports that the older of the two Jews is completely crazy: "What an experience that was! I caught him sleeping in my barn this morning, and I began whacking the big fellow. So he says, 'Thank you.' I keep hitting him and he keeps saying, 'Thank you,' that son of a bitch. 'Thank you, sir,' he says, 'give it to me good, it warms my back,' Ha, ha, ha! That nut!"

Everybody laughs. But the mood is broken by the arrival of young Ceren, the village fiddler.

"Ah," he says when he hears what the subject is. "He was at my place last night with his little brother. My fiddle was on the bed. He asked if he could play it, and he started playing. Just like an organ in church. The Jew plays and he sobs in rhythm. He didn't cry out loud, but kept grimacing weirdly with his eyes. You're right, Szudek, he must be crazy; but he was graduated from music school."

One by one the visitors left. And before my eyes floated a swarm of crazed lice, a sobbing fiddle, frozen Yiddish words, bulging sacks of sugar, and fierce blows that warm the body. I heard violin strains, weeping, 'Thank you, thank you, thank you'—all in Yiddish.

Never mind. What's important is that Jaszko won't be getting any sugar at their expense.

A few weeks later the violinist was back without his ten-year-old brother, who had tragically frozen to death during their wandering. The ground was frozen solid and he hadn't been able to bury him, so he just left him lying there. As for the 22-year-old Jewish young man from Radom, we heard a peasant remark two weeks later that he had surrendered himself to the village headman, who turned him in at the nearest Polish police station, where he was shot.

The peasant, know-it-all Cereniak, added that he knew why: he was unable to go on living. Since he didn't have the courage to take his own life, he made a present of it to the killers, even though he had escaped from their clutches a few times before. Why, at the beginning he even jumped from the train taking the Jews of his town to Treblinka. "Nasty murderers!" Cereniak added, and I didn't know whether he meant the Germans or his fellow Poles, the townsmen or the peasants.

* * *

Felek doesn't like to talk about the destruction of the Jews. However, when he does want to tell the women about some interesting occurrence, he does so in the kitchen, so that the five of us behind the wall can't hear. He speaks in an undertone and our hearts pound. We don't know what's happening this time, whether or not it's something that pertains to us. Afterwards we ask the women, but they won't say a word. That naturally makes us all the more uneasy.

Auntie tells us that Felek is an extraordinary man, with a great sense of honor. He would rather die than do anything to harm a Jew. He quarrels with his wife. Mrs. Felek complains that he doesn't bring home a thing, while all the other houses in the village are fully stocked with goods. The Jews are dead anyway, so why should everybody else have their belongings while they, the Feleks, have only these Jews?

Felek gnashes his teeth. He explains that he can't, but she can go if she wants to. In order to rob a Jew now, you've got to ambush him in the woods and kill him. He, Felek, couldn't do that, and he also couldn't leave a person naked in the woods; that would be like murdering him. Neither can he go into town to plunder Jewish houses during the German roundup "actions"; he's practically blind, and he's afraid of the Germans.

So Mrs. Felek keeps pestering and tormenting him.

Several times Felek told me the story of the Jew whom he found hiding in the underbrush in the nearby oak grove. That was a few weeks before our arrival. The Jew was wearing a pair of fine boots. Felek refused to take the man's boots, though he was urged to do so. Later, other peasants found the Jew, and pulled off his boots.

Felek has a fine, almost new pair of boots of his own. They don't suit the style of dress at all, and when he puts them on, his feet look as though they belong to someone else. I had never suspected him of anything, but something tells me that Felek is dwelling too much on the story of that Jew in the oak grove and his boots. Perhaps Felek has a troubled conscience, and is apologizing to me and to himself. Perhaps he *did* allow himself to be influenced. The very thought makes my blood run cold. No, it isn't so. I mustn't give way to suspicion. We mustn't!

One thing seems unbelievable—that things will ever be different, that things will turn out well. Apart from that, we believe everything. We believe in miracles, in Providence, and even in dreams.

Every morning, when we wake up, we start right in telling each other our dreams: frightening dreams and optimistic ones, dreams that say nothing and those that are full of omens. Most of the dreams are so frightening that they keep us shaking until well into the day. These dreams are a mixture of life and death; but mostly they're visions of red faces and murderous eyes.

We're pursued, we hide, we fall, we're stabbed and shot at; police, SS men in brown, black, green and blue uniforms; manhunts, searches; helmets, foreheads sweaty from murder, and even heaps of hollow-eyed corpses, moving, swaying—

Oh, we recognize them! Frequently we wake up. Or we cry or sob in our sleep. For hours afterwards we worry that someone has heard.

But we also have pleasant dreams. We see our loved ones, we greet them happily, but suddenly they disappear.

In the beginning, shortly after we came to Felek's, we once slept in the attic on a pile of hay. Zippora started crying in her sleep—softly but intensely. I woke her, and she opened her eyes wide at me: "Oh, why did you wake me? Mama was just saying goodbye to me. She said, 'I'm setting out on a long, dark road,' and she was crying."

Esther has dreamed several times that her dead, old, tiny grandmother was sitting in a corner of our hideaway saying: "Quiet, children, quiet, I'm sitting here and watching over you."

Once, when Esther got up, she thought she really saw her grandmother sitting there in the corner. Startled, she woke me. Before she could say anything, I told her angrily: "You woke me right in the middle of a nice dream. I was seeing my grandmother," though I had never seen her alive.

Often we dream about friends and acquaintances. Some of them are people you think about from time to time; others never came to mind before. Some look terrible—wizened, aged—and others look so well—happy, bringing gifts.

Felek is an expert in interpreting dreams; he learned it from his mother, "the witch," the villagers called her. He sighs as we tell him our dreams: "Seeing dead people in a dream isn't a good sign." But try and explain to him that people see only familiar faces in their dreams, and that all our familiar faces are dead!

Recently I dreamed of a friend who, we had heard, was still alive and in hiding. Felek considers that a good sign. But I'm afraid to add words to my thoughts: if he's already come to me in my dream—who knows? Poor man.

* * *

It was Auntie who, right at the beginning of our acquaintance, taught us to take an interest in our dreams and to relate them, first thing in the morning. That was five months ago, two months after the catastrophe.

We were working for the German Road Works Department. Those were days of suffering, pain, and fear. Our circumstances were painful and we were frightened of the future. Daily we learned from the grapevine that we, the last Jews, the Jews of the work brigades, were about to be deported, and that our days were obviously numbered.

We were working, a group of young men and women, the last remnant, the severed branches of family trees. You look at the people around you: healthy, fresh, in the full bloom of youth. However, the work is listless. We all know one thing for sure: "It's bound to happen." But there's nothing we can do. There's nowhere to run. The first person you meet will stop you and turn you in. It's no use even trying. Here? Yet a few more days in the company of other Jews, among the living dead.

On such days you move around aimlessly, do your work, and you don't say a word. Only from time to time you glance at your wife who's also working, silently, absorbed, humming a mournful tune, and you get the urge to embrace her, kiss her, and die with her on the spot, now, exactly six months after our wedding. But we don't kiss and we don't lie. Instead, it seems (or so it seemed then) that our hearts would slowly, gradually, run down. In the meantime, we have to work. Still it's a shame: all that effort, that wasted life; a shame to die, and a shame to live. But the life in me rises in protest:

"No, you've got to save yourself! That is: not yourself alone; yourself also, but *especially* her! But what is she thinking? Does she still care? No, she hasn't given up. Her eyes! She has given up. No, she hasn't. My God. . ."

In the evening, we return to the camp to sleep. It's dark, cold, rainy, muddy. People stand in front of the barracks whispering in clusters. They're whispering in such a way that, without knowing what's happened, I start trembling all over. I listen.

"Today. In the middle of the night. Or first thing in the morning. It's all set. Not the men. Meanwhile, it's just the women."

I don't say a word, only: "Is that definite?"

"Definite!"

It's dark. Esther is beside me. She clings to me.

"Leybl!"

Zippora, her sister, grabs my elbow:

"Don't go!"

"I'm not going. Just for a few minutes."

"Leybl!" I think it was Esther who called my name.

It's cold in the street. A heavy snow is falling. The nearby shop is full of people. I wait outside. Both sidewalks are empty. Even if one passes by, the windblown snow will blind him and he won't notice me.

I go to the back door and I call the shopkeeper. She is a Christian acquaintance. Our families had been on excellent terms through the years. We had been their customers. She was a good old friend, this young, gentle woman.

"Madam," I say.

"Sir," she interrupts. "First let me check if anybody sees me talking to you. All right. What is it?"

"Madam," I say, "you know my wife and sister-in-law."

"Fine young women," she says.

I'm encouraged, and stammer along: "I'll pay. Just one night. It's cold in the barracks. They've caught a cold. Just one night. They'll warm up. Sleep at your place. I'm not asking for a bed. On the floor by the kitchen stove—"

She smiles. "I can't. My husband won't let me. Anything but that."

Nearby I have another Christian acquaintance. A very decent man. A friend. But I'll have to tell him the truth.

He receives me warmly, but he's astonished that I'm ready to endanger his life.

"Sir," I say to him, "you'll hide the two women in the cellar for just one night. There won't be a search."

He stares at me. "I see that you're an enemy of mine."

A third acquaintance sighed sympathetically, but unfortunately tonight he can't, because he's having a party, and his guests might discover us.

Outside, I'm thinking of going back to the barracks. There's nowhere else to go.

"Leybl," I remind myself. "Don't go. Esther and Zippora."

Oh, God!

I didn't scream. But I couldn't go back empty-handed.

I don't know how I got there, but I was inside a courtyard. It wasn't far from our barracks. It used to be a Jewish courtyard. Poor Christians live here now.

I climb the winding staircase to the attic, feeling my way along the walls in the dark. Does anyone live here, or not?

I bang my head against the wall. No pain. Just a slight dizziness. I don't seem to have fallen.

"Who's there?" a woman's voice calls out.

I look around. Light streams from an open doorway. I go inside. Dilapidated walls. Three children are lying in a crib. The mother is in rags. A cat is sprawled on the hot tiles of the stove, flies buzzing up and down around her.

"A Jew!" the woman screeches.

"Madam," I start to say.

"Woe is me!" she screams. "A Jew! Get out, fast! My poor babies!"

"I'll pay you. You'll be able to give them bread and butter."

"Help! He's still here! Jesus! Poli-i-ice!!!"

I don't remember how I got down those stairs. "My poor babies!" rang in my ears.

"Esther. Zippora." I must have been murmuring aloud to myself. I heard tenants talking.

A door opens on the ground floor.

"Who's there? Who is it?" It's a woman's voice. Not young, this time. I'm about to run away. But—

"Esther. Zippora."

"Today, for sure."

Definitely today.

I'm inside a small room. Walls made of dark beams. Cold. A single iron bed. That old Christian woman, isn't she a witch? Her black hairs half gray, disheveled, over her eyes, wild. A tall, skinny figure. Long hands with long, bony fingers. Peculiar clothing.

"A Jew!" But she doesn't scream, just smiles and says softly:

"Oy, Take a seat, you poor Jew. What are you so scared about, eh?"

"Sh-h-h," I beg her.

"Never mind," she calms me. "There's nobody outside the window. Nobody will hear. Don't be afraid. Wretched man. He's frightened, poor fellow."

"Where is everybody?" I ask.

"Everybody?" she says, "which everybody? I'm a lonely old woman, no husband, no children, all alone in the world." Very peculiar, I think. Like a witch.

But I stammer on: "My wife... sister-in-law... sick... tonight... just to warm up... I'll pay."

"Pay-shmay!" she says. "Get them over here quickly, those poor, sick children. There's no need to pay!"

I ran through the streets. I don't know whether it was still snowing, or even whether or not anyone saw me run. But a weird witch ran alongside me, cackling, shrieking:

"Don't be afraid, wretched man, don't be afraid!"

* * *

It was dark in the barracks. Shadows were still whispering to each other. "Today for sure!"

Esther and Zippora clung to me: "Where were you so long? Let's stick together!"

"Yes, my poor children, we're going to be together. Come quickly!"

I went out. They followed me. I took them under my arms and said: "Come quickly, walk tall. We'll speak Polish. We're going out to the street. The gate is unguarded right now, because it's snowing. Quick. Don't be afraid. We don't have far to go."

I told them the whole story. "Just tell her that you have a bad cold. If she knows the truth, she may change her mind."

They ask me if there's a cellar in which to hide. "No," I say, "I don't think so. But maybe God will help."

We made our way to her door quietly and went in without knocking.

"Good evening!"

"Good evening!"

It was comfortable and warm in the room. She had lit the stove to warm us. She began to fuss over us. "I'm sorry that I don't have anything to serve you," she said.

I gave her a coin to buy us something. About half an hour later all of us were eating. Our bodies and our souls seemed to warm up. Then she took out all sorts of old things and spread a bed for us in a corner. We lay down and covered ourselves with our coats. She lay down on her iron bed and soon began to snore loudly. The room became pitch dark.

"Some sort of witch," Zippora whispered in my ear.

"Sh-h-h!" I said. "Don't talk. Just listen to the wind outside."

Esther is nervous, and thanks God that it's so dark in the room.

The "witch" kept waking up from time to time and asking us why we weren't sleeping. We didn't say a word, just shivered at the thought of the cold barracks and the constant exchange of whispers. We couldn't sleep.

A neighbor's clock on the other side of the wall chimed twelve times. Later on it rang out once, twice, two thirty, three, and we were still tossing and turning.

"It's probably too hard for you to sleep," we hear her voice.

We pretend not to hear and start snoring, so that she'll think we're asleep. It really isn't hard; we don't feel a thing. A few minutes later she's snoring again. We toss and turn in the dark. We can't shut our eyes. Then—one, two, three, four, five—

The clock chimed five. We keep seeing the camp. Suddenly a burst of machine gun fire. We huddle together. Another burst of machine-gun fire. We hug each other tightly. Our hearts stop beating: they pound; they stop; they pound again. Another machine-gun burst.

"They're shooting!" the old woman says in her bed. "They're shooting somewhere!"

"Mrs. Gutow," a neighbor shouts on the other side of the wall. "What's that awful shooting?"

"I don't know," our protector answers, "but it seems to be close by."

She asks us if we know.

"We have no idea," the three of us reply simultaneously from our corner.

"Why are your voices so shaky?" she asks softly. "They're not shooting at you."

"Of course not," we say.

"It's over," Esther whispers.

"It's all over!" Zippora repeats after her.

"Our poor brothers and sisters!"

"Who knows whom they killed?!"

The machine-gun bursts continue. The old woman in bed starts crossing herself and mumbling.

"They'll soon come searching here," Esther trembles.

"Where will we go now?" Zippora asks.

Quietly, they repeat after me: "Shma Yisroel!..." "Hear, O Israel!..."

* * *

About half an hour later the shooting stopped.

"Where will we go now?" the girls ask me.

"Quiet! The old woman is asleep. Don't wake her!"

The old woman snores away. Suddenly she wakes and bangs on her neighbor's wall. "Mrs. Lewinska," she shouts, "I've just had a weird dream."

"Let's hear it," the neighbor says.

"I dreamed that they removed the last of the Jews, the workers, from the barracks in the camp and led them in long rows to the cemetery. From every side they shoot them and shoot them and so many Jews fall dead. Boys and girls. They chase them and shoot them from every side."

"That's what's really going to happen," the neighbor interrupts.

"But listen to the end! Suddenly, all those dead Jews turn into officers with leather belts and guns. Strange officers, with long beards. Suddenly there's a whole Jewish army, and they start chasing the Germans. They chase them and chase them and wipe them out."

"A witch!" Zippora says, trembling all over.

"Listen to the eerie way she's chanting that dream," Esther says.

Day began to break outside. We got dressed. The old woman, too.

"Where will we go now?" We were all shivering from the cold.

"Would you like to eat something?" the old woman asked.

"No, thank you. But would you mind going over to the barracks to see whether the Jews are off to work yet?"

She hurried out; we were trembling as we waited for the answer.

She was back in a few minutes: "Hurry up and get washed. The Jews are going to work already."

We didn't wash. I put a few coins on the table. She smiled and thanked me. I asked her: "What's your name?"

"I'm called Auntie," she said.

"Au revoir, Auntie!" We thanked her and left.

We found the Jewish workers at the gate and got into line. They asked us if we knew what all that shooting had been about just before dawn!

There are days of miracles when we believe in Divine Providence, when we believe that an Eye always watches over us. Our neighbor Wacek lost some hens. Wacek is a pauper. Without his hens, that lay eggs in the winter, he would starve to death. So Wacek complained to all the neighbors. He suspects every single one of them. If they don't return his hens right away, he's going to the police.

If the police come, we know, they'll search everywhere, especially at Felek's. Rotten business! But Wacek's threats have no effect. His hens aren't returned.

Felek is overwrought: we might get caught over this silly business! I offer to give him money for Wacek. He can pretend to be lending it to him. But Felek says that will make things even worse: Wacek will become suspicious, and whenever something is stolen they'll come to search his, Felek's, place first. In any case, he has a long standing reputation as a thief.

The hours fly by. We're desperate.

Suddenly, before dark, when Wacek is about to set out for the police station, the hens are back. From where? Who knows? Who cares? So long as they're back. Felek runs in to tell us; "A miracle, a miracle!" he shouts. "You can eat. It's nearly dark outside."

He decides to make us a little party. He tells us to come out of the hideaway, where we're shivering all over from the cold, and warm ourselves by the stove. What a pleasure: It's so warm in the room that the frost on the window pane seems to thaw. Felek says he'll stand by the window to see if anyone is coming.

We come out and stand by that heavenly stove.

Suddenly, we see a tall figure standing just outside the window, looking straight at us, and not saying a word. Felek's guard is really useless. He's almost totally blind, and he couldn't see that a person was approaching the house.

Our first thought was to run back into the hideaway, but we realized that such a move would reveal the location of the hideaway to the person out there.

Felek let out a groan, and Auntie came running from the kitchen. But the look of terror on her face quickly turned to laughter, as she called out: "Good evening!"

"Good evening!" said the voice outside the window. "Who are you? I can't see! Open the door!"

It was blind Pulkowski. Groping about with his hands, he had thought the window was the door. He asked a question and went away.

Soon it became dark. Mrs. Felek hangs her homemade quilts over the two windows, and the little lamp is lit.

That's a good sign. It means that Felek brought home some "reading matter" from the village today, an underground bulletin. He often gets these bulletins, under the pretext that his sister, Auntie, will read them to him.

We all seat ourselves on the floor—me in the center, my group behind me, and Felek, Mrs. Felek and Auntie facing me. Auntie holds the lamp over my head, and I read aloud from the bulletin.

There's sufficient news, political and otherwise. Something about the Jews is included, too, but before reading those passages aloud I skim them silently. First I have to "edit" the material, deleting whole passages and inventing others, sometimes reading the very opposite of what is written—for example, passages that praise Poles who save Jews and say that they will be rewarded. I read the political news as written. But Felek often says that he doesn't understand, so I "explicate": "There are clear signs that the war will be over soon," I say, even though the bulletin clearly reports that the war is dragging on. Better that Felek shouldn't know that. I was about to invent an article concluding that the war would be over in a few months when suddenly we heard rumbling at the window. Although both windows were heavily draped with quilts and I had been speaking very softly, we quickly extinguished the lamp. Auntie went over to the window and moved aside a quilt. Sure enough, someone was standing there. He didn't run away, just stood there staring.

Felek, Mrs. Felek, and Auntie run outside, and the five of us ran back into our hideaway. We hear people shouting outside. A strange voice is shouting, and then Felek is shouting.

But Auntie comes inside laughing, sticks her head into the little door of our hideaway, and tells us: "It's lame Florek's moron son. His father chased him out of the house and he wants to sleep here."

"But why is Felek yelling?"

"The moron is deaf, and he can't hear unless you yell."

That night we had a difficult time falling asleep, wondering what we had done to deserve all of the day's miracles.

Esther is sure that her grandmother is sitting in the corner watching over us. So Zippora's afraid to open her eyes at night. Once, I had a compelling urge to see my wife's grandmother, so I stayed awake all night peering into the corner behind Esther. Several times Grandma appeared in the dark, but each time she looked different. Always in that pearl-studded cap, but each time with a different face, she showed herself and promptly disappeared.

Since that time, I see her even with my eyes shut. I told Zippora. At first she was frightened, but she got used to it; now she often sees her when she covers her face with the blankets, and she isn't afraid.

Once Grandma told me that we don't have to be afraid of the dead, not even of devils, ghosts, and demons. In the otherworld, she learned, they are harmless. The greatest destroyer can do no harm once he is dead. We must rather beware of the living. Among them, unfortunately, the Destroyer has free reign.

* * *

Last night was a nightmare.

At night, all of us sleep on the floor. At about ten o'clock, Auntie spreads several sacks of hay on the floor and covers them with clean bedding. We crawl out of our hideaway and lie alongside each other, our heads on the pillows that lean against the false wall. We leave our clothing in the hideaway. We lie in a row: Ephraim, Froiman, me, Esther, Zippora, and Auntie next to Zippora, beneath the blanket-covered window. We almost never sleep through the night. We doze off, wake up, then doze off again with our hearts pounding.

Last night, at midnight, we heard someone moving in the kitchen where Felek and his wife sleep in a wide wooden bed. We saw that the light of the kerosene lamp had been turned up. Then we heard Felek tiptoe barefooted into our room, and shake Auntie awake. She crawled out of her bed and went into the kitchen with him. They whispered together.

We held our breaths, and pretended to be asleep. Had they heard some voice outside? We listened. Then they softly came back into the room. The two of them bent over us to check if we were asleep. We kept our eyes shut tight.

Auntie and Felek signaled to each other. Mrs. Felek was also there. They entered our hideaway, moved something, then returned to the kitchen. Several times they passed back and forth, each time pausing beside us.

I was hot all over. I opened my eyelids ever so slightly, ready to jump. We dug our fingernails into each other under the blankets.

My heart pounded. I remembered a young man and woman we once knew. In the camp, we heard that one night the peasants with whom they had been staying chopped off their heads with an axe and buried them in the barn.

They were bending over us again. I wanted to jump up, but I lay still. They were in the hideaway again. Were they searching the pockets of our clothes? We were all breathing heavily. They were moving back and forth from the hideaway to the kitchen. After a while it was quiet, and Auntie was once again lying beside Zippora. Felek and his wife went back to bed and lowered the lamp. We were shivering.

Auntie was soon snoring again. I could also hear the sound of snoring in the kitchen.

Towards morning, I dozed off. Suddenly I felt someone gently tapping my arm. Froiman was bending over me. He showed me a trail of flour leading from our hideaway to the kitchen. When we went back into the hideaway, we saw the sack of flour was not as full as it had been.

We all smiled.

Later, Auntie confided in me that during the night, Felek had helped himself to some flour to send as a present to his brother, Janek. She said Felek was too bashful to ask us. In fact, Felek has been staying out of the room today. We sense his sheepish smile as he paces around in the kitchen like an oversized, shamefaced baby.

* * *

Since Auntie's dream that first night in her apartment, I've become a frequent visitor in her little room. Every evening, when we were ready to march back from work to the camp, I got into the last row. When we came to Auntie's house, it was quite dark. After looking around carefully, I would slip out of the line into her courtyard, check from behind the fence to make sure that the rest of them continued to march and that my disappearance hadn't been noticed, and quickly slip into Auntie's room. She always welcomed me warmly, asking me how the sick girls were and offering some words of encouragement. I always found some excuse for coming to her; once I brought some dirty underwear to wash; the next time, I checked to find out whether the laundry was dry; the third time, I collected the laundry. Each time I gave her money and thanked her.

Once I asked her how she subsisted. "A body finds ways," she said. "One trades a little in the market. And this and that. Just to keep a body alive."

Going out, I bumped into someone on the other side of the door. It was very dark and I couldn't make out his face. He couldn't see my face, either. He grabbed me by the sleeve. When he saw that I was a man, he asked if I were coming from Auntie's.

"Yes," I said, my heart pounding.

"Is it worthwhile going in today?" he asked.

"What do you mean?"

"Ah! Which one is there today, the blonde or the brunette?"

"Neither of them," I replied.

"You mean you mount the old lady?" he said, chuckling.

"That's right."

"You've really got it bad!" he laughed. "Let me give you some advice. You can order a young chick from her. She'll tell you when to come."

We left together, because he had no desire to "mount the old lady." But I quickly took off, thanking God that he hadn't noticed my nose and eyes. I smiled as I recalled her answer to my question: A body finds ways.

I slipped in through the barbed wire and went to sleep in the bararck.

As I lay on the straw, all sorts of odd thoughts flitted through my mind: "She's a decent person, the old lady. It's worthwhile going just to her. Something can be worked out with her!"

* * *

The next day was endless. We worked, whispered, listened to rumors. We had a feeling that something was brewing. As usual, my wife hummed as she worked. I was full of plans, all of them involving old Auntie. Finally evening came. We lined up. I was at the end of the line, as usual. We marched through the dark streets. When we approached Auntie's courtyard, I slipped out and went in to see her. This time we had to talk—and not about laundry or other such unimportant things; this time we had to come to the point.

"Why are you so upset," she asked, after inviting me to sit down.

"It's nothing," I said, and started feeling her out.

We chatted about life, about making a living. We talked a long while. She became sad, came over to me, and planted a kiss on my forehead. Suddenly, motherly warmth seemed to course through my entire being. We continued to talk. Then the conversation became more intimate, turning finally into the confession of a lonely old woman.

She told me that she had never married. She was a village girl, but had long ago left the village. She was bored by farm life, by peasants and their petty ways. She had longed for something bigger, for a different kind of world, different people, city people. She hadn't known exactly what she wanted, only that she couldn't stay on the farm, so she decided to leave. Despite the opposition of her parents, she went off to the city and began to search for that other way of life. Every time she thought she had it, or nearly had it, it slipped out of her grasp. She had even tried the convent, but that really wasn't what she had had in mind. So she went on seeking. She even worked for counts because she wanted to see how the nobility lived. But that also repelled her. So she traveled all over the country in her quest but found nothing but disappointment, humiliation and failure. There was no longer any way back for her. She believes in God, but she doesn't understand life. And here she is, all alone in the world, without children, without a family, without a home, without a soul who understands her.

She finished, and I thought that this lonely old outcast would burst into tears. Instead, she started laughing strangely. I didn't really know what to say, so I tried to console her.

"You're not alone. You can have children and someone who will understand you. I mean me, my wife, my sister-in-law. We're also lonely people, so we can all become a family. Rent a place somewhere out of the way, and we'll all live there together. We have some money. We also have some things stashed away by Polish acquaintances, and we'll get them. And when the war is over, with God's help, we'll all survive, and you'll get what you've been looking for all your life. We'll travel all over the world together, find a new home, settle down, and you'll forget all your troubles."

We went on talking for a long while. I remember only the end of the conversation.

"No need to rent a place," she said. She has a brother in her native village. He's over fifty. There's only him and his old lady. No children. It can all be arranged there. And there's no need to talk it over with him in advance. When the time comes, we can all go there together; as soon as she tells Felek, her brother, what it's all about, he'll agree to hide us in his place. Everything's going to be all right!

After I said "Good night" and went outside, I sensed, for the first time in many months, the sweet, fresh air as it coursed through my body.

* * *

After that, I became a regular visitor at Auntie's. I went to visit her nearly every evening, began bringing her our things, and told her to start getting ready.

"Maybe the Lord will help and we won't have to," she would comfort me each time.

"Either way, we're staying with Auntie," I would reply.

After the conversation, her mood changed. She became excited, and took an active interest in our secret plans. She seemed to really look forward to her new life with us.

Then, it came. One evening my wife, sister-in-law, and I slipped into Auntie's apartment. We told her that we had to set out for her brother's place in the country before sunrise; at the camp the end was drawing near.

She didn't get excited. She told us to relax, not to be so nervous. None of us slept that night. At 5 a.m., thinking we were asleep, she said: "Get up, children. It's late. We'd better set out. It'll soon be light."

We dressed, had a hot drink, and got our bundles together. She said: "Yes, children, nothing else in the world matters to me any more. I'm your mother. My life, like yours, is in God's hands. Whatever He does to you, let him do to me, too!"

* * *

It has been three months since we started living at Felek's with Auntie. She plays her role as though born to it. She's already endured quite a lot because of us. We often hear her groaning on our account. But although we anxiously anticipate her complaints, and prepare whole speeches in reply, she always lets us down: instead of our having to persuade and console her, she smiles and comforts us.

Many times she gives us a motherly scolding for being so helpless. She really tears into us. But here she found a new life, she says. Not in the city, in the big wide world, but right here in her native village, which she abandoned many years ago to search for a new life. Her greatest pleasure, she says, is to chat with us in the hideaway for hours on end. Our conversations are medicine for her doubts concerning Jew and Christian, man and beast, life and death, beauty and ugliness. She listens to us and, she says, understands many things that she never understood before. She sits with us for hours, until suddenly she runs outside, calling out, "We mustn't forget to check!"

Sleeping and waking, she won't allow us to despair. Everything will be all right, she's always exclaiming. She just knows it: everything is going to be all right! We just hope that God doesn't disappoint her.

* * *

Our thoughts swirl in our heads like a defeated army stampeding in retreat. Although the retreat route seems to have been wiped off the face of the earth, our thoughts keep wandering back. Shattered images keep reappearing, bits of the recent past, foggy and obscure, like scenes in a hazy dream. And no matter how our thoughts circle, they always return to the same point. The mind just cannot grasp clear images of the reality that was, that once filled our lives with meaning.

I want to remember my mother, the woman who bore me, raised me, and started me out in life. I want to conjure her bright image out of the darkness, bring her warmth into this cold, and store it in my heart. But the image is dim. It's not the mother of my childhood and youth but the war-tormented mother whose face has turned old and wrinkled from terror.

I saw her that last Thursday night before we were separated. I was in my room, downstairs. Suddenly I heard someone screaming. It came from my mother's room upstairs. It was my younger sister's voice: "Mama! Mama dearest!!"

I ran up the stairs. The room was full of neighbors. I pushed my way through the crowd. My mother lay on her bed as though dead, her jaws locked tight, her eyes glazed, her outstretched legs stiff. I pricked her with needles, poured water and splashed brandy on her until a glimmer appeared in her eyes. Gradually the stiffness passed and her jaws relaxed, then all at once she opened a pair of huge, terrified eyes, looked around, and asked me whether it was true that—when "they" come—they shoot on the spot bedridden people who can't walk to the train.

"Mama," I replied, "they're not coming, and you're not that sick." Later, I lay curled up in bed in my room. My head seemed to explode. I felt so impotent that I wanted to bite off my fingers. An ugly thought began to gnaw away at me: I've saved my mother, I've saved her.

I felt the blood rush to my face. I wanted to crush that thought and spit it out! But it kept crawling around inside me like a snake:

Maybe she would have been better off—

No, I'm going out of my mind!

Esther sat facing me, staring into my eyes as though she were reading my terrible thoughts. Neither of us said anything. That went on for a long while. I thought I really *was* going out of my mind.

Later, the ghetto mailman, Shmuel Avraham Popowski, came in. As usual, he smiled and sat down.

"What new, Popowski?"

"Not a thing," he said. "All the men ought to go into the forest and join the partisans."

"But how can we leave our wives and children, our mothers and sisters?"

"They're goners anyway!" he said, adding: "By the time you make your minds up, it'll be too late." After a few minutes, he grinned and said: "Who knows where those partisans are anyway? Maybe they don't even exist."

We sat there a long time thinking, and then I went out with him into the street. We both went to the Judenrat (Jewish community council) headquarters to hear the latest news.

It's midnight. We hear murmuring in the courtyard. Then we see several silhouettes. We recognize the heads of the Judenrat. They're talking among themselves: "What do you think? What do you think?"

That morning, the German district officer told the Jewish delegation that the Jews of Minsk Mazowiecki have nothing to worry about. The chairman of the Judenrat, Moyshe Kramazh, believed him. "He's a decent German, an older person," he said. "No question about it. Also, the police and the Special Police here are bought. Just today they received some nice presents from us. You should hear what they say about Hitler!"

The ghetto hygiene officer, Israel Yoysef Wengel, is holding his five-year-old son in his arms. The child is asleep. Wengel kisses him on the eyes and says: "What a child! What a child!"

Suddenly a roar is heard above the clouds. "Most likely Soviet nightbirds," says the hunchbacked Judenrat member Mordechai Yoysef Kirschenbaum.

Flares in the distant sky, perhaps over Warsaw. The entire sky lights up. A few minutes later the ground shakes. Bombs. It seems that the Soviets are bombing.

"They might bomb us, too," somebody notes. "They've lit us up, too!"

In fact, the flares overhead are lighting us up. In the sudden illumination, I notice Kirschenbaum's eyes looking upward as he says: "Let them blow up the whole city together with us. That's the only way we can avoid catastrophe!"

* * *

Friday. 9:30 a.m. August 21, 1942. Elul 8, 5702. "They're on the outskirts of the city!" "They're here!"

Pandemonium in the street. People run in every direction, with and without belongings, individuals and families.

They're shouting: "Run for your lives, Jews! Run! Get away from the ghettos!"

I feel as though I'm suffocating in the thick smoke. As if in a fog, I run to our house and charge in: "Quick! Everybody! Out! They're here!"

We shut the doors and shutters and run out of the ghetto to the outskirts of the city. My sister Miriam and somebody else carry my mother and run until they're out of breath. My sister-in-law, brother-in-law and his wife, my wife, Esther, and her younger sister and neighbors are also running. I tell them to keep running and hide at the home of a Christian woman whom we know. Then I stop, look back at the city and wonder: Maybe it isn't anything. Maybe it really isn't anything.

People stampede by me. Two children with candy in their hands. Their mother had given them candy and told them to run for their lives. Women hugging babies to their bosoms. Girls with bundles on their backs. Whistles shriek. The Jewish ghetto policeman, Yosl Wiszniewski, comes riding along on a bicycle. "What's up?" I ask him. He waves at me and rides on.

Christians look bewildered as they watch the Jews flee. They don't know what's happening, and they're also frightened.

The wealthy Jew, Yankl Rosenberg, comes running by. "Why are you standing there?" he yells at me. "You won't make it!" He's running to a Christian acquaintance to hide. I turn around and start running.

My family are already out of sight. But I know where they're heading. It isn't far beyond the outskirts of town—the home of a Christian woman acquaintance, Szczepanek. Finally, I'm there also.

A long, narrow, sandy lane, flanked by gardens and houses. Painted picket fences made of narrow wooden slats. The branches of trees hang over the fences. I stand in the middle of the road between two lots. Silence. Not a living soul in sight. Suddenly, I see someone standing in his garden across the road from Szczepanek. I don't want him to see me going in there. I just stand there. He stares at me, then follows me suspiciously. Bursting into tears, I run back to the road.

Suddenly, at the far end of the road, a German death-squad man rides by on bicycle, his sleeves rolled up, his rifle cocked. I hold my breath as he rides in my direction, then I quickly run over to Szczepanek's garden gate. She's standing there stunned. Gaping at me, she lets me into the garden. Her daughter tells me to lie down a furrow among the potato beds, underneath the leaves of some low trees. I lie down. Esther is there. She hugs me.

Esther tells me that her mother, my mother, and my sister fled to Bartnicki, a Christian acquaintance, because my mother was too weak to make it this far. With us here are my young sister-in-law, Zippora, my brother-in-law Sholem, and his wife Chaya. Chaya can't stop trembling, she's so terrified that her extended belly can be seen in the furrow (she's nine months pregnant). The Christian woman points to another furrow, and my brother-in-law takes his wife there.

Suddenly, the din of machine guns everywhere. It's begun! Not far from here! Screaming!

Another burst of fire. Silence.

Heavy footfalls near us. They're searching in the furrows on the other side of the fence.

"Hallo!"

I stretch out on the ground. My wife, right in front of me, clutches my hand. My sister-in-law, behind me, clutches my foot. We cling to the ground.

"Hallo, hallo!"

"*Shma Yisroel*—Hear, O Israel God is one!" My wife repeats it after me and clutches my hand even harder.

They're coming this way!

Sh-h-h!

Cra-a-sh! It's just a few furrows away from us. A girl groans My sister-in-law digs her fingernails into my foot. A rifle shot. Footsteps moving quickly away. Silence.

A burst of machine-gun fire! Heavy banging all around us. Again footsteps near us. Soft ones, this time. It's our Christian acquaintance. She's trembling all over: "Posters! Death for hiding Jews!"

What will happen now, she asks. Jews are being shot and corpses are everywhere. Just three furrows away lies a dead girl. A little farther away is a child with a bullet in her chest. She's still conscious, begging for water, but nobody brings her any. Further away lie several wounded women, still alive and conscious, who beg the fleeing Germans to give them a finishing shot. The Germans ignore their pleas and leave them to bleed to death.

"What's going to happen now?" Szczepanek desperately asks. She stands there meditating for a moment and slips away.

The gunfire is deafening. Every kind of weapon is in use: a cacophony of pistols, rifles, machine guns, automatic revolvers, and hand-grenades.

I hear the distinct shuffle of feet. Someone is speaking to our Christian acquaintance. My wife recognizes the voice: it's

Breker, Szczepanek's son-in-law. He's speaking nervously. Soon he comes over to us, perspiring, full of news. He bends down and offers me his hand. We've known each other a long time (an acquaintance that worries me, in fact). He's just come from town: "You've no idea what's going on there! They're wiping out the Jews. In the marketplace thousands of Jews whom they rounded up are sitting on the ground. Corpses everywhere in the streets. They're taking the people they've rounded up to Treblinka."

He smiles and says quickly it's his nerves.

"The death squad has come with trucks," he continues. "SS, Special Police, Police Guard, Ukrainians, Lithuanians in dark uniforms, and Polish Police. The best are the Minsk Special Police and militia. They know where to look for hiding Jews."

More bursts of gunfire and grenade explosions. Breker listens and says: "Every shot means another dead one!"

We shiver feverishly.

"What about the Judenrat?" I ask.

"The Jew-chiefs?" Breker says. "The Jew-chiefs have to find hens for the Germans. They're crawling around the yards on all fours cackling and collecting hens. Two SS men follow about and crack long whips across their asses."

More shooting.

"Don't be afraid," Breker soothes us. "If they find you here, I'll see to it that you're not shot on the spot but taken to the marketplace, to Treblinka."

Breker ran off, repeating as he went: ". . . to the marketplace, to Treblinka!"

* * *

We were lying in the grass, clinging to the furrows. Overhead we were covered by the thick green boughs of the low trees. Then we heard an uproar. The shrieking of whistles. Bursts of gunfire. Screams. Truncated groans. Bedlam.

We kept on hugging the ground. But the screams were coming closer. Drunken voices screeched. We trembled and dug our nails into each other. They were right outside our garden, shouting, cursing, shooting, running. Szczepanek kept crawling back and forth between us and her house, wringing her hands all the while.

Her daughter came back from town with the news: Thousands of Jews are sitting on the ground in the marketplace—old men, women, and children. They're sitting in the broiling sun with their feet folded under them. People are dying. The SS men run from courtyard to courtyard and drag people out of their hiding places. They use their whips to drive them to the marketplace and to shove them into place. Hundreds of corpses litter the streets: women shot together with the children at their breasts; old men, old women. Germans, Ukrainians, Lithuanians, and Polish policemen scour the houses, looking under beds, in attics, cellars, and chimneys, for people to drag to the marketplace. Corpses lie behind every wall and in every garden. People caught outside the ghetto are shot on the spot; their corpses are spread out in the neighboring fields. Gangs roam the nearby woods and villages in search of escaped Jews. In the village Chochol they shot forty Jews and buried them in a pit. They've done the same in the dunes behind the Christian cemetery and in other places. All the houses in the ghetto are empty. The doors and windows have either been smashed or removed. Inside, the rooms have been ransacked; they look like holes. Every few minutes new groups of people are brought to the marketplace. SS men with flushed faces and rolled-up sleeves crack their whips and fire at the people. The groups are getting smaller and smaller. They keep bringing them from everywhere.

On the marketplace sidewalks stand tables covered with white tablecloths and set with bottles of wine, brandy, and liquor. The officers directing the roundup sit in sofas—which they took from the ransacked homes—stuffing themselves with food and drink. Inside abandoned Jewish apartments, SS men are cooking chickens and geese caught in the same backyards. They twist off the heads and throw the birds whole into pots of boiling water. Then they bring them to the tables outside. The stormtroopers empty whole bottles of liquor at one gulp and devour the meat. They're all dead drunk and giggling. Groups of captured Jews are made to run past the tables. The officers leer at the Jews and, with chunks of meat still in their mouths, they whip them.

Szczepanek's daughter stood for a long time on the other side of the marketplace, next to the church, watching. She saw a senior officer wobble drunkenly, grab another bottle of liquor, gulp it down, and yell: "Criminals! You're nothing but a bunch of criminals getting what's coming to you!" Then he grabbed a rifle and began shooting wildly at the Jews as he screamed: "Criminals! This is the end of you!"

There are rows of corpses with heads blown to bits by dumdum bullets. The people close by are splattered with blood and marrow. They're not allowed to move. A beautiful student—Ruzka, Srulik Edelstein's daughter—went out of her mind. She ripped off all her clothes and started running naked toward the church. A shot dropped her right at Szczepanek's daughter's feet.

"Oh, you can't imagine what's going on there," she said. "They just brought Dr. Greenberg in. The SS men gave him a terrible beating. They said that he'd be worth a lot; they can make plenty of soap out of all that fat." Then she ran back to town.

Her husband, Breker, came running back from town, drenched in sweat. He immediately shouted, "It's bad! I've heard that they'll soon be coming to search us. You've got to leave! But if you have any gold, I'll bribe the Germans before they get here. Better hand it over. If they shoot you, the gold won't be of use anyway. Then they'll pull off your clothes too. Gangs of our boys are running around stripping the corpses. They're also looking for live Jews to hand over to the Germans or to squeeze hush money out of. But I won't let them in here."

Breker stood over us. All the shooting makes the place sound like a battlefield. He helped us to remove our watches, my ring, Esther's wedding band, my sister-in-law's ring. He was going to offer it all to the Germans right away, so they'd leave us alone. But he didn't know whether it would help in the end.

* * *

Later his wife arrived with fresh news. She had been observing the front rows in the marketplace. Grizzly old Kikes were sitting there. She saw a lot of familiar faces. Old Chaim Itzik Berger is there, the one who's been paralyzed in bed for five years; they say that his old woman carried him out on her hands. Probably frightened that they'd shoot him in bed. Shaye Friedman is in a front row, deathly pale, chewing away at his short gray beard—also Shlamka Berkowitz, Leyb Rosenberg and others. Many of them brought along their "shroud"—she meant their prayershawls—which they're holding under their armpits.

She hadn't seen our mothers or my sister. They must still be hiding, or they've been shot somewhere. They're still shooting Jews everywhere. They've just brought over all the Jewish workers from the military and civilian factories. Not a Jew will be left in town. The grapevine has it that tomorrow the Jews in all the outlying towns will also be wiped out.

There's an uproar outside in the garden. Szczepanek and her daughter ran out quickly. We felt that it was all over for us. We buried our faces in the ground and held our breaths.

The noise died down. Old Mrs. Szczepanek comes over to us: We must leave immediately. No arguing!

Breker is back: He needs more gold—or cash. How much do we have? We've got to give everything. The more, the better. He'll take care of it right away. He doesn't know if it'll do any good, but we needn't worry; we won't be shot; we'll be taken to the marketplace, to Treblinka.

* * *

4 p.m. Quiet all around. In the distance, the clatter of machine guns and rifles continues. This time, Breker's wife comes running in with the latest news. It's hell in the marketplace. People are dying of thirst. The living and the dead—victims broil in the hot sun. The whole town stinks. Jews relieve themselves right where they're sitting; anyone caught trying to get up is shot on the spot. They're still dragging people in, only now they're individuals, not groups. They're just brought in the Judenrat man, Mordka Yosek Kirschenbaum. He had been hiding all day with a Christian acquaintance. As soon as he heard that his wife and children were in the marketplace, he handed himself over to the Germans. Now he's sitting at the edge of the multitude, peering out through his glasses as he looks for his wife and children; they're hidden in the dense crowd and can't know that he's in the marketplace too. She didn't see our mothers this time, either; she's been looking for them among the corpses scattered in the streets.

The Poles are scouring their courtyards for hiding Jews. They find them in garbage bins, in outhouses, in pigpens. Landlords are frightened and they're chasing the Jews out. Many Jews won't go voluntarily and they beg for their lives; so the landlords call the police who shoot them on the spot. The landlords have to bury them, but they get the Jews' clothing for their trouble. They also find some money on their bodies. Many Jews have been shot at the river. Both banks are lined with corpses. But our family hadn't been seen there either.

* * *

It has been several hours since Breker left. His wife says that he's in some tavern drinking with the Germans. He'll probably keep them away from here.

The sun has set already. It's Shabbat Eve, candle-lighting time. But where are our mothers? And where is Breker? What is he doing?

We huddled together in the darkness, filthy, digging into the earth. "Leybl, Leybl," they whispered, "we'll be shot!"

Then someone came shuffling through the leaves toward us. Szczepanek felt in the grass with her hands, knelt down, and whispered: "Go away! Go in peace, go with God! You can't stay here!"

We couldn't say a thing. That very evening, she told us some Kikes, like Israel Trafikant and his friends, offered some resistance against the Germans in the marketplace. A young man, a refugee from Kalisz, Mendl Seidel, had jumped on an SS man, grabbed his rifle and cracked it over his skull. But it had been too crowded for him to be able to shoot. If the SS men and the Polish policemen hadn't grabbed him, he's have killed the German. They beat him to a pulp and shot some Jews nearby. In some other places, a few Jews also attacked Germans.

She wrung her hands: "Go away from here! Go with God!"

We heard rapidly approaching footsteps in the dark. Somebody ran in to us. It was Breker, hysterical: "Get out of here, fast! The Germans are heading this way. Go, quick!"

He smelled from whiskey. We wanted to kiss him, but his wife and mother-in-law pressed us to hurry.

My wife and sister-in-law started to cry and clung to the other women. I heard gunfire all around. "Where should we go? Hide us someplace. Save us! We'll be killed out there!" But it was no use. "Get out of here right now!" they shouted.

In the dark, we climbed over the garden gate into an open field.

April 12, 1943:

I'm interrupting my account of what happened that Friday. I wasn't able to write for several weeks. There are several reasons. I don't know exactly what it is. But there's something in the air, a storm brewing.

What's come over Felek? He hasn't been the same old Felek for several days now. He walks around in a daze. He hardly eats and he hardly talks; he just hangs around and mopes. Does he have some bad news? Did he hear them talking about us in the village? Or is it some inner struggle? Lately, Felek told us, he's had a feeling that our days are numbered. We don't know whether he knows something or whether it's just an intuition. We only sense that something is brewing.

Esther and Zippora cry every night. I try to comfort them, but that only makes them feel worse.

But what is Felek thinking? Is he keeping some secret from us? Lately, he rarely visits our hiding place. Through the cracks in the wall of the attic—our new hideaway—we watch him constantly. He always sits on a large rock near the well opposite the cottage, smoking cigarettes and looking pensively into the distance, as though he expects something. Auntie and Mrs. Felek have changed too. They tiptoe around the house and hardly speak. I've asked Auntie a few times, but she always says it's nothing—we're only imagining things.

Last night we were so nervous we almost screamed. Something is going on, and it involves us.

Since we moved into our new hideaway in the attic, we've been keeping guard at night. Each night another one of us stays up to listen for suspicious noises outside and to make sure that we're quiet when we sleep. One night, Esther, who was on guard, heard footsteps outside. She woke us up. Through the cracks we saw a person standing outside. Quietly I slipped into the house and woke Felek. After I returned to the attic, he went outside. Through the cracks we could see the figure run away. Naturally, it was impossible for us to fall asleep again. About half an hour later we once more heard footsteps and made out the same shape right outside our wall. Again I told Felek. He went outside, and again the figure ran away. Later, Felek crawled up to our attic and let out a big sigh. I tried to calm him; maybe it was only a thief. Felek didn't answer, just sat for a long while in silence. After he lit a cigarette, he said that maybe it was the ghost of his brother, Janek. Perhaps Janek is dead—he hasn't been seen for days—and his ghost is coming to haunt us. We all watched Felek's pale, pock-marked face and the whites of his dimmed eyes turn red in the glow of his cigarette each time he drew on it. He sat there a long while, lighting cigarette after cigarette. Only when the darkness began to turn gray did he groan and crawl back down.

* * *

Froiman is making trouble. His nerves are shot. He's always shouting that we're finished, that the villagers know about us. After Felek left us, Froiman urged us to run away immediately; Esther agreed with him. He told us he's seen the figure outside looking up right at us. I disagreed with him and his alleged superhuman night vision; he had only been imagining things. We argued back and forth throughout the night; until I convinced Esther, Zippora, and Ephraim that Froiman didn't know what he was talking about. But they weren't really convinced—neither am I—that we have nothing to fear here. Still, our only choice is to believe.

Froiman seems to be going crazy. When we started to talk about last night's happenings, he denied that he had seen anyone watching us, and accused us of making up stories about him. Now he's sulking in the corner and refusing to talk to us.

We've quarreled a few times lately. Froiman says that we're wasting our energy; we can't possibly survive, despite our pretensions. We won't last long. Each time he says that, I reprove him. The others listen to our debate as though our fate depended on its outcome. They seem comforted by my assurances of survival. They perk up every time Froiman quiets down, crawls into a corner, and dozes off. I can't sleep, though. I know that Froiman is right. But I mustn't give in to him. If I do, then we'll have to turn ourselves in to the Germans.

I've already mentioned our new hideaway in the attic. Eight days ago we had to leave our lodging behind the false wall. It was pitch dark. It had been a jolly evening. We had read an underground leaflet full of good news from the Russian front. Then all eight of us had supper together around the little stove. We had gone to sleep in good spirits. As usual, we placed our beds, wide straw mattresses, in a row on the floor. But just as we fell asleep, we heard banging on the window pane. Half-naked, the five of us dashed into the hideaway (where we always left our clothes before going to bed). In a flash, Auntie removed our bedding and called out: "Who's there?"

A male voice answered in Russian: "Open up, old lady. We want something to eat!"

"Partisans!" Froiman mumbled. We didn't know whether to be happy or frightened.

"She is an old woman and her pantry is empty," Auntie replied.

At that, the window pane exploded. Auntie let out a shriek, and one after another, several men rushed in through the broken window and started to search the house. They beat Auntie and demanded that she hand over the goods she had plundered from Jews. That was a lie, Auntie sobbed. She had never stolen anything. But still the blows came. Standing naked behind the wall and shivering with cold and fear, we could hear them searching, feeling the walls, crawling from place to place. Suddenly, I could hear someone poking and scratching on our little door, and it began to open. A hand holding a pistol reached into the hideaway. I seized it and cried out in Russian: "Comrades!" Then I crawled out, followed by the other four.

It was dark in the room, except for the light of the flashlights held by some of the invaders. They wore long fur jackets and fur hats; automatic rifles slung over their shoulders and revolvers hung in holsters on their hips. They stared at us in shock. I fell into the arms of one of them, kissed him, and said: "Comrade, take us with you. We're going along with you!"

My people started weeping aloud.

* * *

The next morning we were lying in the attic, in the straw, beaten bloody, without clothing. They had taken our clothes, along with everything else in the house. We didn't feel anything, just lay there and waited. We were sure that the bandits would tell the whole village about us.

Esther kisses me. She thinks we should say goodbye to each other; this is our last day on earth, she feels. Ephraim sits there paralyzed. In the house, Auntie lies in bed battered and bruised. Felek has disappeared. Before dawn he had cleaned up the house and the yard, so the neighbors wouldn't suspect. But there's the broken window pane, and the villagers probably heard the intruders firing over our heads.

Felek is back. He crawls up into the attic to tell us that nobody knows what happened during the night. Zippora and Esther groan. Their bodies ache from the beating and they can't move. We were also beaten up when we tried to defend the women. But we're strangely satisfied as we examine our wounds. We still can't grasp the extent of these miracles. This strengthens our confidence a little. Perhaps it's still too soon to give up.

April 14:

We're in our new hideaway, behind a false wall that Felek put up in the attic early in the morning, and we can't forget the night's events. We see that Froiman is right; all our efforts are wasted. Everything is against us. Felek also has come to the conclusion that it's no use hiding; as soon as the Germans are driven out, the Russians will kill us. But we comfort him and ourselves: first of all, they didn't kill us; second of all, they were probably false partisans, bandits, not real Russians. This argument seems to have convinced Felek, but we feel that the floor is caving in right under us. Still, Felek is very depressed and keeps bringing us news that destroys whatever hope we have left.

A few days ago, after a carnival, some young village rascals got into the woods near Zarnowke, piled twigs on a pit in which six Jews were hiding—among them, women and children—and lit a bonfire. The people were burned alive in the crackling flames. The countryside is up in arms against people hiding Jews. Only two days ago Auntie went to the wedding of a butcher in Kaluszyn and came home dejected. There had been talk about "traitors to the people" who give shelter to the enemies of God and the Polish nation—the Jews. One guest, a fat pig-breeder, laughed as he predicted a bad end for these traitors: the Jews themselves would kill them. Later the peasants tell all sorts of tales about captured Jews who give away their Polish protectors to the Germans. Then, those Poles and Jews are shot together. That's the way the Jews repay their benefactors before they die. It's a sin to help them.

Once Felek tried to cheer us up by telling us that he doesn't give a damn, he's not afraid of death. He's risked his life too many times already. Only, he stammered, smiled, and turned pale—something else was involved here. He hopes we're not offended. No, he's not afraid of dying. The problem is the disgrace, the eternal blemish upon his family. If he's killed as a robber or murderer—so what? But if it's said that he was killed for hiding Jews, his family will never, in all eternity, forgive him!

April 15:

Jaszko Odrobinszczak dropped in to complain about his bad luck. "Some people have all the luck," he said. "For example, in Stare Budki just the other day the Peysakh family was caught and shot. So the Peysakhs aren't among the living anymore, either."

One morning soon after we arrived at Felek's, Mrs. Felek told us to come out of our hideaway behind the partition. She took us over to the window, raised the curtain slightly and pointed ahead. In the distance we saw what looked like two dots in the endless snow. Those are the Peysakhs, she said, the sons of a Jewish peddler woman from Kaluszyn. They've been roaming the area, she said. They're only children, sixteen and seventeen, but they're clever boys and can take care of themselves.

How we felt like running out to them, hugging and kissing them, crying and sharing our fate with them. Poor brothers, we are the witnesses of your cruel death, we, a few Jews hiding out like mice.

* * *

As Jaszko recounts the details of the death of the Peysakh brothers, he seems to be bursting with grief. If only he had known about it in time, he might have been on the job. He's angry at the Stare Budki headman for not telling him that a Jew-hunt was on. By the time he found out, it was all over; the police were already there, and the Peysakhs were tied up.

Were their faces white, those two sons-of-bitches! White. Their lips were so parched they couldn't talk. Or maybe they didn't want to talk. The beating they got didn't help a bit. They wouldn't say who had helped them. They certainly were stubborn, those bastards. Just children, and all that stubborn! You should have seen their eyes: sharp as daggers. Until they were shot, they stared everyone down.

Jaszko can never forgive the village headman. According to the grapevine, the headman has a fine fur coat which he was holding for the Peysakhs, and that's why he had them liquidated.

But he won't get away with it. Either Jaszko gets half of the loot or he'll tell the police. That's settled, he's going to get his share!

"Psia-krew! Dog's blood!" he spat, and left, slamming the door behind him.

* * *

A few days later, there was more news about Jews being shot.

This time the narrator is Kuczak from Nowe Budki, where only yesterday some "scum" were caught: a Jew and his wife and two children. Kuczak had taken part in the hunt. The man was a tailor from Warsaw. He had done work for the peasants in exchange for some food. The whole village had been hunting them for hours, Kuczak chuckled, before they finally caught up with them. "Your Jaszko Odrobinszczak was also there. He worked like a horse." Oh, how the woman and her children had cried. Later, when she was shot, the bitch's head had flown across the cottage rooftops. But they were stubborn asses. They refused to tell where they had eaten and slept. They had lived in the forest and ate raw potatoes, they claimed.

"Oh, were we lucky. They could have buried half the village if they had talked. Well, good riddance!"

Kuczak wants to bet that there isn't a village around where some of these types aren't hiding. All you've got to do is search carefully everywhere and you'll find them.

Auntie adds that she'd like to take part in a Jew-hunt. Kuczak acknowledges her words with a friendly slap on the back.

Only after Kuczak draws him out does Felek speak up: "Look, Kuczak, I could never do it. The Lord God says: 'Thou shalt not murder.' I couldn't! Of course, I wouldn't help a Jew, and I certainly wouldn't let one into my house. But kill them? I couldn't do that either. Let somebody else do that."

Kuczak calls Felek an idiot, an animal. "If you don't kill a Jew, he'll kill you!"

After Kuczak left, Felek came up to the attic and said to us with a cunning smirk: "Maybe Kuczak is right, eh? Maybe you'll kill me yet, eh?"

April 16:

It seems that in the village they know something about us. Did it come from those partisans? Yesterday, Felek ran into Logidzak carrying a heavy sack on his shoulder, and he joked: "What are you carrying there, Logidzak, a sack of gold?"

Logidzak retorted: "Where would the likes of me get gold? I'm not keeping any Jews. . . ."

Felek didn't want to tell us about it. But later, Mrs. Felek revealed the secret.

And what of the stories that Kalesz brings to Felek every day about partisans rampaging in the area and uncovering Jews?

The village deputy headman also asked Auntie whether she knows anything about partisans discovering Jews somewhere around her, and finding a large quantity of gold on them. Auntie laughed it off. She even makes fun of fearfulness. "First of all," she says, "he doesn't know that it happened in our house. And even if he did know, Kwiatowski (the deputy headman) is a decent fellow, and wouldn't tell a soul. Besides, nobody around here would dare to snitch. Felek has a reputation for being a bandit, and nobody wants to take the risk of informing on him. We can all relax!"

April 30:

Good news: Auntie has been to Minsk, where she found out about a camp of Jews at Rucky's metalworks. Nearly one hundred Jews are working there. At our request, she went there again the next day. She returned in the evening with some letters from our friends. Froiman's two sisters and two brothers are there, too.

We jumped for joy. Immediately we discussed it with Felek, and decided to prepare a fresh hideaway here for a few more Jews. However, since there was some chance that people knew of our presence here, Felek said he ought to talk to his brother Janek about fixing up a new hideaway in his cottage. (Felek's intuition had been wrong; Janek was alive.) But meanwhile, he'll allow those few Jews to come here.

Froiman and I promptly wrote to his sisters and to our friend, Yisroel Greenberg, about preparing to come here. Auntie has already been to town several times and discussed it with them. She says that she puts her life in danger every time she goes there. The area around the factory is crawling with suspicious-looking faces, plainclothes police on patrol. So she remains there awhile, with her palm outstretched, pretending to be a beggar; when she sees that nobody's watching, she signals to the

Jews to come over to the fence. "They look like skeletons, not human beings," she exclaims.

Each time she comes back with notes from friends and acquaintances. When we finish reading them, we're depressed for hours. Most of the people seem to be passively awaiting their fate. Some think of going to Warsaw. They write that tens of thousands of Jews are still living in Warsaw. Yankl Schiffman writes that Jews in the Warsaw ghetto are manufacturing "eggs"—homemade hand grenades—and getting ready.

Israel and Froiman's sisters keep postponing the date when they are to join us. Several times Auntie went to see them determined to bring them back with her but each time she returned alone. They're not ready yet, they write. "Are they afraid to make the trip?" Felek and Auntie ask angrily. She says she's not going to them again; she can't understand why they're dragging it out. They finally wrote that they're definitely coming on Tuesday, April 27. But on Tuesday, Auntie came back alone. They keep putting it off. I write to warn them that they might be too late if they delay any longer.

They've just written that they're definitely coming on June 7.

May 1:
Today is May Day, the workers' holiday. On this day tens of thousands of Jewish workers used to march with their slogans about liberty and equality, and their cries mingled with those of millions of workers around the world. What happened to international solidarity? Where are the mighty Jewish masses? What happened to all those noble dreams?

It's spring outside. A gentle sun warms everything. The treetops are beginning to green. Shafts of sunlight penetrate the cracks of our hideaway. We feel more at ease and stirred by vague feelings. The world is coming to life again. Our hosts are in a good mood today, festive, no longer depressed. Is it the influence of springtime? Or is it the new suede suit we gave Felek for agreeing to take in the new people?

* * *

May 2:
The peasants are talking about an uprising in the Warsaw ghetto. Cereniak has remarkable news about the Jews of Warsaw. He says that a thousand Germans have already fallen in the

ghetto, and the Jews are setting their tanks on fire. The Germans don't know what to do; the Jews have all kinds of weapons and there's heavy fighting in the streets. And leading it all is some Jewish boy, a hero who's only in his twenties. But the Germans are burning the ghetto—they're setting fire to all the houses, with the people in them!

Felek just reported that all of Warsaw is burning. The villagers say that last night they could see the flames of Warsaw forty miles away.

May 3:

Auntie was at the camp at Rucky's metal works yesterday. We asked her to try to persuade Yisroel and the others to wait no longer, to come right away. But she brought back only some more letters.

They're all so engulfed in defeat over there. They seem to expect catastrophe any day now. The Jews have been liquidated not only in Warsaw, but also in the camps at Mrozy, Siedlce, and Lukow. A few Jews from Rucky's factory were working in the Minsk railroad station when some Jewish workers on a passing freight train dropped them a note: "Save yourselves! The last 200 Jews of Lukow were slaughtered yesterday. Our days are also numbered."

Indeed, two days later we learned that the last Jewish workers in Siedlce had been liquidated. A fourteen-year-old boy from the Garwolin camp ran to Rucky's factory to report that the last fifty Jewish workers had been shot. Among them was Shmuel Roth, one of the heads of the Minsk community; before his death, he said his prayers and encouraged the others to think of the end of their suffering at last. Some of them attacked the Germans with knives and iron bars. A few hours later they were all shot. The fourteen-year-old boy was the only survivor.

What is Yisroel waiting for? Why is he putting it off till June 7? He writes that he wants to bring his father along. But his father doesn't want to come; he'd rather stay and perish with the other Jews, because he thinks nobody will survive. Yisroel says that their jobs are assured till June 10, so he'll come on June 7: he hopes to convince his father by then. They're all waiting for his father.

May 25:

Felek likes to tell us stories about thieves, bandits,

highwaymen, and partisans who carry on in the nearby forests. He tells about their heroism, how the Germans pursue them and can't catch them. He's completely engrossed in these adventure stories. He knows all those thieves and bandits personally, referring to them by name and speaking of them in awe. A kind of holy fire is kindled in him as he tells the stories.

As we listen to these tales, we can feel a narrow trap about to spring on us. Where does Felek get those stories? He's a responsible, careful person, but he likes to play with fire. Taking risks charges his imagination.

Today Felek is depressed. He heard in the village that the Germans caught a band of partisans in a nearby stable; in the battle that followed twelve partisans were killed. "A pity about those fine boys!" he said. "They made trouble for us, but they also gave the Germans plenty of trouble." He's really taking it badly.

* * *

May 30:
Days go by in the hideaway when none of us utters a word. We feel all alone in this vast Gentile world. After all, in the camp, Jews are with other Jews. Here we're surrounded by alien murderers.

The cuckoo sang a sad song in the forest today. It sticks in my mind like a dirge. The peasants say that the cuckoo foretells the future and gives signs. You decide in advance how many cuckoo calls will be a good sign and how many a bad sign, and then you listen and count. But we're afraid to try. Whether a good or a bad omen, that cuckoo today keened away in an elegiac tone that stabbed at our hearts. It flew away, but its echo remains.

June 10:

I don't understand what's happening to us. Some mysterious hand seems to be guiding us. What we've gone through in the last few days! Auntie is sick in bed, one of her hands in a cast, and she has become very depressed. It was a nightmare. The Jews of Rucky's factory are no longer among the living. That includes Froiman's sisters and brothers and Yisroel, and all those friends and acquaintances. Our own lives had hung by a thread and only a miracle saved us. Is it really our destiny to go on suffering and be witnesses to it all?

It all began on June 5. At 12 midnight, Felek gave us a signal to shut ourselves in tight, because there was a commotion in the village. Suddenly, we heard the noise come closer. A few minutes later our cottage was surrounded. We heard Russian spoken. They came into the house and asked where we were. Felek replied that we had taken off long ago, since we had run out of money to pay for our upkeep. He had no idea where we were—probably somewhere in the forests. The cottage began to shake. They ripped open the door of our former hideout, searched everywhere, and began beating Auntie to make her tell our whereabouts. "I don't know, I don't know!" she kept screaming.

Suddenly we hear noise in the dark passage near the ladder leading up to the attic. We're freezing. They're soon searching in the attic. We don't dare to even breathe. Through the cracks we see flashlight beams. It's all over for us!

They stand near our wall, they bang on it, test the planks and search for a door. That went on for several minutes. They're raving and cursing.

They're going down the ladder so it seems. We're still afraid to breathe.

They're in the room below. Auntie starts screeching. We can hear the blows. Later, just behind our wall, outside the house, we hear them appealing to Felek, as a Christian and a Pole, to hand us over to them. They don't want a thing. He can keep all our possessions. All they want to do is shoot us.

When Felek swears that we're not here, they threaten him, shouting: "Traitor! Judas! Aren't you ashamed to save the Jews?!"

After they left, Felek crawled up to the attic. He lay down and didn't say a word. Then he confessed that he'd come up this time to grab us and throw us out. He won't and can't take it anymore. He can't look at his sister Auntie lying there beaten and bloody. With their knives they jabbed at her private parts. He just can't take it any more! So help him, this time he really came up here to grab us by the scruff of the neck and throw us out. But—but he just can't get himself to do it.

He starts stammering and groaning. Each groan tears at our hearts. We don't say a word. Only when he got up to leave did I start talking it over with him. Our conversation made no sense. Eventually, we got around to the rising price of tobacco. With some coins in his hand to buy tobacco, Felek went down the ladder smiling.

Later, I went down to pay Auntie a sick call. She was groaning. I wanted to kiss and comfort her. But she said: "I mustn't pamper myself. The day after tomorrow, Monday, is the 7th, and I have to go to town to bring those Jews here."

My tongue stuck to my palate. I couln't look her in the eyes. I only know that nothing is comprehensible, neither good nor evil. Fate is playing strange games with us.

* * *

On Monday, June 7, before sunrise, Auntie mustered whatever strength she had left, packed some food, said goodbye to us and urged us to pray for her, and set out for Rucky's. The dawn was bright; it was going to be a nice day. In our hideaway we started getting things ready. Froiman awaited his sisters with excitement. Soon the sun lit up our little space. Now we were pleased with the events of last Saturday night, even the visit of the so-called partisans. Now we would have some peace around here; those bandits will probably tell everybody that we aren't at Felek's anymore. We didn't know whether to cry for joy because we had narrowly escaped death, or to be glad over the security of our hideaway. But we saw in the way things had turned out a sign that the new people would get here safely. As was his habit lately, Felek sat on the stone beside the well as he puffed away at a cigarette and gazed blindly into the distance.

Then suddenly, we heard someone groaning, the moans of a woman coming closer and closer to the house. Felek jumped up. Cart wheels creaked. He rushes over to the cart. Now we can clearly hear Auntie groaning. She is brought into the house and place on the bed. I hear a doctor move around, the noise of people, crying. What happened?

A few hours later, when everyone had gone and it was quiet in the house, I went down and found Auntie in bed, her hand in a cast. Smiling gently, she told me that on the way to town, an automobile crashed into the cart in which she was riding. Nobody was hurt, except for her broken arm. She had been in terrible pain. She was taken to the hospital, where her arm was put in a cast. Then they brought her home. But she still worried: "Those poor creatures at the factory. They must be waiting for me. After all, I promised I'd be there today. Now they'll have to wait. But as soon as I'm better I'll go and bring them!"

In the nick of time I heard voices approaching and rushed back to the attic. Peasants were talking around her bed. They had come to pay her a sick call, but they also had some news. We were unable to make out what they said, except that it had something to do with Jews.

Half an hour later, Mrs. Felek poked her head into our hideaway and reported: Last Saturday evening (the night of our latest visit by the "partisans") the last Jews in town, those working at Rucky's factory, were slaughtered.

End of June:

It's one big nightmare—everything that's happened until now. How good it would feel to at last get a good night's sleep and wake up the next morning to find out it had all been only a bad dream.

We often recall what Esther said that terrible Friday night when Szczepanek chased us out of her garden. We fled through the fields, over the corpses scattered in the potato beds. We heard gunfire everywhere; and feeling nothing but the choking wind in our ears and eyes, we kept running in the dark toward the nearest village to a wealthy farmer we know, Kontraktowicz. It was just after midnight. Kontraktowicz was sitting in front of his house listening to the sounds of gunfire that came form town. At the sight of us he crossed himself: "You're still alive?"

He was almost in tears. Soon his entire family, his wife, father-in-law, mother-in-law surrounded us and was begging us tearfully to have mercy on them and go. "Better hide in the forest," they said. "They'll shoot us all yet, and burn our property!"

We stood there speechless. There was nowhere to go. Hundreds of corpses were scattered in the forest. Then my wife begged him to hide us. She offered him half of her mother's property, which he was holding in his safekeeping. She appealed to the friendship that had bound our families over the years. Finally, Kontraktowicz led us cautiously into the garden, sat down on the grass with us, and told us the latest news.

At six in the evening they brought all the Jews to the railroad station. They are being taken to Treblinka to die. The road from the marketplace to the railroad station is littered with corpses and severed limbs, hands, feet, heads; and with blood-stained clothes, hats, shoes, coats. The town looks like a battlefield. Both banks of the river are piled high with corpses—men, women, children, and babies. The Judenrat and the workers from the German labor camps have also been taken away, except, he thinks, for one group. Now they're conducting a house-to-house search. People found hiding are dragged out and shot. They say that tomorrow there's going to be a roundup of Jews in all the neighboring towns and villages.

Esther embraced me, kissed me, and pleaded: "Let's poison ourselves, Leybl, let's poison ourselves! I don't want to be shot by them!"

I calmed her down. We thought then that our families were still alive.

Kontraktowicz later hid us in a haystack in the field. But only after we promised that we'd tell them we had gotten here on our own, without his knowledge, if we were caught. He lay there with us for a while and told us what was happening.

The Jews were all waiting at the loading platform of the railroad station for the freight train to take them to Treblinka. They're squatting as searchlights aim down at them, and they're shot at from every direction. The guards keep dragging out the women and raping them. "Yes," he smiled, "women—girls from age twelve, thirteen, and up. The girls cling to their mothers. They're raped right before their mothers' eyes! The pavement and walls are splattered with the brains of babies. SS men compete with each other to kill the most children the fastest; they pick them up by the feet and smash their heads against the wall.

After he left, Esther again pleaded with me to poison ourselves. We keep remembering her words. Perhaps she is right. We didn't have the courage. We still don't. We want to live. In any condition, to live like a dog, but live!

Yes, we want to live, even under the worst conditions. We grasp for all sorts of reasons to justify our desire to live. Now we tell ourselves that it's our duty to go on living, so that our dead won't be forgotten; only we can truly remember them. Sometimes we seem to hear them commanding us: "Survive, and take revenge. Survive, and tell the world what happened to us, how we suffered and how we died!" At such moments, how we want to live!

Many times, sensing the miracles that keep protecting us, I feel as if I've been selected for some mission, a sacred mission. It seems that we're destined to be among the last witnesses. We must store every detail away in our memories and tell it all to posterity. But perhaps these are only rationalizations for our shameless will to live. We want to live now, when the last Jews of Warsaw and the camps are being incinerated.

That Saturday night a German dog sniffed us out in the haystack where we had been smothering for two nights and a day. I barely managed to escape and make my way through side roads to the Rucky work camp, where a few Jews still remained. When I learned that my mother and little sister had been taken to the marketplace on their way to the railroad station loading platform, I wrung my hands, banged my head against the wall, and howled like a wounded animal. I realized that I would never see them again. "Mama! Miriam!" I screamed in my loneliness. I had a feeling that Dina and Esther, my sisters in Radom, and Meir, my brother in Paris, were also no longer alive. I banged my head against the wall, bit my fingers, threw myself on the ground, and chewed the dirt. I felt like exploding.

Since then I've had no peace. If only I could have seen them for a moment longer, said at least one more word to them, kissed them and even died with them.

Poor Mama! I can imagine your last moments as you led your daughter to her death. Who can avenge your grief? And you, my dear Miriam, I can sense how you felt in the end, trapped and gasping for air. How you wanted to live! Poor child, what did those murderers hold against you, what harm had you done in your innocent young life, why were you so mercilessly cut down?

July 1:

Felek's brother, Janek, is here. He hasn't seen us yet. We see him all the time, through the cracks. Tall, dark, skinny, piercing eyes. Whenever he's in the yard, he looks up at our wall; he moves around as though he feels unseen eyes watching him. Frequently he lies down on the grass beside the well with Felek and Auntie, and the three of them talk. They smile and speak nervously. Is he plotting against us? Or is he upset that nothing has come of the plan for a hideaway at his place for our people from Rucky's metalworks? He's probably jealous of Felek because of the suede suit we made him.

The suit! It may be our downfall. We beg Felek not to wear it in the village. The other peasants know very well that Felek couldn't have bought that suit out of his own income. Every Sunday he decks himself out in the checked brown suede suit and the partly silk shirt we made him, and goes strutting off to the village, to church, happy as a child. He knows that it might be the death of him. In any case he has already raised the eyebrows of all the villagers by his new lifestyle

Shortly after we arrived here, we asked him to go to the village to buy bread. At that time he refused, arguing that he can buy bread only in town, where he isn't known. Here in the village, everybody knows that he doesn't have the money to buy bread, and it might raise suspicions that he's hiding Jews. We were pleased that he was so cautious.

Now? The whole village is murmuring that in Felek's house they eat wheat dumplings fried in fat every day. Whenever some peasant would like a good meal, he just happens to drop in at Felek's house at lunchtime and he's promptly invited to have a bite. What's more, this spring Felek hired someone to plow and sow his field. And now he's planning to hire a person to reap the hay and, later, to harvest the crops. Yet, it doesn't help when we tell him that a good meal is nobody else's business. Felek knows that he's endangering his life. He knows that the disaster with the "partisans" was a result of reports about the good life at Felek's. We know that people are talking in the village, and that all their guessing leads to one assumption: it all comes from the Jews. I don't want to talk against Auntie, but every day she parades about in the new dress we made her. We can't restrain her enthusiasm.

She's also wearing new dresses that didn't come from us. Esther and Zippora know that they're made from material which their mother gave for safekeeping to Kontraktowicz and other Poles, and which we've asked her to pick up for us. We've long suspected that she was bringing us only a small portion of the goods handed over by those Poles. In spite of the fact that we don't use any of the things ourselves, it all goes for the upkeep of the house.

We wouldn't mind, but we're afraid that one fine day, when the materials run out, and there isn't any more to send for, they'll throw us out, or worse! We have to make sure that they don't use up all the material at once, that enough is left to whet their appetites.

July 9:

Janek is drunk most of the time. He spends every day drinking with a different gang, and generously picks up the tab. For the past two days he's been wearing a sharp new suit that gives him the look of a city person. He travels around the villages selling all kinds of goods. Auntie says that someone in town gives him goods on consignment, and he sells them for a commission. We pretend to believe her, and we even give him things of ours to sell. In exchange he buys food for us: flour, buckwheat, and potatoes. We also got Felek to let Janek do some of the household shopping; this way, people will think that Janek is buying commodities for re-sale for his trade in the villages. Everyone in the village knows that each week bread is baked at Felek's, while the other peasants bake only once in four or even six weeks. We got them to do the baking in the middle of the night, but only for a while. Now they're baking again in broad daylight, and peasants and their wives come to watch and spread the word.

July 14:

With every passing day it's becoming clearer that Janek and Auntie are playing games with us. And now we also know how my brother-in-law Chaim died. We soon understood the cause of his death; only we didn't want to believe it. It was shortly after we came here from Auntie's place in Minsk. Esther's twenty-year-old brother Chaim was at the other camp in town. He was supposed to come here with us.

The night before we were to leave I went to get him. He wasn't able to leave just then; but he begged us to go, because things were too active in our camp and his camp was relatively quiet. He would join us in a few days. At that time, we weren't sure whether Felek would take us in. If he did, Auntie promised that she would go to fetch Chaim. And sure enough, the day after we got to Felek's, she went to Minsk. We waited and waited—for two whole weeks we waited—until she showed up one evening alone, with some letters from Chaim. She hadn't even seen him; someone had brought her the letters. She apologized to us for the delay: someone had broken into her place in Minsk and stolen the material we had left there; she had been too ashamed to tell us about it. It so happened that she wore a new dress and kerchief made from that material. Yet we had no choice but to believe her. She had neglected Chaim, but we couldn't afford to indulge our suspicions. Besides, we had no time for that. In his letters, Chaim called for help. He was no longer at the camp in Minsk. They had all been driven to Kaluszyn, to a fenced-in field packed with thousands of people from dozens of camps. We had to save him before it was too late. He couldn't hold out much longer, he wrote. All of them had been stripped of their shoes and warm clothing. It rained all the time; they were sleeping in the mud under the driving rain, and the worms were chewing them up.

Auntie said she was tired and it was late, but first thing in the morning she would go to Kaluszyn and bring Chaim back.

That night we lay awake shivering in the pile of hay in the attic. Outside, the wind howled, ripping shreds from the straw roof and nearly blowing away the entire cottage. The wind seemed to sob and wail. Terrified, we dug into the hay. We kept seeing Kaluszyn: the black night in the open field, the naked people whipped by the wind, cold, rain. The night seemed to drag on forever, and the wind kept howling. At dawn, I heard knocking at the cottage door. Some peasants brought the news that during the night, all the Jews rounded up in Kaluszyn were loaded on freight trains: hundreds of corpses were left on the barbed-wire fence, in the fields, and on the roads.

We had missed by just one day! Now we know, Chaim: You died on account of a stupid bit of cloth. We can see you searching for help, looking out for our messenger.

* * *

But that bit of cloth is keeping us alive. I hope we won't lose our lives because of it.

From time to time we send notes to those Christians who are holding our goods in safekeeping. We tell them that we're in the forests with the partisans, so that they, our Christian acquaintances, will be afraid of us. There were quite a few incidents lately in which messengers coming to collect things for Jews were turned over to the police, who tortured them until they revealed the Jewish hiding places. So we write that we're roving the forest with the partisans. And each time Auntie mails our letters from a different town. Our scheme seems to be working, for each time Auntie is sent out to fetch some cloth, she receives a small package. She always tells them that we meet in different spots, that she has no idea where we are, and that we're heavily armed.

Some of them really seem to believe her, and are afraid that if we are harmed our fellow partisans will take revenge against them. Others throw Auntie out and tell her that they'll hand her over to the Germans if she dares show up again.

So we really worry each time Auntie goes to town, and we're at our wits' end until she returns. Many times she doesn't return the same day, and we're sure it's all over with us, that she's been caught, and that they're on their way to get us.

When she gets back the next day, she's always a little drunk. We make sure to say our prayers.

July 16:
Today we met Janek. He came up to the attic, knocked on our little door, and greeted us as if we were old acquaintances. At the sight of our hideaway, he grabbed himself by the head and exclaimed: "Jesus! How can you live here?!"

He gazed at the moldy straw on the floor, the dusty, cobwebbed walls, our rags, and ghostly pale faces.

Soon he calmed down, however, and came to the conclusion that we were paying for the sin our ancestors committed thousands of years ago. "Yes, that's your destiny! Maybe you're personally not to blame, but the Lord takes revenge forever. Besides—well, maybe you're good Jews, but the others—"

He started talking about Jews who got caught, and how ungrateful they are: they always betray the people who hide them.

Then he pulled some illustrated pamphlets out of his pockets. They were being distributed throughout the countryside. The drawings depict Jews crucifying Jesus and burning the Host. One of them shows a mob slaughtering Jews in the streets in revenge. Each illustration has a caption calling for the death of the Jews, "the enemies of God and the people."

I explain to him that it's all German propaganda printed in Polish. He laughs and tells me to stop talking nonsense. Why, he remembers that in 1920 Jews shot at Polish soldiers. And the Jews even use the blood of Christian children to bake matzos.

While Janek was talking, Felek crawled in to the hideaway, sat down, and listened. He smiled all the while and didn't interrupt. But after Janek repeated that the Jews had crucified Christ, he smiled again and said: "So if he's God, why did he let himself be killed?"

Janek started down out of the attic, and Felek began to speculate: "I don't know whether all those stories are true. But there must be some truth in them! I really don't know. What do you think?"

After all, Felek is a practicing Christian, goes to church regularly, and loves the priest.

Once, after a bitter argument between his sister, Auntie, and his wife, Felek came up to us very gloomy. He told us he had decided to hang himself, because he couldn't take the two women any more. They're driving him insane with their endless quarreling.

It's been this way since we came here. They're constantly at each other. Mrs. Felek already threatened a number of times to report us to the police if we don't control Auntie. When we talked it over with Auntie, she told us to have no fear—her sister-in-law was only threatening. Besides, she, Auntie, wasn't to blame; it was all Mrs. Felek's fault. The same scene repeats itself every few days.

Felek says he can't take it anymore. They're both to blame. They're both constant agitators, and he's helplessly caught between them.

He confides in us that he's planning to tell the whole story, about us, also, to the priest. "He won't tell a soul," Felek assures us.

We plead with him not to do that. But he insists. What's more, we can't tell him why we're afraid of the priest. We've been telling him all along that only faithless mobs kill Jews, while intelligent, religious people secretly help them. "So why are you afraid of the priest?" Felek asks.

We pleaded and argued with him until I had an inspiration. I told Felek that priests don't want to know about such secrets, and they only become angry with those persons who confess them; they themselves are afraid of being reported to the Germans. Still, I said, the priests secretly bless people who hide Jews. Didn't Felek's own priest give us all his Christmas blessings right in this very house?

Felek broke into a big smile. He was satisfied. He wouldn't go to the priest. But he was going to hang himself. Absolutely!

July 18:
Esther is the only of us whom Auntie can't bear. She imagines, for no good reason, that Esther has a low opinion of her. And God forbid that she should find Esther sitting beside me. When Auntie finds me sitting between the men, Ephraim and Froiman, she's delighted, she tells them to move over, and sits down next to me.

The first few times that she found Esther sitting beside me, she scolded and scolded us for having sleepy eyes, and left in a huff, without so much a "Goodbye." Now, we avoid sitting together; instead, the men sit between Esther and me.

On the other hand, Felek seems to have taken a dislike to me. It began when he started to visit us after dark and sit down beside Esther. He sits there a while, until, it seems, he is overcome by certain emotions—and then, Esther suddenly must tell me something and she comes to my side. Felek sits there moodily for a few minutes and then leaves. Afterwards, we sense his mute resentment of me, and we're certain that no good will come of it, just as no good can come of Auntie's loyalty to me.

Esther hasn't been well lately. She was running a fever. We didn't dare let Auntie find out; she'd have stopped bringing up the daily bottle of black coffee I asked for to quench my thirst.

But our thirst has cost us dearly. A heat wave is raging, and here in the attic the heat is unbearable. From drinking cold water, Froiman caught cold and coughs constantly. We're afraid that they'll hear him. He buries his head in the hay to stifle the cough, but that only makes things worse. So he drinks more water, to weaken the cough, until he's coughing and choking once more.

Several times I refused to give him water, and I refused Ephraim too. But they complained that I was dictatorial, and I had to give in. Now we have constant coughing up here day and night. They bury their heads in the quilts, but the noise carries. Who knows whether they're not talking about it in the village? Our fears keep us awake at night; with each cough, we hold our breaths.

The days are long. Each day drags like an eternity. In the morning we wake up in a fright. Outside, the sun is shining. Everything looks fresh and peaceful. The fields wear a bright green smile. The nearby woods seem to issue a call to life. People, refreshed, calm, walk leisurely, drowsily to work their fields. Our heads ache from the stuffy hole; the closeness makes our temples pound. We feel all dried up. There's no space, so we curl up together. Our limbs ache from the hardness of the attic boards. Although we change the straw many times, it's soon ground to bits under us. At first, it feels like threshed hay; then it's more like a dung heap swarming with fleas and bugs. Our clothes are torn and decayed. And the sloping straw roof, moldy and damp, closes in on us. The two walls, thin as funeral boards, are covered with cobwebs. Our limbs seem to be twisted into immobility; will we ever be able to stretch them again. Our hair is disheveled, gray with dust and dirt, our faces pale and drawn. Dark blue cavities engulf our piercing eyes. We try to yawn into our palms. Our hearts pound harder and harder all the time. But the day drags on endlessly.

Below, the house is stirring. Strange voices. We put our ears to the floorboards. What are they buzzing about? What's happened? They stay around a long while. By the time they leave, the sun is high. Auntie hands us two bottles of water, for washing and for the day's drinking. We're about to wash, when someone comes into the house. More news. We wait. When they leave, we wipe our eyes with our fingers and hand down the pail of dirty water. Felek rushes out to see if anyone is coming. Meanwhile, Auntie spills the dirty water into a pit behind the stable and cover it up with dirt. Mrs. Felek brings us a loaf of bread and a bottle of coffee.

By noon the sun pierces the cracks in the attic wall, and singes our flesh. We inhale puffs of dust that stick in our throats. The still wet hay on the outer side of the attic wall gives off a sharp odor that makes our eyes tear. The heat is becoming unbearable. We sweat for hours, until Auntie hands us a fresh kettle of water. Our throats are parched and we're choking. Felek warns us to be careful. Police have arrived in the village. We stuff rags into the cracks between partition and attic. Down below, peasants are coming and going. They tell about Jews who were caught, by chance, during a hunt for unregistered hogs. Through the cracks of the outer wall we can see the paths leading to the village. Everyone coming this way seems to be wearing a green police uniform; any moment now, polished jackboots will be stamping about. We hear motors whistling. Our hearts are pounding. But it wasn't anything!

Time seems to stand still. Auntie sends up a pot of cooked food. Our hole fills with steam, and our eyes mist over. The liquid in the pot is still bubbling. Big half-raw oat dumplings float inside. They stick to the gums and palate and are impossible to swallow. We sit around the pot and our disheveled hair gets stuck in the cobwebs that cling to the straw roof. We work hard with our spoons. Gradually the food disappears.

Soon someone moves the pot aside. His stomach is turning. He grabs the pail, bends over it, and groans; he's drenched in sweat and his eyes bulge. Another person's stomach begins to churn. The pail is passed along quickly. Somebody else is becoming even sicker. The person on guard keeps an eye on the crack, shakes back and forth, and pleads: "Hurry! Hurry!"

Mrs. Felek comes up to retrieve her pot. She asks if we enjoyed the meal, and is pleased to hear that it was excellent. "It's very hot today!" she says, as she grabs the full pail and warns us to be careful; the night is a long way off, and the German swine may yet show up.

Before we shut our little door, Mrs. Felek, holding both pot and pail in her hands, mentions the bad dream that her neighbor, Mrs. Rechniakow, had told her just this morning: our cottage was surrounded by police and heads were flying. "Very bad," said Mrs. Felek.

We smile bitterly. She winces, lets out a sigh, and disappears. We're shaken. Never mind the dream! Was Mrs. Rechniakow hinting that she knew something?

The sun moved along to the west, casting shadows our ways. It's turned chilly, and we're shivering. Our teeth chatter. The shadows engulf us as we inhale some fresh air that seeps in through the cracks.

"Another day nearly safely over, thank God," someone murmurs.

We each take a deep breath. We have no strength left. We lean our heads against the sloping straw roof. It's quiet. The deep shadows swallow us until we fade into the darkness. Our bodies are heavy and sluggish, like corpses. Someone starts snoring. Another long and dreadful day lies ahead.

* * *

Yes, I've talked it out of me a little, even if only on paper. It seems to provide some relief.

I've asked Janek to bury my writings somewhere in the village, in earthen vessels. If the worst happens, he should hand all of this material over to Jews after the war. I've assured him that he'll earn a fortune, and he's agreed to do it.

July 20:
There's some action at the front, and a bit of hope creeps into our hearts. Ever since Stalingrad, "their" end is clear, their downfall approaching. However long it may take, their miserable end is certain. May we only live to witness it!

July 22:
Konyak is back. I haven't mentioned him yet. For the past several weeks, a Jewish boy of about sixteen has been prowling around in the neighborhood. The peasants call him Konyak, after his father. He is the son of Khone, the Kaluszyn tailor, who used to do sewing and patching for the peasants.

He was here for the first time a few weeks ago. One morning we heard Auntie and Felek talking in the kitchen with a stranger. Frightened, we listened very closely, then calmed down. It was a boyish voice. We didn't know who he was. When Auntie asked him if he prayed to the Lord to keep him alive, he answered: "No, I've stopped praying. Our God doesn't listen to our prayers anymore." He sat in the kitchen for a while. He had aroused our curiosity, and we pressed against the cracks in the wall waiting to catch a glimpse of him.

Finally he left. He passed under our wall and remained standing there: tall, gaunt, pale-faced, with dark, misty eyes. He was wrapped in rags. A torn shoe on one foot, and on the other an old oversized boot tied with rope. Like a cornered animal he glanced in all directions, extended a foot, and then drew it back.

We were bursting with frustration. There he is, on the other side of the wall, just a few steps from us. If only we could have a word with him. If only he knew we were here.

He vanished into the nearby woods. Later, the peasants told all sorts of stories about him. We learned that only a few evenings ago the Wiszniew village headman got hold of him, and locked him in a stable, posted four peasants to guard him through the night, and first thing in the morning called the police. When the police opened the stable, it was empty. It seems that several boards in the roof were missing. The police whipped the four watchmen for their negligence, and the angry headman ordered a manhunt. The villagers caught another Jew, who had strayed into the neighborhood, and locked him up in the bakery. But when the police came to get him, they found him dead; he was hanging by his suspenders.

The village headman is furious. When he caught another Jew, he made sure to remove his suspenders, belt, and shoelaces. But the man slipped right through his hands. Now the headman plans to vent all his fury on Konyak. With the help of the regional governor, he got an order out for Konyak's arrest. This time he's handing him over to the Germans alive. The peasants have already staged several manhunts in the vicinity. But no Konyak.

We've spoken to Felek about saving him. But he insists that even our own days numbered. He finds all kinds of excuses for doing nothing. Our place is crowded enough as it is. The other day he even drove Konyak away from the door. Later, he explained that they might find us, too, when they come looking for him. We asked Auntie to think of something.

Today she hid him in Janek's barn, deep in the hay. When nobody's watching, she brings him food that we've stashed away in the attic.

July 25:

The last few days Felek has been depressed again. Once more he sits on the rock by the well puffing away at his cigarettes. They must be talking about us in the village again. Felek is full of secrets. We've known about Felek's inner struggle since January, when we were still behind the false wall in the house.

It was a frosty evening. The window panes were thickly coated with ice. Nobody outside could see into the house. We took advantage of that to warm ourselves around the stove. No lamp had been lit, and the room was dark except for the glow cast by the firelit oven on the walls and ceiling. Felek entertained us with funny peasant anecdotes and stories. The women were in the kitchen making supper.

There was a knock at the door. Quickly we crawled into the hideaway. Mrs. Felek opened the door and in came Maczuszak's son-in-law, Paltyn. He had been sent to Germany as a slave laborer and had escaped a few days ago. He told how the German women were mad about foreign men, especially Frenchmen, and submitted to them at once. He spoke in a loud voice, and Felek and the women laughed.

Later, after the women returned to the kitchen, his voice dropped to a whisper. He suggested that Felek and he do a little "night job" at a certain farmer's potato bin in a nearby village.

Felek stammered something and tried to hush him. But Paltyn pressed on: "We'll work quietly. Come on, I don't have a single potato left at home!"

They went out into the yard, where they whispered for a while. When Paltyn left, Felek returned to the house and murmured to the women: "I'm not going! May the Lord punish me if I go on a job today!"

"What did you tell him?" Auntie asked.

"I said that my foot hurts and they'd hear us."

A few days later Paltyn came back with the same proposition. But Felek complained that he had a stomach ache. Paltyn kept coming back, and so did Szudek, Logidzak, Odrobinszczak, and other peasants.

Recently, Auntie lamented that Felek had been out on "jobs" several times. "He has to, because otherwise," she explained, "they'll start wondering what he's living on. But that Felek's a fool. I have to keep pushing him, he doesn't want to go. Without him they don't know what to do. Although he's blind, he works better than the whole lot of them."

Felek has found out that we know about his work; so, he's stopped pretending with us. He's even telling us about his "jobs." He's been in and out of prison many times over the years. Practically every time there's a big "job" somewhere, the police come to search him as the most likely suspect. "It's bad either way," he explains. "If I don't steal, the boys will start suspecting. If I do steal, the Lord will have it in for me: stealing when I've got plenty to eat! Besides, the police will come here for sure!"

So Felek shuffles around deep in his moody thoughts. "No," he says, "we won't survive."

But we have a feeling that something else is really bothering him. We don't know what it is, but we feel it has something to do with the village—and with us.

* * *

We relaxed a bit: Mariszka and Garwolinski were shipped off to Germany in the latest labor transport.

Mariszka, Felek's cousin, is a chubby peasant girl with rosy cheeks and squinting eyes. She's the one who stole peat from Felek's barn every time she came to visit. She used to come here every day and sit for hours waiting for Garwolinski, Felek's crony from Wulke. Garwolinski has a wife and children, and also a mother-in-law, a real devil, Mrs. Danielov. He used to have trysts with Mariszka here at Felek's.

He discovered us shortly after we got here.

One evening, before our partition hideaway was ready, we were sitting downstairs in the dark. Suddenly, the door between the kitchen and the other room swung open, and he stood there. I quickly turned to the window, to block his view of my face, and I blocked the others with my body. He quickly withdrew, shut the door, and left without a word. Felek assured us that Garwolinski wouldn't inform, that he was "one of our boys." We stayed up all night wondering what to do. We decided that Felek would "confide" in Garwolinski that he had been visited by a suspicious character who spoke both in Russian and in some queer language, undoubtedly a partisan. The visitor, Felek would say, had slept over and left before dawn.

The following morning, we overheard Felek give Garwolinski that explanation. "He's a sharp one, that fellow. I knew it as soon as he turned around to the window," said Garwolinski. And he really didn't tell anyone.

Two days later the whole village was aroused: there are Kikes in Felek's house. Mrs. Szudek had passed by in the morning, looked in through the window, and seen curly Jewish heads. That evening the village headman came to warn Felek. We worked all night putting up the partition. Hiding behind it for several days, we left all the doors and windows wide open, for all to see that there were no strangers in the house. Curious peasant men and women came by and looked in. That went on for a few days.

Later, we had a reliable witness. Mariszka told everyone that she spent whole days in the house and saw nothing suspicious.

It was Christmas eve. Garwolinski and Mariszka decided to celebrate "the Lord's birthday" in Felek's home. The tables were to set right by our wall. At the proper time, we went up into the attic and lay down on the hay. Felek told us not to budge, because any sound upstairs is heard downstairs.

After dark the guests came and the banquet began. Dishes clattered and glasses clinked. The "Nine Delicacies" went on for hours.

At about midnight, they were all drunk. Garwolinski gaily sang Christmas carols and Mariszka laughed lustily. Gradually the rest of the company dozed off; but we can overhear Garwolinski asking Mariszka to go up to the attic and lie in the hay for a while. We shivered.

I thought for a moment, then I crawled away, and a minute later handed the others some poles.

"What's that?"

"The ladder."

When Garwolinski led Mariszka to the hallway beneath the attic, they just stood there gaping. There was no way for them to climb up.

When I told Felek about it in the morning, he slapped me heartily on the back and complimented me for the quick thinking which had saved us; it meant that I was "one of the boys," an expert, he said.

* * *

Whenever they talked about us in the village, we found out about it from Mariszka. She always reported the discussions and laughed at the "blockheads" who suspected there were Jews here. Since she left, we no longer learn the village gossip.

The other day Staszko, chatting in the kitchen with Auntie, Felek, and Mrs. Felek, flung open the door to the main room and humorously shouted: "Out, damned Jews!"

Everybody laughed. But clearly Staszko hadn't meant it as a joke. He was sure he was about to catch some Kikes.

A while ago the village headman told Felek that Staszko keeps warning him that Felek is hiding Jews, and that the whole village would yet burn as a result. But the headman assured him that only Felek was in danger. Still, Staszko continues to agitate, and whenever he comes around he snoops in the kitchen to see how much food, for how many people, is being cooked.

But we openly cook as much as we please, in a big pot, and ignore him. Froiman suggested adding potato peels to the pot to make it seem we're cooking for the livestock. So whenever Staszko lifts the lid of the pot, he's disappointed: he sees potato peels for the cow.

July 27:

Today Felek rushed home from the village full of news, and came right up to us in the attic. He said he had just been to his cousin, Jozef Guczak, a cobbler, and had found him making a pair of soles "with the Jewish God." I didn't understand.

Felek raised his eyebrows at me: "You don't understand? With the Jewish God! From the scrolls. Jozef says that the parchment is very strong and lasts longer than leather."

Felek told Jozef that he couldn't do such a thing. True, it's Jewish, but still a God. Jozef cursed him and they quarreled. Now he was afraid that in the village they would say he had defended "the Kike God."

We explain that it isn't the Jewish God but the sacred scriptures, a Torah scroll, containing the Ten Commandments that say, "Thou shalt not murder." Now Felek understood why they were tearing it up. "They don't want to be told that," he said.

He left the attic, and I could imagine burning Jews and burning Torah scrolls. Rabbi Hanina ben Teradyon, and Moyshele, Chava's son, leaping into the flames of the Kopernik building in Minsk holding the Torah scroll.

They're burning the Jews together with the book. But, as in the case of Rabbi Hanina, "the scrolls burn but the words hover poignantly in the air." The words of the command, "Thou shalt not murder," linger on.

July 30:

For the past few days a suspicious character has been coming here each evening, and he and Felek spend quite a few hours sitting on the grass near the oak wood opposite our cottage. We don't know what he looks like, since it's dark and we can only see his silhouette. They whisper and gesture to each other.

Today Felek told us what it's all about. The visitor is a bandit chieftain. He has organized some groups of bandit partisans, and he wants Felek's help. While talking to me, Felek removed something wrapped in a rag from his pocket and handed it to me. I unwrapped it: a revolver and a clip of bullets. "It'll come in handy," Felek said. "Only don't use it to 'thank' me, they say that's how Jews thank people."

The bandit had given him the gun. Before that, Felek brought us a dagger that had been buried in the ground. He said we ought to be ready: if the Germans catch us, we should kill at least one of them. He'll help us. He told us that he had hidden a few weapons in the ground near his farmyard. "It'll come in handy. I can let you in on all the secrets. After all, you won't tell anyone, will you!" He laughed.

When he left the attic, we examined the gun and said a prayer.

August 3:

It seems that Felek was right about his days being numbered. He is no longer among the living! On July 29, Felek was out in the yard until very late at night, refusing to go to sleep. He sat on the grass outside our wall with his brother-in-law, Zhelenski, a wealthy farmer who was guarding his harvested crops in the field that night. It was a hot, humid night. They sat in their undershirts, talking about the Jews. Every few minutes Zhelenski got up, ran to check his piles of harvested produce, then ran back to finish his statement: ". . . Absolutely not! Helping bandits is a crime! In fact, they should all be killed."

But Felek insisted that when the Lord said "Thou shalt not murder," He meant all people. I know one thing: 'Thou shalt not murder,' If they were all meant to be killed, why didn't our ancestors do the job? Why must it be our job?"

Zhelenski retorted that Felek was an oddball, and an ignoramus to boot. "Didn't the Jews kill Our Lord?"

It was after midnight when Janek showed up. Zhelenski took off for the field and Janek asked about us. He said that Zhelenski is right. Felek got angry, stood up, and walked away. After he got into bed, we heard him say to himself: "The Lord said, 'Thou shalt not murder,' and that's it!"

At 5:30 in the morning, Ephraim, who was guarding, woke us up. His face was pale. "Police!" he barely gasped.

I peeked through the crack. The yard was full of local police, Polish police, and Russian soldiers from General Vlasov's army. We were surrounded. Just behind our wall stood several Mongols in German uniforms and helmets, their guns ready to fire. Below us in the house, they were searching and shouting orders.

We grabbed our quilts and stuffed the cracks between our wall and the attic, so that no light could enter. A few minutes later, we hear heavy treads on the ladder. We all embrace. Esther strokes my hands: "Leybl!"

"Let's say Confession!"

"*Shma Yisroel*—Hear, O Israel! . . ."

Ephraim and Froiman are pale as ghosts. Then Ephraim starts shaking, first his lips, and then the rest of him. He begins to convulse. I can feel my blood congeal, my heart pound. Through a crack I catch sight of the oak wood. "In another minute they'll shoot us there."

Esther and Zippora want to get dressed. They don't want to be led out half naked. But I don't let them budge.

"This is it, people. We have to share the fate of all the others: parents, sisters and brothers, all the Jews." I feel as if I'm going to burst.

One more minute! One more minute! The words spin in my mind.

"Hush, children. *Shma Yisroel!*"

There are some men in the attic. They're turning everything inside out. They're banging on our wall. We all embrace, hold our breaths. Fingernails dig into my flesh.

"*Shma Yisroel! . . .*"

A minute later they all left the attic. Once more we hear gruff voices in the cottage below. Now the voices are out in the yard Suddenly we see Felek, wearing the velvet suit, being led in chains past our wall.

"Till we meet again," he murmured as though to himself.

We sat there several hours not knowing what to do. Should we run away? Auntie isn't here, and Mrs. Felek drifts around like a ghost. We don't know what's happened or why Felek was taken away.

Mrs. Felek comes up to us. She has no idea either. He's been taken for questioning, but she doesn't know whether it has anything to do with us.

We think it might be related to the recent visits of that bandit. Could he have been an instigator? If that's the case, they'll soon come looking for the gun!

Janek's barn was searched, too. Luckily Konyak ran away last night; Janek had come back, and he was afraid to stay. They also wanted to arrest Janek, but let him go at the last minute.

What should we do? We're afraid that Felek might break under questioning and tell all. Esther says we should run away right now. The others don't know what to say.

Suddenly, a scream and wailing in the yard. Auntie runs in, wringing her hands and crying: "Woe is me! Felek! Woe is me! Felek!"

They've shot him in the next village.

Later, Felek was brought home in a cart. He lay there in his bloodsoaked suede suit. They laid him down on the grass beside the rock next to the wall. Peasants hurried by too frightened to stop. Auntie and Janek ran to the village for the death certificate. Mrs. Felek drifted around aimlessly, weeping and wailing. The village was silent. Not a soul was in sight. It seemed that everything had died. Only terror remained.

A few hours later Auntie and Janek returned with a long coffin on a wagon, accompanied by two peasants. The peasants lifted Felek like a sack of flour, put him into the coffin, and quickly rode off with him. Mrs. Felek, Auntie, and Janek followed on foot behind the cart, and chanted dirges. The five of us burst out crying.

* * *

Already rumors are flying in the village about Felek's death. At first, they said he had been shot for hiding Jews. But the headman denied that; he was right there when the police were searching, and no Jews were found at Felek's.

He was probably shot as a robber. The Germans are wiping out robbers and bandits for collaborating with the partisans.

We sit and count our miracles. Another miracle occurred when those fake partisans discovered our hideaway, and we had to move to the attic. Otherwise, this morning the police would have found us sleeping downstairs.

Perhaps now there will be an end to the rumors about Jews hiding in Felek's house. Still, something undefinably heavy hangs over the house, something that bodes no good.

Late August:
An oppressive stillness inhabits our cottage since Felek's death. Everything here—the oak wood, the field, the stable—seems to know what happened and to have sunk into mourning. The scattered houses in the neighborhood gaze with menace in our direction, looking smaller than before. They seem to be hiding behind their fences like frightened creatures, and their looks are secretive and threatening. The neighbors seldom show themselves, and then only for a few minutes; averting their eyes and quickly vanishing inside. Neighbors sneak in to visit each other, and sit together for hours; they seem to be

hatching plots and, at the same time, cowering in fear.

The deadly silence doesn't cease. Then, one afternoon, Mrs. Felek opens her door, goes out, stands on the threshold staring, and suddenly bursts into a shrill cry that pierces the air. She weeps like a baby, into space. But the silence seems to deepen, the distant cottages shrink and seem to sink into the ground. Eyes peer out from window panes and quickly withdraw in fright.

Mrs. Felek sits down on the rock beside the well, buries her face in her hands, and starts moaning; she stops for a moment, then starts wailing even louder. She continues to sob, pant, and cry that way for several hours. Then, when she's tired, she gets up, wipes her eyes with her blue apron and shuffles back into the house.

It's quiet again outside, until about dusk. The sun begins to set. In the distance we can see barefooted peasants coming home from the fields. The men are wearing floppy hats and dark shirts that hang out over shrunken trousers; their scythes are slung over their shoulders. Peasant women in white kerchiefs are carrying baskets; boys driving cattle home from pasture play tunes on their wooden fifes.

Auntie comes into the yard, observes the scene, and cries out suddenly in a broken voice: "Felek, Felek! Come home! Everybody's going home. You've worked long enough. Supper is ready, potatoes and cabbage. Fe-lek!"

Her words, accompanied by a sobbing wail, frighten the peasants, and they hurry along till they vanish in the dark. But she stands there a while and cries out:

"Fe-e-lek! Fe-e-lek!"

Something stirs among the trees. And it seems as if any moment he will appear, Felek. He'll float out of nowhere and eat the potatoes and cabbage.

Night descends upon the village. The huts scattered in the fields seem to wink at each other in conspiracy; candles flicker in their windows. Auntie is still calling: "Felek, Fe-e-lek! Felek, it's dark! Why are you still in the field? Come home! Come, let's light a fire in our house, too."

We hear someone creeping around in the attic in the dark. There's a soft knock at our door. Mrs. Felek asks us to open up. She drags herself into our hideaway and sits down, but doesn't say a word. We are also silent. She sits that way for a while, all choked up. Outside, Auntie, sensing that Mrs. Felek is up in the attic with us, calls out even louder, more nervously: "Felek! Fe-e-le-ek!" And she weeps into the darkness.

In the village dogs are barking, and an owl begins to hoot. Mrs. Felek starts up, listens, and trembles, calling out: "Death, oh death! He's knocking at our door again!"

But Auntie will bring us an even greater catastrophe, she seems to be saying to herself. Felek may yet take revenge on us. Ghosts don't like it when you call them, when you don't let them rest in their graves. "Woe, she'll be the end of us yet! Yes, that's what the owl was just saying!"

Meanwhile, Auntie has crawled up to us and sat down. Mrs. Felek becomes quiet. Auntie is silent, too. It goes on that way for several minutes, until we hear shuffling in the attic. We're not as cramped as before. We grope about with our hands, sure enough, Mrs. Felek is gone. Auntie lets out a deep sigh from the bottom of her heart. Suddenly she starts crying: "Fe-lek! Fe-lek!"

She stretches out in a corner, hiccoughing. Then, sitting up with a start, she says that no one is to blame for Felek's death, no one but his wife, that is. She drove him out of this world. No one but she. She tormented him to death!

* * *

Mrs. Felek keeps issuing dire prophecies. She tells us her bad dreams. Once she plainly saw a torn shoe. And didn't old Maczejowa see torn shoes in her dreams for several nights before she passed away? Mrs. Felek also had visions of a dead pig and of her sainted uncle Waclaw.

We try to explain that this is all superstition, but Mrs. Felek gets angry and calls us unbelievers. She reminds us about Mrs. Rechniakow's dream a few weeks before Felek died: police encircling our cottage and heads flying. Well, hadn't she foreseen Felek's end? And Mrs. Rechniakow had a similar dream just a few days ago. She confided in Mrs. Felek that she had seen heads flying around our cottage.

I tell Mrs. Felek that they might have been hens' heads. A hawk may yet rip off the heads of a few hens. She seems to accept my explanation, and starts mourning the fate of "those poor hens," precious, quiet creatures; it's such a pleasure, the way they're laying eggs!

* * *

The conflict between the two women gets more serious every day. At first, after Felek's death, they didn't talk to each other. Now, they're always trying to spite each other, and their shouting bouts are heard all over the village.

Mrs. Felek accuses Auntie of stealing eggs and butter, and helping herself to sour cream from the jug. She says that it's all our fault: if not for us she would have thrown the old witch out long ago. Let her go back to her whore business in town! She, Mrs. Felek, can't take it any more. Either we send Auntie away or leave together with her.

I beg her not to make a fuss, and tell her that I'll pay for anything that's missing. But it isn't so much the eggs, butter, and sour cream that bother her; she just can't stand a thief and a spiteful person in her house. We've already told Auntie that she must be more careful with her sister-in-law. But she says it's not her fault; "that one" is always starting with her.

The last time that Mrs. Felek accused Auntie of stealing, I begged Auntie to do something about it. But she let me have it: "Juzek, do you really believe that I'm stealing?"

"Of course not," I said. "We all know it's a lie. But just to prove to her that she's only imagining things. we'll give you the money to buy butter, eggs, and whatever else you need, so that there's plenty of everything in the house, and she'll see for herself that—"

Auntie laughs and protests: "You know me, Juzek. Do I need butter and eggs? I don't need any money or delicacies! What we need is bread; there must always be plenty of bread!"

* * *

Indeed, since Felek's death the bread situation hasn't been so good. Even though they've been baking twenty inches of bread a week, we always go without bread a few days each week. Auntie says that Mrs Felek steals bread for her cronies, and Mrs. Felek insists that Janek is taking bread home with him.

Janek has become bossy lately. From time to time he comes up and hands me bills. The expenses have almost doubled since Felek's death, and the food is worse than ever. Auntie says that under no circumstances will she cook for Mrs. Felek, and she stays away from the stove for days. She goes off with Janek for hours. When she gets back, she comes up to the attic and smacks her lips. But Mrs. Felek won't cook for "that whore." So every day she cooks just enough for herself; when she's finished eating she curses Auntie in front of us: "That old witch—stuffing herself at Janek's and letting you starve!"

Mrs. Felek curses Auntie, "that witch," of robbing her, embittering her life, and spiting her in every way. Then she cries and cries until she comes to the conclusion that it's all our fault. What does she get out of slaving for us? "That one is robbing you and having a good time with Janek. What am I getting out of it?"

Suddenly she remembers that she's running out of hay for the cow, and she starts to complain. We seize the opportunity; she gets money for fodder; and we all agree to keep it a secret. "That old witch mustn't hear a word about it!"

* * *

The harvest is in full swing. The entire village is hard at work. Fields only yesterday full of corn and wheat are now stripped bare. It makes me melancholy: Another summer nearly gone, and we—

All day long busy peasants labor in the fields. They swing their long scythes, and stalks topple like fallen soldiers. Women tie up the sheaves and stand them up to dry in the sun. Cows are grazing everywhere. In the yard fertile hens strut about with their chicks and wage war against sterile hens who try to steal grain from them. The oak wood is green and cool. Barefoot children splash in the pond, holding up their pants to keep them dry. The air seems to carry a melody—of field, of corn, of wheat, of tall grass on which one can spread out and rest and breathe in the fragrances of ripening fruits. The smells of apples, plums, and wild pears fill the air. It's evening. Every living thing comes home. A peasant leads his family home. Calves romp behind aging cows. Hens lead their chicks to the farmyard. Birds fly back to their nests. Peasant girls gather in front of their cottages—washed, shampooed and combed, flowery new summer dresses, colorful ribbons in their hair. Young girls take each other by the arm and stroll through the lanes. The village is full of girlish singing accompanied by boys on harmonicas. Esther and Zippora lie in their corners pale, disheveled, stuck all over with slivers of straw. They glance through the cracks and sink back exhausted. A peasant girl starts to sing:

Youth, youth is a beautiful thing.
Nobody can have it but us.
Life, life is a beautiful thing.
Beautiful, beautiful as us!
In the distance a harmonica joins in:
You're my girl so beautiful,
Youth is really beautiful,
As life itself is beautiful!

September 1:

Only now do we realize how much Felek meant to us. How things have changed in the three weeks since his death. We felt it also in today's raid in the village.

It was about 7 a.m. when we heard strange noises coming from the village. We looked outside: from every direction, men and women were running toward the woods. In the fields, peasants dropped their scythes. Barefoot girls and young women carrying babies run by, their faces drenched in sweat. From every direction, we can hear them shouting, "Oh, Jesus! Oh, Jesus!"

We secure our door with boards and rods, and cover the partition with dark quilts.

The distant roar of motors tells us the village is surrounded. People are fleeing in terror. Soon there's no one in sight. It's so quiet we can hear the flies buzz. The calm before the storm. No signals from Auntie or Mrs. Felek downstairs.

Suddenly, huge hounds, followed by German police on bicycles, followed by Polish police. All helmeted, rifles swung over their shoulders, pistols at their sides. We bite our lips. Commands fly in German.

They've passed! A few minutes later—shouts in the nearby houses, wailing women, crying children. As soon as one section becomes quiet, cries for help come from another one. The motors keep roaring and honking. The sounds of gunfire are everywhere.

There's a commotion in the oak wood. Green uniforms move among the trees. Shooting! We hear screams in the distance; now they're almost directly upon us. Heavy footsteps and coarse voices. We can make out the German: "*Kreuz Donnerwetter, verflucht!*"

They're in our yard! It's quiet in the house below. Laughter outside the attic wall. They've gone by! More running, screaming, shooting.

This lasted for several hours. In the afternoon, the motors started up again. Gradually the vehicles faded into the distance. Half an hour later some old women and small children could be seen calling to the others to leave their hiding places and come home. A throng of people crawled out from the woods. Everyone was talking at once, describing the miracles that had happened. Some wept. Women tore their hair and screamed: "Oh, Jesus, Jesus!"

They realized the worst was over.

We started to breathe more freely. But we were in a daze. That evening, someone crawled up the ladder to the attic. It was Mrs. Felek, who wailed as she told us what happened:

Bad news. The whole village was surrounded. They went from house to house and ransacked every attic, cellar, and barn. They were looking for young men to send as forced labor to Germany. There was no hiding from them. They smashed walls and found camouflaged bunkers. They searched everywhere, omitting only three houses: two on the other side of the village and ours. We'll be caught yet.

This wasn't the first raid on the village. We've already lived through several dozen such searches. They always last about a day, and they've always skipped our cottage. When Felek was alive, though, we felt more secure. He would fill the attic with straw, cover our wall with hay, and force himself to remain in the house, tinkering with some chore; he didn't let the women go out either. "It'll be worse if they don't find anyone home," he would say. "They'll search even harder."

Today the women ran terrified from the house. Mrs. Felek fled all the way to Kaluszyn, and Auntie wandered boldly around the village observing the manhunt. They didn't come home until evening.

Janek spent the day drinking in a nearby village. All of them deserted us; and still we felt the presence of the Guardian of Israel.

* * *

"The Guardian of Israel does not sleep or slumber"—we repeat this psalm each night before going to sleep. It makes us feel better. We feel that a great, watchful eye is protecting us. We give thanks for today, anxiously wait for tomorrow. When we pray, we're in touch with our friends who are also in hiding. We ask the Guardian Angels to watch over them, too: "On my right, Michael; on my left, Gabriel; before me, Uriel; behind me, Raphael; and above us, the Presence of God." But, my God, there are no more Jews left! We are only a pitiful vestige. Oh, please watch over this remnant of your people.

On Saturday at dusk, we eat a bit of bread and softly sing the Sabbath parting song: "We long to behold Thy purity Thy Grace. . ." It's dark outside and shadows seem to swallow everything. We huddle together, singing: "My soul is lovesick for Thee. Please, God, please heal by revealing Thy sweet Glory!"

Later, in the pitch darkness, we wish each other "a good week, a week of life!"

Mid-September:

Another raid, and again they skipped our cottage. But we were very worried. Our neighbor, Wacek, had some pointed words with Janek. It was early in the morning. Wacek is working in our yard today. He's helping Mrs. Felek load the barn. While they were working, they received the news that Germans surrounded the village. Then Wacek whispered sharply to Janek: "It's dangerous to be on this farm!" Wacek knows that something is up here.

But Janek reassures us: "Wacek knows how to keep a secret, especially when he isn't sure. However, you must be very careful not to make a sound, very careful. Because then, it would be very bad, terrible, it would be the end!"

* * *

But what's the use of our being careful, when Janek's own behavior can provoke the most fantastic rumors? He's a free spender at every opportunity. And you can hardly recognize him; he's become years younger. Auntie is also radiant. Gaily she goes off on day-long excursions. She's mentioned in several places that she has "a few foolish thousands" somewhere. When she comes home, she feels guilty; she knows this can come to no good.

Recently, Auntie has been disappearing for several days at a time. And it's made us very uneasy. Mrs. Felek says that the villagers are having a good laugh about Auntie: "An old woman like that carrying on love affairs!" It seems she has two lovers.

Auntie boasts to us about her successes. She praises the organist of the Wiszniew church very highly: Oh, he's a real intelligent one. She wouldn't even be afraid to tell him about us.

Then, there's Frank Kuczak, of Kaluszyn; he's a real man. A pity that she can't invite him here sometimes. Mrs. Felek wouldn't allow him in.

Once Auntie sighed that some people have all the luck. For example, those city ladies are always wearing silk underclothes. The fellows say there's something about the flesh of a woman dressed in silk. She herself could use at least two silk blouses. If we promise not to tell anyone, not a soul, she'll let us in on a secret. No, it has nothing to do with us. All right, all right, she'll tell us; but we mustn't tell Mrs. Felek. She, Auntie, menstruated until she was sixty! So help her, until sixty! Let Esther and Zippora judge whether her body isn't as fresh as a virgin's!

September 20:
Since Felek's death, Mrs. Felek feels all alone in the world, and surrounded by enemies. "Everyone is sucking my blood!" she screams.

The peasants look at her with contempt in their eyes. And she freezes them with angry looks in return. But she lets it all out on the hens that stray into her vegetable garden and poke around in the seedbeds. She throws stones at them and chases them with sticks. Then, peasants, their wives, and children run out at the sound of the clucking hens and shout curses at Mrs. Felek. She screeches and curses back, and the tumult can be heard through the next neighborhood. Afterwards, the neighbors take it out on *her* hens when they grovel in *their* seedbeds. They break their wings with sticks and smash their legs. The battered fowl flee for their lives. At the sound of their yelping, Mrs Felek comes running out again, and half the village is in an uproar.

The peasants all hate her, and we're afraid that this could yet be our undoing. At the slightest suspicion, they'll go running to the authorities; Felek is dead now and there's no one to be afraid of.

When Mrs. Felek isn't home, the peasants walk by our cottage angrily, as if they wanted to burn it down with their looks.

After she left the house today, we saw a neighbor, Maczuszak, looking this way as he loitered in the field opposite the cottage. He moved around for a long while without taking his eyes off the cottage. Finally, he came closer and peeked in the windows.

We were certain he was looking for us, making sure we were there. But, all of a sudden, he left the window, sneaked back into the field, and plucked up some big tobacco leaves; then he stuffed them into his pocket and dashed off.

So he doesn't suspect that we can see him, that we're hidden in the house. We were practically delighted with his stealing.

Also, Klesz's wife, Mrs. Rechniakow's daughter, comes here often after Mrs. Felek has left for the village. She rips out vegetables from the garden, tucks them into her basket, and runs away.

No, they can't imagine that frightened, watchful eyes behind cracks in a wall keep track of whatever they do.

Mid-October:

After several days in Warsaw, Janek has some news:

So you think there are no Jews left, eh? Well, there are plenty! There isn't a place in Warsaw where Jews aren't hiding. But now they're out to get them: they're staging raids everywhere. They seal off whole neighbor hoods and search from house to house, from apartment to apartment. They stop the trolley cars and check the identity of every passenger. Whoever is found at the railroad station or riding the trains is checked. And in every raid they land a few Jews.

Actually, it's hard to tell who's a Jew nowadays. The women bleach their hair pale blonde, powder and rouge their faces, and they wear fancy clothes. At first, they used to cover their faces with mourning veils. But people soon realized that those were Jewish women hiding their eyes. Now, even Christian women in mourning—true Aryans—are afraid to wear those veils.

Once, they discovered some Jews in a five-story house on Chmielna Street. It was midnight when police detectives came to get them. However, they grabbed only three of them. The others, a young mother and her baby, and two eighteen-year-old girls, jumped out of the window, from the top story. Their smashed bodies were left in the street. Everyone in Warsaw ran to have a look.

With his own eyes Janek saw them leading away six captured Jews, among them a young man and a girl, they looked like a bride and groom. She kept grabbing his hand. He kept stumbling. They were all handcuffed. Many children and even some adults ran along with them all the way. I wouldn't have known they were Jews. They wore such fancy clothes. Not at all like the people running away from the ghetto half a year ago.

At that time, when the ghetto was burning, they also caught quite a few people, who had tried to escape to the Aryan side through the sewers. But you could tell right off that they were Jews: ragged, pale, bulging eyes, running barefoot and looking frantically for a place to hide. They were immediately caught and shot. With his own eyes Janek once saw two ragged children climb out of a manhole in Wilcza Street. You couldn't tell whether they were boys or girls, but he thinks one was a boy and the other a girl. They resembled each other, like brother and sister. They could hardly walk. A mob gathered around them. A twelve-year-old boy soon arrived with two SS men. The children didn't cry. Their faces turned white as chalk. They drowned the girl immediately, in that very sewer. An SS man grabbed a long broom from a streetcleaner, threw the girl down the manhole, and with the broom forced her down into the water. Then he laughed and said, "It's all over." The boy tried to run away. He took a few steps, limping on his skinny little legs, and everybody laughed. The second SS man let him take a few more steps, and burst out laughing. Then he hugged the boy and began caressing his face. The German laughed: "Don't worry. Nothing will happen to you." Then he slowly drew the pistol from his holster and shot the boy right in his mouth. "I gave him some candy," he told the mob, laughing.

The newspapers say that those who help Jews are traitors, enemies of the Polish people. During the last few weeks, the Polish press is up in arms against people helping Jews. Every day they print letters from readers that call for a strong punishment for those who hide Jews. It's not enough to kill only the guilty one; but those who help Jews should burn together with their families, and in public, to teach everyone a lesson. Many Poles are really frightened, and are turning out the Jews they were hiding. Those who report Jews on their own aren't punished.

Oh, were those Jews rich, says Janek. Their belongings are still scattered all over the streets of the burned ghetto. You can't tell those were once streets. All you see are rubble and piles of bricks. It looks like a garbage heap. People with sacks are crawling and digging everywhere, and the air is so heavy with soot that you can hardly breathe. A stench of smoke and rotting corpses sticks to you. Skeletons, skulls, armbones and legbones are everywhere.

It hurts: all that property, all those lonely things, destroyed. In many cellars, which were turned into bunkers, there are packs full of flour and groats, cakes, and all kinds of food, enough to last for years. The Jews stocked up for a long stay. Now everything's spoiled. The Germans flooded the cellars with water and drowned the Jews, or pumped poison gas into them, so everything stinks. God's gift gone to waste, when Poles are having such bad times!

* * *

Once, after coming back from Warsaw, Janek said he thought he had seen the Kaluszyn shopkeeper Pesakh's wife, Mrs. Pesakh, in the street.

You wouldn't recognize her: an elegant lady with blonde curls, trimmed eyebrows, and painted lips, wearing a fancy coat and carrying a handbag under her arm. She wore black stockings, as though in mourning, and it occurred to him that she must be a Jew in mourning for some relatives. He was eager to see her face, so he rushed past her, turned around, and looked directly at her. He immediately knew from the eyes that she was a Jew. True, she was walking boldly, but he knew she was only pretending. The eyes were frightened. Then it struck him that she was "Mrs. Pesakh." He thought of stopping her to say that he recognized her, but she quickened her pace. He followed for a while. At almost every corner she paused briefly, turned around, and looked back. When she saw Janek, she would walk ahead even more briskly. Each time she came to a gate she paused, as if debating whether to go inside. Then she came to a church whose doors were wide open. In the interior, candles glowed on the decorated altar. It was Sunday, and people streamed into the church. She went in with the crowd. He followed her inside. There he looked her again in the face, now lit up by candlelight. She knelt, and made strange movements with her lips. She must have been praying in Yiddish, to the Jewish God, because a few times she buried her face in her hands. When she caught sight of him, she looked worried. A few times she glanced at him. then quickly turned away, crossed herself. She must still be mourning for the two sons who were shot in Budki last year.

* * *

We had heard many times that Pesakh's wife was alive. The peasants who come here often talk about it. She was also seen in the villages around here. She comes to collect debts from former customers, to have something to live on.

Staszko Kuczak's looking forward to her coming to Budki or nearby. When she does, she won't be making the trip back, the whore! All the people in the village owe her money. He also owes her a few zlotys. "We've talked it over among ourselves. Just let

102

her show her face! We'll 'pay' her, all right. First, we'll 'line up' on her—ha, ha—like we used to line up at her shop on market day. Only she won't live to give birth to any bastards, oh, no! The police will finish off the party, and the boys will have a hot time, like with the Moszko woman."

* * *

We heard about how "the Moszko woman" died a few weeks ago, right after the harvest. We learned about her indirectly, from Konyak. The week after Felek's death, he came to stay a few days in Janek's barn. We told Auntie to ask him if he knew about any other Jews. At first, he said that he hadn't seen a living Jew since the last Jews in the Kaluszyn camp were wiped out. But after a few days' rest in the barn, after Auntie gave him a change of underwear and a pair of heavy pants that Esther had made out of Felek's old trousers, he told her he'd been wandering around with a Jewish woman, a Mrs. Moszko. They're sharing a bunker in one of the nearby forests. She stays in the bunker all day while he forages in the villages for food. She's about thirty. They've been together since they met in the forest.

He's worried about the coming harvest. Now, during a manhunt, they leave their hole and hide in the tall grain. The grain fields are vast, and good for hiding. But after the crops are harvested...

Right after the harvest we heard that Mrs. Moszko had been murdered. Peasants in the nearest village informed the authorities that Konyak was hiding out in their vicinity, and one morning a group of police and soldiers went into the forest. They found the bunker, but it was empty. The two had already escaped into a nearby field and were hiding in the furrows between the potato beds. It was quiet for half an hour, and they thought they were safe. Then suddenly they heard footsteps and voices. The police spread out through the field. Apparently, they had followed the footprints that led from the bunker to the potato field. Konyak raised his head a bit and saw a huge wolfhound running ahead of the police. The dog headed straight for the furrows where they were hidden. Konyak buried his head in the dirt. He was afraid they could see the soles of his shoes. Almost directly above him he heard German voices. Then the dog pounced, and he heard Mrs. Moszko scream. He could hear the beating and pounding, and the Germans shouting. Through the

potato leaves he could see the German's boots: one step back-
ward and the man would fall on top of him. Konyak held his
breath. They were beating Mrs. Moszko to force her to tell them
his whereabouts. She screamed that she didn't know. Her
screams carried through the early morning stillness to the surrounding villages. He was frightened that they might hear him
trembling. A few minutes later he heard two shots, a gagged
scream, heavy footsteps. The voices were far away now. It was
quiet. He didn't know whether she had been killed. He was lying
there for a long while, afraid to budge. Then, again he heard
voices and footsteps. Again he dug in. Among the plants he saw
a policeman leading a few peasants; he took them to Mrs. Moszko and told them to "bury the corpse." Then he left. Konyak
saw the peasants drag out Mrs. Moszko from the potato beds.
Her arms and legs were stiff. Blood ran in trickles through the
damp red hair, over her glazed eyes, into her open mouth. Two
peasants grabbed her hands and dragged her body aside. A
crowd of villagers quickly gathered—peasants and their wives,
girls and little children, and they began to dig a pit. One young-
ster pulled off Mrs. Moszko's clothes and hurled them into the
air over the crowd. People started to push and shove. The wom-
en fought a tug-of-war over every garment. The boy watched the
spectacle as he threw one thing after another to the mob—first a
skirt, a blouse, a scarf, a shoe, another shoe, and—

"Attention! Look here!" he called out.

Off came the undershirt, then the bloomers. The mob burst into hysterical laughter. Women screeched, almost had a fit, as
they rushed to grab the bloodstained slip and bloomers.

"Hey!" a tall youth shouted. He grabbed the corpse by the feet
and with one swing stood it up. She hung there, head and hands
on the ground, feet in the air. She seemed to be standing on her
head. "Hey there!" he yelled again, spreading her legs apart.

The crowd doubled over with laughter. The women screeched
and laughed till tears ran down their faces.

"Hey! Look!"

* * *

By some miracle the front lines seem to be coming closer; the
Red Army has advanced several hundred miles. The villagers say
that the war is nearly over. The Germans are on the verge of collapse. These reports give us some hope. It can't be too long now.

After each report of a German defeat, we feel a change in mood around here. Janek, Auntie and even Mrs. Felek become cheerful and friendly; they even pat us on the back. Then they want to know how we'll pay them back later; it better not be in the "Jewish style."

Every Thursday, Auntie brings us the whole week's newspapers from Kaluszyn. She wants to know how much longer the war is going to last. We "prove" to her that it's only a matter of two or three months at most. Auntie isn't really convinced. "Every time we ask," she says, "you say 'two or three months at most.' Still, this time I believe you."

Auntie starts to tell us what it will be like after the liberation, and what important people we will be then. "They say there's a Jewish army and Jewish generals. They say that the English and Americans are all Jews, especially the generals and the officers. And of course, the Russians." We always confirm these "facts" for them. Froiman's uncle, they know, is a very high officer in the King of England's guard. And all our uncles and aunts abroad are practically ministers. These fairy tales have been our salvation more than once.

Mrs. Felek lets out a groan. It better be in three months, she says; in any case, it doesn't look as if she'll survive.

Later, after they left, we felt depressed. Maybe it will only be three months? Is freedom really calling us already?

Freedom—how we long for it, how we dream of it, how we fear the days after the liberation! All our wounds will open up then.

We experienced something like that during the Rosh Hashana that just passed.

It's the first day of Rosh Hashana. We're sunk in our thoughts. This is the Day of Judgment! Memories of past holy days come to mind, of home, of parents, sisters, brothers, a world filled with Jews! These are the High Holy Days. The Days of Awe—awful days in an awful time.

Suddenly we hear the news: the Germans have surrendered. "Definitely!"

The peasants get drunk, celebrate. The news seeps through the cracks into the hideaway. We can't believe it: Are we really free?

We're stunned and confused, and instead of celebrating we sit down and weep: Where shall we go? No Jews are left! To the graveyards, to the mass graves?

We each stretched out in a corner and didn't say a word. We just wanted to sleep—to sleep like this forever.

Later, Janek told us that it had only been a rumor. Our illusions evaporated as fast as they had appeared. The old terror was back.

October 25:
It's been cold for several weeks. It's late autumn. Patches of snow cover the stripped fields. The bare trees sink into the mud. It's dark in here. The damp boards have expanded, sealing the cracks. We can barely see each other. Although now the wind doesn't blow in so hard, the cold pierces our bones. We sit all day in a circle with our feet under the covers. Our bedding is moldy and swarming with worms and bugs. The fleas chew away at us; our bodies are bitten and scratched.

Summer was even worse: fleas in the straw beneath us spread out all over the attic, the rooms below, and even the yard outside. Suspiciously, visitors would ask: "Where do all these bugs come from?" Now that it's cold, the pests have congregated in the attic and they don't let us rest. They crawl over our faces and into our mouths and we inhale them with every breath. Each time we clench our fists we squash piles of them. Like leeches they're sucking our blood.

The cold brings us temporary relief. Although it freezes the ears, the nose, the fingertips. We keep shifting position. When the bugs bite, we flee into the cold for relief. And when the cold begins to bite, we flee under the straw, to the bugs. . .

October 27:
Another uproar between Auntie and Mrs. Felek today, and as usual, we were the victims.

Early in the morning, Mrs. Felek went off to church in Wiszniew. Before leaving, she locked the jug of sour cream in the laundry chest. After she left, Auntie arrived. She started looking for the sour cream everywhere, but couldn't find it; then it came to her that it had to be in the laundry chest. Without thinking about it, she lifted the chest, turned it upside down several times, and went out for a stroll.

When Mrs. Felek returned, she found sour cream on the floor, and the garments in her chest soiled and sticky. She came up to us screaming hysterically. We begged her to lower her voice, but she cried even louder; she pounded her head with her fists, crying that she wanted everyone to hear "once and for all": today it was coming to an end!

Then we hear somebody moving about in the house below. But Mrs. Felek goes on screaming and cursing as she crawls down the ladder.

The "visitor" turns out to be Auntie herself. They start to yell and curse. Mrs. Felek tells her to go to the devil together with us. Auntie answers that she'll go to the devil first, because we're staying in her house, not Auntie's. Mrs. Felek rushes up to tell us that we'd better leave now, or she'll pack up, take the cow, and tell the police about us. Auntie shouts up to us: "Don't believe her, she won't do it, she loves herself too much! She's only threatening."

Mrs. Felek ran back down, and soon pots, rolling pins, and stools started flying below. They screamed, tore each other's hair, slapped and beat each other: "Police! Police!"—we heard them both shout.

* * *

By some miracle, nobody came running to see what the uproar was about. Later, Mrs. Felek went off to the village and Auntie came up to us, sat down in a corner, and burst into tears. If not for us, she told us, she would end this misfortune once and for all. She would kill her sister-in-law, set fire to the cottage, and—that would be it!

She went down. We sat for a few hours, wondering what happened to Mrs. Felek. Each time we heard footsteps near the cottage, our hearts seemed to stop beating.

Finally, Mrs. Felek returned. She asked us for our decision. She wants to know right now; she'll wait for the answer. She's not going downstairs until that "cadaver" goes. She's not staying in the same house with her. Mrs. Felek groans, pinches her cheeks, tears at her hair, then starts swaying and wringing her hands: How miserable she is! All alone in the world. No Felek. No children. Not even an animal. If only she had at least a piglet to raise! Oh, how she love little pigs! By coincidence, she saw just such a piglet in the village today, and it occurred to her that such a creature would bring some comfort into her bitter life. It only costs a couple of hundred zlotys. Oh, if only she had some money! "You?! Oh, no, I'm not taking any more money from you! You have to get out of here anyway! Well, if Mr. Juzek insists on being so generous—all right, I'll buy it. Such a sweet little pig! You'll like it too."

Of course she won't tell that old hussy that the money came from us!

October 26:

There's a celebration in the village today: Mrs. Staszko gave birth to a daughter. Staszko is in his fifties already, and this is his first child. Two years ago, after his first wife died, he married a young woman. Cynics said it was no use. Despite them, she gave him a baby, and the whole village is jumping. Some say that a third party had something to do with it. But be that as it may, Staszko is celebrating.

Staszko's house is near our cottage, and we can hear the happy commotion, the rejoicing over the new life. First we heard the screaming of the new mother as the baby shoved its way into the world. Now we hear the baby crying at night, and it makes us nostalgic.

"Oh, God, a baby!"

We remember so many Jewish babies. Where are they now?

The last time I saw them was in the camp a year ago, when the SS men snatched the children from their mothers and took them away. Children from two to fourteen years of age; the sound of gunfire muffled their crying. They tried to get back to their mothers. The mothers, who were lined up on the side, waited and banged their heads against the wall. They wanted to go with their children; but when they struggled with the guards, they were forced back into the barracks. The children were lined up four abreast and ordered to march. The older children led the younger ones by the hand.

I see little Yitkele, our neighbor's daughter, that golden child with long blonde hair and blue eyes. When she used to play in the grass in our garden, she looked like a sun-drenched flower. Yitkele toddled out of the line and cried: "Mama, I'm afraid, I don't want to go!"

The gates were slammed shut. The half-crazed mothers sunk their teeth into the fence in desperation, rolled in the dirt, rubbed their foreheads into the ground until—about an hour later they heard grenades exploding in the cemetery.

Mrs. Staszko's baby is crying—

Perhaps she's thirsty. I can no longer tolerate a baby's hunger pangs. I want to run away from them. Israel Aaron jumped from the train bound for Treblinka because he couldn't stand the crying of the thirsty infants in their mothers' arms. It drove him crazy, the mothers, too. I'm haunted by the cries of the thirsty children on the death trains and by the grief of their helpless mothers. Each time I take a sip of water I feel their thirst.

There's joy in our neighbor Staszko's house today; I remember the joy in our house when my sister-in-law, Chaya, entered her ninth month. She stayed up nights sewing little sheets and pillows, her eyes glowing with secret happiness. We were all getting ready to celebrate. A week later she had been shot, and lay in a pool of blood in the camp compound. We watched from the side, where we had been lined up, and bit our fingers. A German wearing a silk shirt watched over the dying girl, his rosy cheeks puffing up with pleasure at every last gasp. She writhed and convulsed that way for several hours, her eyes wide open, fingers digging into the ground, kicking her naked, bloody feet. Finally she was still, her jaws locked and fists clenched. Her belly was still moving when she lay in the pit and the first shovels of earth were thrown over her.

Mrs. Staszko's baby is crying—

I recall the time in the ghetto, during the German bombardment, when seven-year-old Shimele's big brown eyes were sealed by plaster that fell from the crumbling walls. He kept rubbing his eyes with his hands; he wanted to rip them open. They no longer had pupils. He cried that he couldn't see. We all knew that he would never see again—not daylight, not the other children, nothing. And he asked from time to time: "Mama, when will I be able to see?"

After that, I always stared into the eyes of all the ghetto children and felt their light. The day before the roundup, I saw dozens of them in the big synagogue compound. They were playing, as if nothing had changed. The sun was shining. We, the adults, felt that our days were numbered. We roamed aimlessly through the streets and courtyards, our hands dangling limply at our sides. I would stop to gaze to the children. One boy was crying and wiping his eyes.

Two days later a hush lay over the ghetto and the synagogue compound. It was after the slaughter. Only dogs scampered about licking blood from the cobblestones. The German sentries casually marched by.

Mrs. Staszko gave birth to a baby, and its cries are so sad.

November 8:

Auntie returned to the cottage today. She had run away two days ago. She hasn't any peace here since Mrs. Felek bought the pig.

Mrs. Felek has come to life again. She's busy with her little pig from sunup. For breakfast she cooks him potatoes and *farfl* fried with sour cream. They both sit down by the stove (because of the cold outdoors, she keeps him in the house) and the two of them eat from the same bowl. How clever and handsome he is, she tells us. She's even brought him up to the attic a few times. She kisses him on the snout, babytalks to him, and hugs him to her breast.

Auntie was in a rage. She cursed Mrs. Felek relentlessly, and threatened to move back to her place in town. We had to appease her with a new dress, on the condition, of course, that Mrs. Felek didn't find out about it. Then Mrs. Felek went wild about Auntie's new dress, and accused her of robbing us to make herself new clothes. Auntie grabbed a stick to beat the piglet and shouted that she wasn't a thief, we gave her the dress as a present. On the other hand, Mrs. Felek was certainly a thief: where else did she get the money to buy herself that filthy swine?

"If you must know," Mrs. Felek said, "they bought me the piglet!"

Auntie crawled up to us, pounded her head with her fists, and told us to go to the devil "right this second!" Then she stormed out of the house.

She was gone for two days. We expected disaster at every moment. For two nights we couldn't sleep a wink. But Mrs. Felek told us not to worry. "If only," she said, "I could be as sure that the thief won't come back as I'm sure that she *is* coming back!" But we knew that this time it was a serious matter.

Auntie came back today. She slunk into the house so quietly that we didn't hear her. Mrs. Felek brought us the news. In the afternoon, Auntie came up, and sulked for a while, saying: "I wouldn't have come back. You don't deserve it. But it's silly. The war is nearly over anyway."

November 14:

Lately, before leaving the house, Mrs. Felek brings the jug of sour cream up to the attic and hides it somewhere in the hay. I come out from behind the wall to make sure that Auntie doesn't help herself. I also keep an eye on the eggs the hens are laying in the hay.

I'm on guard for the sound of unfamiliar footsteps. The others also keep watch from the one crack in the outer wall through which we can still see. As soon as they notice anyone in the distance, they give me a sign and I quickly crawl back into the hideaway.

My vigilance is working. A number of times already Auntie came up to the attic for a fresh egg. But when she catches sight of me, she pretends to look for something in the dirty laundry. She asks me what I'm doing here, "Getting some air," I say. She goes down, comes back a few minutes later to see if I'm still around, leaves again, and returns; this goes on until Mrs. Felek comes home.

The hens are used to me, and they lay their eggs in the hay right near me. When they've finished laying, they just climb back down. I've also befriended the mother cat and her kittens. The kittens prance on my arms, my lap, and even my head; the mother cat sits by quietly enjoying the sight. We regained her trust after she had her second litter. Or perhaps she's just forgotten the scene she caused that night.

It was in the summer, after she delivered four kittens in a corner of the attic. At midnight, we heard a peculiar wail in the attic. Something was charging at our little door. We were startled out of our sleep, and suddenly afraid. But after listening for a moment, we realized it was the mother cat. We took it for a bad sign; she seemed to be going berserk. Her charging at the door became furious, her howls deafening. This continued for nearly an hour. At last, we heard footsteps in the attic. The cat leaped away from the partition and howled like an infant. Mrs. Felek knocked on our door, and we opened. With a leap the cat burst in, but Mrs. Felek grabbed her and held her tight. Then she lit a candle and searched in the hay. The four kittens lay dead. A tomcat had killed them in the mother's absence; it seems he was jealous of losing her attention. The mother cat kept on howling and trying to charge at us. "She thinks you killed her children," Mrs. Felek explained.

That night, the cat became our enemy and abandoned our

hideaway. For days on end she lay in a corner howling. She couldn't forget. At night her howls filled the attic. Sometimes she would gnash her teeth and hiss. This went on for some weeks.

Mrs. Felek explained that animals have a powerful maternal instinct; they don't easily forget.

November 18:

Lately we go for weeks without any hot food. Auntie eats lunch in the village somewhere and Mrs. Felek cooks only enough for herself, the cat, the little pig and the hens. First thing in the morning they hand us a chunk of bread and a bottle of half-brewed coffee for the whole day; in the evening they hand us more of the same.

We're thirsty and parched, and need something to revive us. Esther and Zippora speak in rasping voices. Ephraim's heart races from time to time. He could use some milk. Several times I've given Mrs. Felek money to bring us some milk, a few eggs, or anything to perk us up. But she takes the money and "forgets" about us. She's even told me that she'd gladly help us, but she knows that we want the food for Auntie; and for all she cares, Auntie can eat rocks. We also give Auntie money to buy some nourishing food. She does her eating in the village, so that Mrs. Felek won't know about it. Mrs. Felek sells her milk, sour cream, butter, and eggs in town. Our money has already supplied her and Janek with cellars full of potatoes, and both their barns are stocked with grain. But Mrs. Felek's cow and Janek's hens must also eat potatoes and grain. So we must make do with bread, and sometimes even without that.

We are at least partly to blame. At the outset, when Felek was still alive, we were afraid to eat rich food. We ate only what was needed to stay alive. We thought we couldn't digest anything rich; that it was sinful to eat rich food in these times. So we ate dry bread and avoided foods cooked in fat. Then there were two diets: one, for our hosts below, that included fats; and a special diet without fats for us. Now we can't do anything to change it. We're getting skinnier by the day.

The money is running out too. The goods we left with some of our Polish acquaintances have been collected and sold. Others are refusing to hand over our things. As for the rest, who knows how long they'll continue supplying us? Each time Auntie goes to see them we worry: What if they've decided to end this business?

November 19:

Something terrible just happened, and I haven't fully recovered yet. Half an hour ago. Auntie knocked at our door, and told me to come out of the hideaway. Sitting down in the hay, she told me how things were quiet at the fronts. In the village they say that the war is dragging on.

I tried to assure her that they didn't have the right information; they never even read the papers. It won't be long now. A miracle may happen and it'll be over any day now.

"But how long at the most?" Auntie asked.

"At the most?" I said. Maybe two months, three months, maybe—

Auntie exploded: "Bastard! That's too long, too long! Understand, son of a bitch?" Then she jumped on me, tore my hair, and pounded with all her might on my head. "Get out of here, damn it! Two more months? Three more months? Enough!"

Mrs. Felek and Janek heard the rumpus and hurried up to the attic. Mrs. Felek was trembling: "That bastard! Do you hear, Janek? The war—two more months, three more months!"

Janek told me to get back in the hideaway. He took Auntie by the hand and led her down the ladder.

November 21:

It's two days since Auntie's attack, and we still haven't recovered. We've lost all hope. The others look on me as a martyr. Yesterday, we sat in our corners without saying a word; we couldn't talk. In the morning, Froiman said that perhaps we ought to leave.

Today, Ephraim tried to paint a rosy picture of the future. If we survive, God willing, all the suffering and trouble will have been worthwhile. The world wants us to survive, especially the Jews abroad. We must think of ourselves as front-line soldiers, bear it all, and stay alive.

His words at least gave us a little encouragement.

Mid-December:

Janek was here today. It's been a month since we last saw him. He didn't show up since that incident involving Auntie. Lately, he hasn't even visited her. He's avoiding our cottage. On the other hand, Auntie spends entire days at his place. We think she's ashamed of the rumpus she raised. She comes up to see us often, but something has changed. Her talk is guarded, and she can't look us in the eyes.

Perhaps her conscience is starting to bother her just a little, because she's cooking us lunches again. She boils a big pot of potatoes, adds some wheat dumplings done in fat, and brings it up to us. She herself eats at Janek's. She says that Janek is impatient for the war to end; we also sense that he's fed up.

But today he gave us each a hearty handshake, smiled, and apologized for not coming to see us lately. After giving us the latest news from the village and the town, he began to complain about the war dragging on and Christmas coming! Practically everybody, he said, is getting rich, doing big business, but some people are still poor. So many people have been wiped out—all the Jews—and yet some people are still so poor they don't have money for the holiday. He could use some yard goods to make dresses for each of his two daughters, who've really blossomed in the past year. They're real young ladies! They already have suitors, and they need to be properly dressed.

"No," Janek said, "the world isn't standing still. The years fly by. Only yesterday they were little girls, and now they're real young ladies. I must get them new clothes. The young generation today has gotten used to living well, eating and drinking well, dressing well, enjoying life. My girls have to keep up with the rest."

* * *

Mrs. Felek came up to ask what "that thief Janek" wanted. Most likely to cheat us! He doesn't come just to socialize!

Two brothers, she said, and such a difference! Take her Felek of sainted memory: he was a thief, stole from people, frequently sat in jail, and even paid with his life. "Now I ask you: What did he steal? Some food for himself and that dumb beast of a cow in the barn. He was a cripple, couldn't work, blind, so once in a while he brought something home at night! Did he harm anyone? He always took only from the rich, who have plenty. He never touched a poor man. He didn't have the heart."

She remembers late one winter, when there wasn't even a lick of hay in the barn for Losza, the cow. And there was no place to get any: the rich masters lock everything up tight. And here your cow is wasting away on you for lack of a bite, a chew. Every night, Felek of sainted memory ran from barn to barn, for nothing. Everything is sealed tight. So what happens? One night he finds an open barn filled with hay. The owner forgot to lock it, and it's all there for the taking. Take as much as you want! Felek stood there staring into the dark, feeling the hay, and thinking hard. And what did he do? He left, that's what. Just walked off without taking a thing! Came home emptyhanded! He didn't have the heart: the hay belonged to a poor orphan, the Michaelow girl. May God punish him, he said, if he takes anything from a poor orphan! If he can't get anything out of the rich, he certainly won't take anything from the poor. If the cow starves to death, he said, they'll cut her up and eat her meat. But he's not ruining an orphan on her account!

"That's the sort of man he was! Such character! And him they murdered! And that bandit Janek is robbing the whole world, swindling everybody, and they all think he's such a saint. He comes and goes as he pleases! He should only drop dead!"

New Year, 1944:

The new year is here. What does it have in store? Hideous new deaths for the last Jews alive, or—Maybe we'll wake up one fine morning and find ourselves free. The newspapers write of a major offensive by the Russians. Maybe in the winter, or in the spring?

Even Mrs. Felek and Auntie are pleased with us today. They're still drunk with holiday joy. And they're both feeling victorious: each is sure that she alone received Christmas money from us. Mrs. Felek got several hundred zlotys and promised to prepare us all a good meal. But Auntie said that people shouldn't be celebrating in these bad times; we have to thank the Lord for what piece of dry bread there is. A bitch like her sister-in-law needs to feel the taste of war. Still, we must be starved so she thinks she ought to make a festive meal! She'll prepare it at Janek's. Mrs. Felek won't know that the money came from us. When she brings us the food, we're to tell Mrs. Felek it's a present from Janek. And, above all, we're not to give Mrs. Felek even a taste of it. She's not worth it!

Mrs. Felek prepared several pounds of lard, meat, jellied feet, and a few big cakes. On Christmas morning, as soon as Auntie left for church, she put it into a few bowls and brought it up to us. She wished us a happy holiday and told us to eat. As for Auntie, let her explode.

We sat for several hours unable to touch the food. Our throats were clogged. We kept shoving the bowls at each other. At last, Auntie came, loaded with "Janek's present"—several big pots.

Again lard and jellied feet and many slices of cake. First she carried it downstairs, so that Mrs. Felek could smell it, and only then did she hand us the pots one by one. She was pleased to see that we hadn't touched Mrs. Felek's food. "That one's cooking can make a person vomit" she said. She kissed us all and wished us a happy holiday.

She accepted our invitation to eat the meal Mrs. Felek had brought us, and before she left, she tucked it all under her apron, saying: "You shouldn't eat that vomit. It's not fit for humans. I'll feed it to the horses in the village."

"Janek's present" also stood there for a long time, until Mrs. Felek came up and said that she understood; after a meal like hers, how could we have an appetite for Janek's vomit? If we like, she'll take it down, without that old witch knowing, and feed it to the cat and the pig.

* * *

We just can't eat greasy food. The thought of it repels us.

The next day, when Mrs. Felek brought us hot milk porridge, we helped ourselves to a few spoonfuls. We kept passing the bowl around, each of us claiming to have no appetite. Froiman swallowed a few spoonfuls, which revived him a bit, and handed me the bowl. I passed it to Esther and Zippora, but they said that Ephraim's heart was weak; they could manage without it. Ephraim passed the bowl back to them, and said it would pick them up. They, in turn, passed it back to me. Meanwhile, the food was cooling off.

Esther had two spoonfuls and swore that she simply couldn't swallow any more. Zippora had a few and ordered Ephraim to eat; he was sick and needed food. Ephraim gulped down a bit of porridge, but said he would spill it all out if we kept on pestering him. I grabbed the spoon, but I couldn't swallow.

Meanwhile, Mrs. Felek came up to get the bowl. She was shocked that we hadn't finished the porridge. Didn't we like it? she asked.

January 2, 1944:

Mrs. Felek and Auntie are both very pious, and go to church in Wiszniew several times a week, especially on Sundays and holidays. Mrs. Felek stays in church from eight to ten in the morning, for the early Mass. When she returns, Auntie goes for the late Mass. They're both spiritually uplifted by the priest's sermon. Oh, what holy words he spoke! Every word of his is gold! Why doesn't everybody see things his way? What a different world it would be! People wouldn't fight and curse. People would forgive each other.

Mrs. Felek can't understand why Auntie can't learn a lesson from the priest. And Auntie can't understand why Mrs. Felek runs to hear the priest, since she doesn't listen to a word he says. She, Auntie, would like to hear Mrs. Felek's explanation. Would Juzek please ask her why she goes to church so often? And Mrs. Felek would like Juzek to tell Auntie once and for all that it's better not to go to church at all than to go and do just the opposite of what she's told.

Immediately after sundown, Auntie calls me out of the hideaway, sits down in the hay with me, and tells me the latest news from the village: she tells me how everyone despises her sister-in-law for her meanness. Even in church they know about it; even the priest knows! Juzek must tell her that even we're on to her tricks.

We hear Mrs. Felek bolting the front door. Then we hear her climbing up the ladder. "It's her!" Auntie exclaims, pinching me. "She doesn't know that I'm here. It's dark, she won't see me. Ask her now. I want to hear what she says."

By some miracle, Mrs. Felek bumps right into Auntie in the dark. *"Psia-krew!* Dog's blood!" Mrs. Felek exclaims, and falls on top of me. "Ha, you're here, Juzek?" She sits down beside me and begins to groan.

Auntie also starts complaining that the world is too terrible—nobody listens to the priest. She doesn't understand why that riff-raff goes to church at all!

Mrs. Felek groans louder and starts pinching me. I pretend not to notice. She pinches harder and searches for my ear. At the same time, Auntie pinches me on the other side and whispers: "Why don't you tell her off now. This is a good time."

Mrs. Felek whispers: "Well, Juzek, speak up!"

I let out a sigh and start groaning. Meanwhile, the two of them talk about love of humanity, goodness, God.

"But," I say, "what's the use of the priest's fine sermons if people don't listen to him? The priest preaches, and the peasants do as they please."

They're both silent and I become bolder. "Yes," I say, "the peasants do as they please. I don't understand: If they don't want to learn anything, why do they go to church? They really ought to stay home. In any case they're evil—fighting with each other, cursing each other."

Again they started pinching me, one on each side. They're both delighted that I told the other one off, and each pinches me to thank me and to get me to say more. I'm about to continue my sermon when Mrs. Felek lets out a curse: *"Psia-krew!"* It seems that her pinching hand had encountered Auntie's pinching hand.

" The plague!" Auntie cries out. They both leap up and follow each other down from the attic.

January 18:

Last Sunday I had another scene with Auntie. Again she beat me.

It all began a week ago Sunday. At about 9 a.m., Auntie went off to town to see Frank Kuczak. Before leaving, she ordered us not to let Mrs. Felek cook us lunch. She'll be back soon and cook us something. Mrs. Felek, she said, is irresponsible and careless. Someone from the village might come in, see the big pot of boiling on the stove, and it all will be over with us!

At about 12 noon Mrs. Felek came up to ask if we were hungry. She's going to cook for the hens, so she can cook for us at the same time.

We say that we're not hungry and have no appetite. She leaves somewhat insulted. But she's back in two hours, announcing that she's "about to cook." We suggest waiting for Auntie to come back. We're fools, she says, because that one won't be back till evening, and maybe not before tomorrow. "When you go to your lover, you don't come back so soon. Besides, the hens are hungry."

We beg her to wait two more hours, because Auntie will be angry and she'll take it out on us. Mrs. Felek left sulking, not saying a word. We prayed for Auntie to hurry back.

Several more hours pass. It's getting dark. At about 4:30, Mrs. Felek tells us angrily that she's cooking now, no matter what!

Half an hour later we hear the clatter of bowls below. Mrs. Felek is about to bring us our food. At that very moment, Auntie returns.

She stepped into the kitchen, but only for a minute. When she saw the pot of cooked food, she threw off her outer garments, and in a leap and a bound was up in the attic. She called me out of the hideaway and demanded an explanation: Why had I let Mrs. Felek cook? I started stammering something, when down came a slap on one cheek followed by a slap on the other. "Bastard!" she shouted, snatching a bale of hay and throwing it at me. When I came to, she was gone.

The incident wasn't mentioned all week. Auntie, though, came up every day, as if nothing happened; we took it as a sign that she was sorry.

This Sunday she again went off to Frank, but this time without saying a word. At about 11:30 a.m., Mrs. Felek was up here. She asked if she could make us something to eat, since in any case she was cooking for the hens. Again we pleaded with her about Auntie. She's very angry. If Auntie tries to hit me again, she says in a rage, I should punch her right in the face—one, two—and that will be a lesson for her! But she *must* cook. She's waiting two more hours at most!

Meanwhile, Auntie came home. When she saw the clean sink, she dashed up to the attic and asked me why lunch wasn't ready. She is starving. She was sure that when she got back from town, I would have arranged to have a bite of lunch for her prepared.

I stammer: "What do you mean? Have you forgotten what happened last week? I deliberately didn't let her cook anything."

At this, Auntie pounced on me and started beating me all over—on my face, my head, and the rest of my body. "But Auntie!" I pleaded. Then she seized me by the hair and yanked at my scalp, screaming: "Get right out of here! Finished! Robber! You want me to starve to death?"

Mrs. Felek came up and shouted: "Lunatic! You don't eat lunch here anyway! You stuff yourself at Janek's!"

She shoved me into the hideaway, and the two of them went down to the yard yelling at each other.

January 25:

A few days ago, our neighbor killed our mother cat. It was because of their hatred for Mrs. Felek. They were always trying to take it out on her animals. They hated the cat ever since she gave birth to kittens. She used to run around the village hunting for provisions, and she always snatched something from the cottage entranceways. She also used to snatch mice for her kittens. The neighbors set a trap for her. Then Mrs. Felek found her corpse lying outside our hut. Now Mrs. Felek weeps and curses the neighbors for stabbing the cat to death. We had the feeling than an arrow aimed at us had struck the cat.

During the last few days, a falcon swooped down twice and each time strangled one of Mrs. Felek's hens. She's stunned and confused. She cooked the dead hens and offered some to us, but we declined. We considered the dead hens to be scapegoats.

February 15:

Esther is very sick. She has had a high fever for two weeks. Her body aches, she feels strength draining away. We can't keep out the fierce wind that blows from all directions. She lies in a corner covered with a rotting quilt and a few threadbare overcoats. We watch her suffer and can do nothing to help her.

Auntie mustn't find out. If she does, she'll accuse us of pampering ourselves, and she'll even stop cooking our miserable lunch.

We've already asked Mrs Felek to sell us some milk and eggs but she refuses. She's angry because Auntie won't let her use our wood for kindling. Three weeks ago, Janek sold us some bales of wood from his section of the oak grove. We wanted to keep enough for cooking and heating. But Auntie won't let Mrs. Felek use any of it. She said "that witch" couldn't use Janek's wood. She's got warehouses full of timber, besides the trees in her section of the grove.

Mrs. Felek approached us and made a fuss over it, so I gave her (without Auntie's knowledge) a few hundred zlotys to buy herself some wood or to have some of her own trees cut down. She took the money, but didn't bring a fresh supply of wood. She said she still had plenty on hand; it only bothered her that Auntie, "that witch," should be the boss over our lumber supply. So she must use our wood in order to spite Auntie.

Esther can't eat. Her lips are parched and feverish. But we have no liquids to give her. The old women have stopped making us coffee. Each demands that the other use "her own" lumber for kindling.

One evening, when Esther was burning with fever, she begged for a drink. I pleaded with the women that we were very thirsty and that Esther was very sick. Each of them told me to ask the other, saying: "She's got plenty of wood."

Later, Auntie crawled up to our hideaway, sat down in a corner, and started smacking her lips to show she was thirsty. She's passing out from thirst! I'm to call her sister-in-law and tell her to brew some coffee!

I went out of the hideaway, and begged Mrs. Felek to make us some coffee. She refuses; it's because she thinks we really want it for "the witch" who's sitting in there with us. I swear it's for us, for Esther. Finally, she agrees to make the coffee, but just a little, just enough for us.

Auntie is pleased that Mrs. Felek has to boil the coffee with her own fuel. I whisper to Esther that she'll soon have something to drink.

Meanwhile, Auntie realized that Esther was sick. She shoved her hands under the overcoats and felt Esther's burning face. She began asking questions. She could hear Esther's feeble voice. She scolded us for neglecting ourselves and catching cold. Anyway, Auntie added, it's foolish to make a fuss over it. She herself has a cold, she coughed a bit as proof, and she isn't making a fuss. People shouldn't pamper themselves. By the way, she's dying of thirst! Let Juzek hurry and bring the coffee!

Just as I went to get it, Mrs. Felek appears on the ladder and hands me two bottles of black coffee. I give one to Auntie and one to Esther.

Auntie takes a sip and starts cursing: the coffee is lukewarm! Mrs. Felek is too stingy to put more wood in the fire! And before we know what's happening, she snatches Esther's bottle and pours the contents of both bottles into the hay. Phooey! "That's not coffee, that's vomit!" she yells. Juzek must go right dowm and tell Mrs. Felek to boil up some fresh coffee, but this time boiling hot!

I whisper to Mrs. Felek that the coffee was excellent, and we're very thankful; but we'd be grateful for some more, and could she make it hotter this time?

Mrs. Felek starts cursing us: Go to the devil together with Aunie! Some nerve—to spill out the coffee she made us! The house below is swimming in coffee; it's dripping down through the attic floor, and everything is soaked!

I crawl back inside. Auntie is smacking her lips: "I'm dying! Coffee! A sip of coffee! Robbers! You have no pity! I'm sick and I

121

must have a hot drink! Oh, Jesus, I'm dying!" She starts coughing: "Oh, I'm choking to death!"

I beg her to go down and boil some herself. She starts sobbing:
We're cruel. We only want the coffee for ourselves. We don't
care a bit about her. Finally—groaning, smacking her lips, and
coughing—she crawls downstairs.

February 18:

A few days ago, Losza, Mrs. Felek's cow, who calved two and
a half months ago, started mooing so sadly that it broke our
hearts. As though she were suffering from some terrible
Weltschmerz. She kept us awake all night, wouldn't eat a thing
during the day, just kept mooing sadly all the time. We thought
she was dying. Besides, her mooing seemed to have a bad omen,
as if the dumb creature could sense an imminent danger that
would affect us all.

Last night we couldn't sleep again. Esther was still feverish
and begged for something to drink.

First thing in the morning, Mrs. Felek appeared with a glass of
milk for Esther. She agreed to bring a quart tomorrow morning.
Losza was refusing to eat, she said. She's pining away for the
bull. It's nearly three months since she calved, and, well, she
wants a male. There's a healthy bull in the next village that will
cost half a hundred. If Mr. Juzek likes, she can bring milk for
Esther every day. But she just doesn't know what will become of
the cow. She's liable to get sick. She has to be taken away right
now. Only there's no money. Thank you very much! She'd better
hurry now and take the cow right over to the next village. Her
heart is breaking for the poor, dumb animal! Thank you very
much for the fifty *zlotys!*

February 23:

Esther is better. We don't know how it happened. Her temperature dropped, she regained some strength, and she's more
alert. Now there's only some pain and tenderness in her sides.

We don't know how to thank God. We could do nothing for
Esther—only pray and drive away bad thoughts.

February 27:

Yesterday we had a double dose of miracles. It had just turned
dark. We all seemed to merge with the darkness as we sat there
shivering from cold, not saying a word. Suddenly, Ephraim be-

gan to scream. We were shuddering from fright. But then he began growling like a wounded animal. We grabbed him and held him tight. He became quiet, dropped into Froiman's lap like a dead weight, and lay there motionless. We were shaking and pinching him, but he didn't stir. His arms, legs—his entire body was stiff, and his lips were covered with a thick froth.

Zippora ran for some water. But Auntie and Mrs. Felek, who had heard the noise downstairs, were already in the attic. Mrs. Felek quickly climbed down and brought up a pail of cold water. Again we began to pinch Ephraim and to shake him; we forced open his clenched teeth, but nothing would help. We poured water on him, and he began to writhe, but soon he became rigid again. We held down his head, wiggled his hands, and applied artificial respiration. But again he writhed and let out a bizarre roar. We held his mouth shut with our hands. Auntie screamed: "Good God!" Mrs. Felek rushed outside to see if anybody had heard. But Ephraim kept on howling; then he nearly bit off our fingers as his teeth clenched around them, and he collapsed into unconsciousness.

For ten minutes we kept on pinching him, shaking him, and dousing him with cold water, until he was writhing and yowling once more.

Auntie went outside this time, and again we had to stuff his mouth shut. Once more he struggled with us, and once more he became rigid.

Somebody got an idea: We doused him water and piled on bedding and overcoats. Beneath all that, he continued to yowl until he fell asleep.

All night he snored and cried out in his sleep. He just woke up and can't remember a thing. He's drenched in bloody froth, feels a sharp pain in his chest.

Mrs. Felek and Auntie assure us that nobody heard a thing.

March 6:
We're very disturbed about Ephraim. A week has passed since his attack, and we still shudder when we think of it. But we don't believe it was a freak happening. His behavior has been worrying us for a long time. Every day we notice changes in him, and not only physical ones. For days on end he sits stonily in a corner, completely withdrawn. There's a queer look in his eyes. He seems weaker and more depressed every day. Something is dying inside him. He seems to sense it also and is struggling to pull

himself together. But each day he becomes more remote and more withdrawn. I try hard to draw him into our conversations, but he's lost interest in everything and wants only to sleep.

Today, for the first time in weeks, I succeeded in making him smile. We were talking about the new front that would be opening up in the west. Enthusiastically I described those days that would determine our fate. For the first time in a long while he seemed to wake up and pay attention; his eyes lit up, and he smiled. But although Esther and Zippora hold and support him, he goes limp again. He needs food. We've spoken about it to Mrs. Felek. Twice she brought something, but she seems to have "forgotten" again.

March 7:
It's more than a year since I started keeping this diary. Who dreamed that it would drag on so long and that we would still be alive?

This is the sixteenth month since we made our way here with Auntie. How things have changed! Felek is dead, and Auntie has changed beyond recognition; she's not the same person. I often think about these people, but I can't understand them. I shiver when I think that fifteen months ago Auntie brought us to hide out in the house of a bandit who (as we've recently learned) had terrorized the entire region before the war. Yet Felek was like a father to us. And who knows the story of his sudden death?

I remember the first weeks, when there were only three of us behind the wall downstairs, Esther, Zippora and me. After the terrible days in the camp, everything here was new and peaceful—especially Auntie! We had put our fate in her hands.

We'll never forget that horrible, pitch-dark winter night when we were told that 218 Jews, "unfit for work," had been shot in the Kopernik camps — feeble men, women, and children. We virtually gave up hope for Ephraim, who had remained among those awaiting their death.

Auntie saw how we were suffering, and that dark, freezing night she went to town to see about him. In the middle of the next night she tapped softly on our window. Then she came in with a peasant girl dressed in rags—several layers of skirts and a woolen scarf around her face. The "girl" was Ephraim. It seems that Auntie got him out of the camp in the nick of time. A few days later everybody there was burned alive.

That night we didn't sleep. Auntie sat on the floor, with all of us around her, and told us how she smuggled him out of the camp, out of the city, over the roads, on foot and on the carts of peasants, both acquaintances and strangers. She had introduced Ephraim as her brother's daughter, who was a deaf-mute and a half-wit. Some of the peasants cast pitying eyes at the unfortunate "girl," and others made fun of "her" and laughed at her.

Ephraim sat in a daze, not yet recovered from the trip. He didn't seem to know whether to remain here or flee back to the camp. He was shocked and afraid.

At Adamow, the village headman stopped them and asked Auntie if that deaf-mute wasn't by any chance a Jew girl. Did Auntie knew her well? He even asked for documents. Auntie made such fun of him that the peasants with whom they traveled began to laugh at him too. The "dimwit" tried to hide "her" eyes, even though "her" face was wrapped in a scarf, and "her" terrified gaze couldn't be seen in the dark. And she had to push away the peasants' groping hands.

Auntie laughed as she told the story.

We had a hard time convincing Ephraim to stay with us. He kept shouting that he wants to return to the camp, that it's safer there. He begged us to let him go, to persuade Auntie to take him back. That went on for a few days, until we received the news that the Jews had been burned alive.

A short time later, Froiman came to us. He had been hiding out with six other Jews in the Mrozy forest when the Germans discovered them and blew up their bunker. By a miracle he survived and wound up in a camp. When we found out about him, Auntie set out to bring him here. She brought him to us on the main roads, in broad daylight!

When we think about these things, we feel like kissing Auntie all over! What's come over her since? Though even now she forgets herself sometimes, and we feel her sympathy. Is this what reality is all about?

March 21:
During the last few weeks things have been quiet between Mrs. Felek and Auntie. They're still angry at each other, but instead of quarreling they avoid contact. Every day they come up to see us separately and pour their hearts out to us. Each still would like to drown the other, or at least to strangle her.

Auntie doesn't understand why the Lord permits such a worthless creature as Mrs. Felek to stay alive when so many good people are dying all the time. Mrs. Felek, for her part, would like "that witch" to break both her arms and legs and be taken to the hospital for at least a year. Mrs. Felek is very sad these days. What a miserable life! What can a lonely woman do in this world? No husband, no child, nothing but that plague, Auntie, in the house! How different things would be if she had somebody to confide in, a man: "After all, a man is a man!"

She has often thought about it. Spring is nearly here, sowing time. Her piece of ground, even though it's small, needs a master. Then there's the cow. And the piglet has grown into a proper hog. Then there are the rooster and all those hens running around in the yard. But what will the new master say about us? Isn't it dangerous to let a stranger in on the secret? Though actually, it's none of his business! But it's spring already, and it's possible to live in the forest. Konyak is managing! Maybe she ought to talk to him. He'll find us a hiding place. Maybe even with him.

Oh, no, it certainly isn't too early to talk about it. No, we've got to get ready. She won't be able to manage otherwise. Of course, "the witch" has to go with us! Or, let her go to the devil, or wherever! It's none of her business where Auntie goes. But she can't stay here!

From time to time Mrs. Felek likes to consult us about the matches being proposed to her. "What do you think of old Cereniak? He's a decent man, but a fool. Staszko Kuczak would be fine. But he's got a wife. She's sick though. Maybe she'll die."

She sighs: If not for "that misfortune" in the house, everything would be different. A person would be able to visit her, and she wouldn't be alone, a forsaken dog!

Auntie comforts us: Nothing will come of the whole matter, since there's nobody in the countryside crazy enough to marry such an ugly, evil woman. Besides, it will never come to that. Leave it to Auntie. As soon as she knows who the intended is, she'll have a long talk with him; that'll put a stop to it. So long as she's alive, that one won't get married! Ha, ha, ha! She herself wouldn't mind getting married, but she's not. And how much older is she than that one? Not even ten years!

* * *

Mrs. Felek is unhappy that no match is developing. If somebody serious does turn up, a few days later he suddenly changes his mind. She never has any luck! Lord Jesus seems to want her to remain a widow! Felek must have a hand in it, too. He doesn't want her to marry. He wants her to mourn him forever. So she'll have to remain alone in the world. But it's a pity about the fields and the farm. There's no one to take care of them. You can't rely on strangers—they cheat and steal, and their work isn't worth anything. Besides, it's very expensive to hire strangers. What, Mr. Juzek will pay for it? Well, all right. Mr. Juzek is really a generous man. Mrs. Felek will never forget us.

March 23, p.m:

We worked all day today. We were drenched in sweat, and now we lie in our corners exhausted. Early in the morning, as Esther was crawling out of our hiding place into the attic she lost a needle that she had stuck in her lapel. She was very upset: should Losza, the cow, swallow the needle, our lives won't be worth a penny.

I started searching carefully in the hay. I checked practically every stalk and put it aside, groped in the dark with my fingers, and felt around for the "friendly" prick of a needle.

I labored for several hours, but no needle. When I returned to the hideaway, Froiman went out to search. He was at it for several hours, and was followed in turn by Esther, Zippora, and Ephraim. They, too, exhausted themselves searching—but no needle.

Mrs. Felek comes up several times a day to get a basket of hay for the cow. God help us if Losza chokes on the needle! And we dare not tell Mrs. Felek that we've lost a needle in the haystack.

Again we took turns searching, separating the hay in small piles, tossing it from side to side, groping, squeezing, each of us in turn. And still no needle!

It was evening when I went out to try once more. I sifted the hay in anger. Suddenly I felt a prick, and then another one. I shoved my hand in and pulled out a threaded needle. Triumphant, I crawled back into the hideout.

March 26:

Mrs. Felek has come up with a plan to bring over her brother's son, a sixteen-year-old peasant boy, from his village in the

Wengrow district. Since she doesn't have a child of her own, she would like Wacusz to live with her. He'll even come in handy. He's a healthy boy. They say that he can do the work of two people. She won't have to hire strangers to work her field.

We know the boy. Last summer, when Felek was still alive and Wacusz spent several days here, the whole village was buzzing about the Kikes at Felek's. Wacusz had noticed how cautiously food was cooked in big pots, and he concluded that Jews were hiding out here somewhere. He searched in the rooms, in the stall, in the barn, and in the cellars, and finally headed for the attic. Felek noticed and stopped him. But Wacusz always found reasons for going up there. Finally, they had to hide the ladder in the cellar.

One day, peering through the cracks at high noon, we could see Wacusz lying in the grass directly opposite our wall, playing intently with a small mirror; he was turning it in every direction, catching and reflecting the sun's rays, and staring steadily at our wall. Suddenly, he was directing the sun's reflection of rays right at the cracks in our wall. We quickly moved away and buried ourselves in the corners.

That day the village was buzzing that there were Kikes in Felek's attic: Wacusz had seen them with the help of the mirror.

Felek sent the boy home and hid us in the cellar for several days. He dismantled the partiton in the hayloft and brought up the village headman and peasants to see for themselves that not a living soul was there. Afterwards, he replaced the partition and we returned to our hideout. But that alone might not have helped. Meanwhile, however, Felek was killed, the militia search in the hayloft and throughout the premises and found nothing. That convinced the villagers that Wacusz was a liar and a troublemaker.

But now Mrs. Felek says that she must bring him here; she has no other choice. It will be like having her own child with her. Auntie says that the moment the bastard sets foot in here, it will be the end of us all!

In the past few days we discussed the matter over and over again with Mrs. Felek, gently and with threats. First, I assured her that she wouldn't have to work the field alone: I'll give her money to hire someone. The boy isn't needed. He'll only steal produce and send it to his parents. Furthermore, it's not only our problem: if he sees us, he'll surely inform on us, and she'll be executed!

Mrs. Felek becomes distressed. She left and returned a few hours later. In that case, she said, we must leave before Wacusz gets here. The weather is turning warm. She'll arrange with Konyak to make room for us in his bunker in the forest.

Today I put a fright into Mrs. Felek. I told her that we're ready to go into the forest. Only she must let us take the weapons that Felek buried on the farm; if the Germans discover us, we'll be able to fight back, since one gun isn't enough. As I spoke, I showed her the revolver that Felek gave me before his death.

Her eyes opened wide with fear: She didn't know that we had a weapon, or that "that fool of sainted memory" had given it to us. I must tell her where the rest is buried, and she'll get rid of it. If the Germans should find out, they'll burn down the house and shoot her!

I handle my revolver and tell her that I solemnly pledged to Felek that I wouldn't reveal the hiding place. She'll find out only when we leave for the forest and I dig it all up.

Mrs. Felek stares at the revolver, and then at me; she's suspicious that after we leave, we'll let the police know—by an anonymous note—that they can find weapons at her place. She starts groaning: Well, she didn't actually say that she's bringing Wacusz here. Maybe it *is* a better idea to hire someone. But can Mr. Juzek afford it? And we mustn't say a word about Felek's weapons to Auntie. That witch might inform, and she'll hold it over her as a threat. Still, she herself would like to know where they're hidden.

"No, I swore to Felek that I wouldn't tell."

She looks at me respectfully, then asks me to put the gun away. Her eyes are burning as she crawls down from the hayloft.

March 30:

Nevertheless, we've decided to arrange another hideaway. We asked Janek if he would dig a pit for us in his barn. (It's empty anyway; he has no cows.)

At first, he wouldn't even hear of it. He's afraid of Mrs. Felek. We said that we have no intention of using it now. We only want it in an emergency, for a day or two. In any case, it's a good idea to have a hideaway ready: these days, it could even come in handy for him and his family. Besides, why should he mind digging a pit that he can one day use for storing potatoes in the winter, or as a cellar.

Janek agreed: we're right, it may yet come in handy for him

and his wife and children. Such times! It breaks his heart to think of his daughters. Such fine, well-developed girls! And so pretty! He made them dresses from the wool we gave him for Christmas. Beautiful! But now summer is coming, and you can't wear woolen clothing in the summer. Oh, how they could use light dresses! We can go right ahead and dig the pit. What fine girls he has. They keep growing out of their new clothes.

* * *

Before daybreak Froiman and I climbed down to Janek's barn. We started digging with our spades. Janek and Auntie kept watch in the yard. At 11 o'clock it was done: 8½ feet deep, 6½ feet high, and 5 feet wide. Janek handed us sticks and boards. We fastened the walls and made a "roof." We place the roof beams 2½ feet below ground level and piled that much earth on them. The remaining earth we spread 10 inches high around the barn. So our "roof" was underneath about 40 inches of earth. Janek and Auntie jumped on the "roof" and pounded their feet on it to make sure that no one walking in the barn could notice the hollow in the ground under foot. We then carefully camouflaged the opening, the width of one person, through which we could lower ourselves into the pit. When we returned to the attic after dark, the others greeted us with hugs and kisses. We made a wish that we'd never have to use our new hiding place.

April 1:
Today is Esther's birthday, she's twenty-four. This is her second birthday in the hideaway. May 16, Lag B'omer, will be the second anniversary of our marriage in the ghetto. That was one of the last Jewish celebrations in our town. The catastrophe came three months later.

Many times we take pleasure from the thought that both our mothers lived to bless us under the wedding canopy; both our fathers were no longer alive. That was a blessing, a farewell blessing.

That was only two years ago. Now we feel like old people. All of us do. Though not one of us is even thirty. Froiman, the oldest, only recently turned twenty-nine. I'm twenty-six and Ephraim is twenty-two. Zippora is going on twenty. Konyak, dressed in rags like an old beggar, told Auntie on his latest visit that he just turned sixteen.

He recently hid in the hay in Janek's barn for a while. He can barely drag his feet. Esther made him underwear and thick cloth shoes, and we sent him some money to buy proper shoes. Auntie delivered the money to him, but he said that he cannot and must not buy any shoes. First of all, he has no place to buy them. Secondly, his ragged appearance is his salvation. If he had new shoes, he'd have been murdered a long time ago, if only because someone wanted to steal them.

Konyak says he owes his life to those rags and to lice; their constant biting kept him from falling asleep and freezing to death on those winter nights in barns and his bunker in the forest. And all that scratching and scraping kept his blood circulating and his body warm.

He confides in Auntie. Once he told her that he has met other good people. Only recently he met one such person, a farmer who couldn't stand to see him suffering; out of pity, he wanted to beat him to death with a club. Konyak declined the favor and ran for his life.

Auntie refused to believe that the farmer acted out of pity. Konyak swore that it had been nothing but pity; he knows that farmer. No, it was pity. Because, he said, he wouldn't be telling a story about someone just trying to kill him. Every day peasants try to drag him to his death.

* * *

If only we could help Konyak somehow! Each time he goes away, we fear we'll never see him again. And we're ashamed that if anything happens to us, he'll learn about us and will never forgive us for hiding from him.

A few times when he was staying in Janek's barn, we thought of stealing over to him at night. But then he would have known that we were hiding here. And to lie to him would have been even uglier.

April 5:

Early this morning, after Mrs. Felek went off to the village, we heard someone banging on the ceiling directly beneath our floor. Then Auntie started shrieking: "I'm dying! Oh, Jesus, I'm dying! Juzek! Juzek! Save me! I'm dying!"

I ran downstairs. All the doors and windows were wide open, and Auntie stood in the middle of the room stark naked.

"What's wrong?" I shouted breathlessly.

"Nothing," Auntie laughed. "I just wanted you to tell me whether I have a nice body. Well, Juzek, what do you say?"

I ran from window to window, imagining that the whole world was watching.

"Don't worry," she said. "Nobody's watching. I checked carefully. Well, Juzek, am I pretty?"

I barely slipped out of her reach and dashed back up to the attic. I hadn't quite caught my breath in our hideaway when I heard her once more knocking on the ceiling and shouting: "Fool! Juzek is a fool!"

We were all afraid that someone had seen me through an open window. But Auntie kept on banging upon the ceiling, laughing, and shouting.

Meanwhile, Mrs. Felek returned. She stood in the kitchen listening to Auntie call up to me. When she came into the room and saw Auntie stark naked, she screamed: "You old cow! You old mare! Old bitch in heat like a girl!"

Auntie *has* been carrying on like a girl lately. She has dyed her hair blonde, and every day she runs to her rendezvous with either the organist or Frank Kuczak of Kaluszyn.

132

Mid-April:

The village seems to be buzzing with rumors about us again. Auntie and Janek deny it, but we have solid proof. It seems to be serious this time.

It all started a week ago. Our neighbor, Maczuszak, sold Felek a piece of land fifteen years ago. Now he decided that he had sold it for too little, and he told Mrs. Felek that he was repossessing the property. When Mrs. Felek made a fuss and protested, he shouted at her: "Just try and stop me, you Jews' slave you!" And when she turned away and entered her house, he was still shouting so loudly that dozens of peasants gathered to watch. "I'll teach you, you Jews' slave you!" he shouted.

Everybody laughed, including Janek and Auntie, who even egged him on.

Mrs. Felek was distressed, and asked us what to do. Afterwards, Auntie tried to reassure us; she said that Maczuszak only meant to imply that Mrs. Felek had worked as a maid for Jewish families in town when she was a girl. We calmed down, until Sunday's episode.

Late Sunday afternoon, Konyak was in the village. A gang of young toughs from Wolka saw him and ran after him. He fled into our cottage. The boys wanted to drag him out, but Auntie blocked the doorway and Mrs. Felek went after them with a broom. But they surrounded the cottage, demanding that she hand him over; if she agreed, they would take Konyak to the police but wouldn't report her giving him shelter. If she didn't hand him over, they would call the police, which would be worse.

The gang charged at the door and windows, and created such an uproar that within half an hour dozens of boys and girls of all ages were rioting in the yard, shouting: "Hand over the Jews! The police are coming! Mrs. Felek's hiding Jews! Here come the police! Hand over the Jews!"

When it got dark, the children left and Konyak fled.

Janek and Auntie assured us that they had meant only Konyak: Those young punks can't even talk properly, so they yelled "Jews!" Besides, they were only having some fun; it will never get to the police.

Janek went to Wolka to get the latest news. He came back in a good mood, bringing details about the Soviet winter offensive: they've chased the Germans another few hundred miles west and caused them heavy losses. The Russians are already well into Poland. They're just the other side of Kowel. People say they're about to launch an even bigger offensive. We'll soon be free. That business with those young punks? No need to worry, he didn't hear a word about it. We cheered up a little, and were even close to tears.

But this morning, the headman of Wolka was strolling along the path near the oak wood with Mrs. Felek's niece, Wacusz's sister, who's staying in the village. We noticed him stopping a few times to stare at the cracks in our wall. The girl also was staring right at us. They seemed to be whispering to each other. We figured she was telling him about her brother and the mirror, or about the riot on Sunday.

In the afternoon, they walked by again, and again they paused several times to look up in our direction. Will something happen now, precisely now, when salvation is so close?

April 27:

I've been sick for the past few days. I feel tired and hot all over, although I've got the chills. I can feel my blood raging and my heart pounding. My head is heavy and a deep listlessness keeps putting me to sleep. The others look at me sadly. They're also resigned, as if merely waiting for the end.

Easter just passed, and the village celebrated gaily. All the cottages were rejoicing. Our neighbor, Maczuszak, had guests from Warsaw, his daughter and her husband, Kapusta. At night we heard them whispering outside our attic wall; we recognized the voices of Kapusta and Maczuszak's daughters. They stood there silently for a long while, then began to whisper, became quiet again, and were soon whispering once more.

The next morning they gathered again outside our wall and peered through the cracks. The beams had dried up and contracted, so the cracks had widened. We hid in the corners of the attic. But they ran away as soon as they heard Mrs. Felek open the front door to go out.

Since then, we've noticed every passer-by from the village staring up at the cracks. It's been confirmed by Auntie and Janek, who hid in the oak wood to observe what was happening. Now they admit that Maczuszak's threats, the incidents with the Wolka children and the Wolka headman weren't just accidents.

They've been in a terrible state since we told them about the latest episode. Yesterday evening, Mrs. Felek and Auntie went out, separately, to the village. They left the front door open. Suddenly, we heard someone climbing the ladder to the attic. Quickly we covered the cracks in the wall and held our breaths. Someone moved around in the attic for a few minutes. A good thing that the other side of the wall is stacked high with hay. Then we heard the person climb down the ladder. We looked out and saw Maczuszak's youngest daughter, Mariszka, nineteen, emerge from the cottage into the yard. She paused beside our wall and looked up.

Later, in the evening, Auntie visited Maczuszak, spoke with Mariszka, and felt her penetrating glance.

Janek tells us to do something. Auntie blames us; we must have been seen through the cracks. Mrs. Felek curses both Auntie and us. She says that Auntie's behavior has aroused suspicion. Auntie, in turn, blames us and Mrs. Felek, because the whole world can hear her screaming at us. Janek says that both women are to blame. Even he can hear them yelling when they come up to the attic.

Today Auntie staged such a scene that Janek had to come up to the attic with a stick and drive her out. Then Mrs. Felek let us know that the villagers had probably found out about us. Auntie was always banging on the ceiling with a stick and calling up to us. But she, Mrs. Felek, had no intention of suffering because of us. She won't be shot because of us. We must leave immediately. She started crying so loudly that Janek had to drag her out of the attic.

Now she's downstairs crying and in a shouting match with Auntie. Janek says that he'll throw both of them out together with us, and burn down the cottage. This has to finish once and for all. He's fed up.

I can feel my temperature rising. I'm dizzy and everything's spinning before my eyes. I can see the cottage burning, and we're floating in the air over an abyss. The others just sit there frozen. A storm is raging outside. Eerie sounds rise from the depths; huge paws grab at us. They're coming closer and closer. They're inside the attic. They grab hold of us. They're clutching our throats, and choking us.

May 2:
We've just been through some turbulent days, and it's hard to believe that we're still alive. The whole village was in an uproar over us. We are no longer in Mrs. Felek's attic. Our hideout was discovered. We're in the pit in Janek's stable.

On the evening of April 28, we heard noise and shouting coming from Maczuszak's cottage. We could make out Mrs. Felek's shrill voice. We heard enough to know that it was about the tract of land that Maczuszak was appropriating. The shouting went on for hours. Downstairs, in our cottage, it was deadly silent. Auntie was also at Maczuszak's taking part in the argument.

We couldn't sleep that night. We sensed that the worst had come to pass. Early in the morning we heard shouting again. This time it came from downstairs. Janek was cursing Mrs. Felek: because of her, "now everybody knows." She shouldn't have made that scene with Maczuszak. She should have let the matter pass. "Now it's all over. The police will soon be here!"

We felt a pit open under us. Our ashen faces broke into a cold sweat. Esther and Zippora dug their fingernails into their cheeks. My eyes misted over. Someone was in the attic. Auntie knocked. "Bad!" she said. "Bad!" Last night Mrs. Felek threatened to tell the police about Maczuszak's unregistered hogs. So Maczuszak shouted, in the presence of about half the population of the village, that Jews were hiding in Mrs. Felek's attic, and tomorrow they would all burn together.

Janek asked us what we were going to do. He doesn't advise us to run away now, since we'll be caught immediately. The peasants will catch us and turn us in. Maybe someone has already gone to report us. We must leave the attic at once, because the police might arrive any minute. Since we can't show ourselves in the village in broad daylight, he suggests that we go down to our former hideaway temporarily. In the evening, if everything is all right, we'll think of what to do next.

Janek and Auntie left, and we started tearing down the partition and spreading the hay. Half an hour later we were behind the wall downstairs.

A strange silence exists in the house. Nobody is home. There's nobody to camouflage the false wall by hanging clothes on it; to hang a rug over our little door; to move the bed back into place. It's so quiet that we can hear the flies buzzing in the house as well as a medley of sounds from all over the village.

Our foreheads are pressed against the partition. Our hearts and temples are pounding; we're keeling over. The minutes drag on like hours, years. Ephraim feels faint, he needs air. He can't stand any more; his feet aren't used to it. My legs won't hold me up either. Esther and Zippora gasp for air. There's hardly enough room to stand up in here; and it's impossible to move our hands. We're squeezed in between two walls. Froiman's stomach is churning. We're going to pass out.

We hear noise in the distance, footsteps. It's Mrs. Felek. She moves around in the kitchen, sighing and passing back and forth. She comes into the room and tells us to open the door. She's terribly frightened. It's too quiet in the village, she reports. People are avoiding her. They stare at her suspiciously. The calm before the storm. But nobody found out anything from her, she says. They've known for some time. Auntie must be to blame. But it may even be better this way, out in the open. All those secrets would have brought the police here, and they'd have found us right in the attic. Here, behind the wall, they may not find us. Let it be night already! Those scum, Janek and Auntie! They ran away from the village. What do they care if we all get shot?

Mrs. Felek quickly camouflaged our little door, moved the bed against the wall, arranged things in the attic, and left the house.

* * *

Janek and Auntie came back in the evening. Janek says that we can't hide in the pit in his barn, because it's filled with water. We have to hide in the cellar of Mrs. Felek's barn. It isn't camouflaged, but it can be covered with straw and sticks. But Mrs. Felek says that the policemen all know her cellar; it was the first place they searched after a theft in the neighborhood. We'd better hide in the forest.

Janek tells her not to be silly. As soon as we get to the forest, the peasants will catch us and hand us over to the Germans. They'll beat us until we tell everything, and that will be the end of them all, Mrs. Felek, himself, Auntie. No, we can't leave!

So Mrs. Felek agreed to hide us in her barn cellar. But she's going off to another village to sleep. She will not stay at home!

An hour later, when it was pitch dark outside, we were taken to the cellar. Mrs. Felek ran off immediately, followed by Janek and Auntie. We lay in that dark hole on a pile of potatoes. The air stank with mildew and rot. Rats ran and leaped around us. Esther and Zippora were groaning; Ephraim was in a daze. Froiman was afraid that in the middle of the night, Janek and his cronies would hack us to death with hatchets, leaving no trace of us.

"What are we going to do?"

"Maybe we ought to run away."

"Where to?"

"If at least Konyak were with us!"

We thought of all our neighbors in the village, one by one, to see if we could find one who would shelter us in exchange for money for even a few days.

Esther thinks that it's a bad idea. If we ask the peasants for shelter, they'll probably turn us in to the police. At best, they'll refuse us, and then spread the word through the village.

But one name occurred to me: Wacek, who lives nearby. He seems to be decent and trustworthy. Even if he won't hide us, he won't gossip to everyone, and he certainly won't turn us in. We can take a chance with him. Besides, he's very poor, and maybe he'll hide us for the money.

The only problem is that Paltyn, Maczuszak's son-in-law, is living with him. Paltyn's wife, Maczuszak's daughter-in-law, took part in the screaming match with Mrs. Felek; and she also accused Mrs. Felek of hiding Jews in her attic. Ephraim says that with Paltyn there, it's too risky.

We couldn't make any decision. Half an hour later I jumped up and announced: "I'm going to Wacek!"

Esther and Zippora grabbed hold of me, started crying, and begged me not to go. But I appealed to their common sense: "Staying here means certain death. Just to run away is also certain death. We must take a chance. Maybe Wacek *will* help. He's a pauper, and his children are sick. We'll offer to help him out."

Esther began to shake and tear her hair. "No, I'm not letting you go! I'm not letting you go alone. I'm going with you!"

We kissed the others. I put the revolver in my pocket, lifted the cellar door, and we went together.

* * *

It was a bright night, lit up by the snow-covered fields. The village houses huddled together in a single bloc close to the ground. Their windows were curtained and dark, except for the few scattered cottages where some lights still flickered. It must have been close to midnight.

We took a side path to avoid the neighboring cottages. We hoped to cut through the oak wood and end up right at Wacek's door; we knew its appearance from descriptions we had heard: a white plastered cottage, with Wacek's name on a plaque on the doorpost.

We were in the woods. Esther took short, deep, heavy breaths, unable to inhale all that fresh air at once. I could hear her heart pounding. Her head spun. I felt intoxicated; I wobbled and couldn't see straight. A few more steps, and Esther had to stop; her feet wouldn't obey her. She couldn't even stand up straight. The ground was covered with snow, there was nowhere to sit. She leaned against a tree, and I supported her.

A few minutes later we started walking again, but Esther tired quickly. She complained that she couldn't go on, that she wanted to go back. She wanted only to lie down; she couldn't take another step.

We started back, but she couldn't move. She needed some rest. I found a tree stump, brushed away the snow, and sat Esther down on it.

Light shone in a nearby window. I came closer: a white plastered cottage. It was Wacek's! I kissed Esther, took the gun out of my pocket, and checked to see that it was loaded: then, my heart pounding, I slipped out of the woods and approached the window. It was light inside.

A farmer aged about forty sat by the stove warming himself. In a nearby bed lay a woman and a few children. She was chatting pleasantly with the people in the other bed, a farmer and his wife. In the third bed some more children were sleeping. A kerosene lamp was burning on the table. The man by the stove was half undressed, about ready to get into bed; he was finishing his cigarette as he joined in the conversation. From time to time he smiled at the other man's jokes.

I didn't know who was Wacek and who was Paltyn. I checked the plaque on the door: sure enough, it was Wacek's cottage. My heart pounded. In my head I rehearsed my little speech, then tapped a few times on the window pane.

"Who's there?" they all said at once, startled.

I couldn't answer. I wasn't used to talking out loud, and my tongue seemed to stick to the roof of my mouth. Finally I managed to blurt out: "Wacek!"

"Who's there?" a frightened woman's voice asked.

"One of us!" I replied in a voice I didn't recognize.

"Who?" They all jumped up in their beds.

"One of us!" I forced the words out. "I have to speak to Wacek!"

"The Lord have mercy!" one of the women moaned.

I tried to calm them: "It's nothing, really. Don't be afraid. Open up." I went to the door and knocked softly.

A few minutes later the door opened. A husky peasant stood there gazing at me. Then he saw the revolver and said: "Please, sir, we haven't done anything, have mercy!"

"Don't worry," I said. "You have nothing to fear. I won't harm anybody. Just tell me your name."

"P-palt-tyn," he stammered.

I asked him to calm the women. Nothing would happen to them. I only wanted to speak with Wacek. Let him tell Wacek to come right out!

Paltyn's voice quivered: "How many of you are there?

"We're in the woods," I said.

He went back inside. I went to the window. I heard him say that a band of Jewish partisans wanted to speak with Wacek. Mrs. Wacek started pounding her head with her fists and shouted: "No, Wacek! Have mercy! Don't go! Have mercy!"

Wacek sat on the bed confused. He was scratching his head.

"Don't go!" his wife cried again, hugging and kissing him. "Oh, Jesus, have mercy!"

Wacek started to get up from his bed. But his wife jumped up, her blouse slipping off her shoulders. She cried: "Oh, merciful Jesus, don't go! I'm not letting you!"

I called Paltyn out again and asked him to calm everyone down.

"Have mercy, master!" he begged. "I've got little children!"

But Paltyn came back outside to say that Wacek wasn't coming out. Warm air streamed at my face.

Mrs. Wacek, a woman of about thirty, was trembling. Nearly naked, she knelt and bowed before the icon, wringing her hands all the while. The others were shaking in their beds.

I stepped towards Mrs. Wacek. "Relax, madam," I said. "I won't harm a soul."

She stood up, turned to me, and began kissing my hands. "Have mercy, sir!"

I stroked her hair and shoulders and said: "Madam, go back to bed. Nothing is going to happen to him."

Gradually I calmed her down and she returned to bed.

I asked Wacek to step outside with me for just a few minutes. I wanted to discuss something with him privately.

"Sir," he pleaded, "have mercy! I'm not going outside!" He began to shout: "You can kill me, if that's what you want to do, right here in bed! I'm not going out!"

The women and children were hysterical.

"Just for a few minutes," I pleaded. "I have to tell you something in private."

"No! Tell me here! I'm not going outside!"

Having no choice, I told him within earshot of everyone: "We're a group of Jewish partisans. We have orders to get through to the Eastern Front. Someone gave us your name and said you would let us spend the night in your stable. We'll be on our way before dawn."

"But we don't even have a stable," Wacek whined.

Paltyn suggested that we sneak into Mrs. Felek's stable. He told us where she lived, and even offered to take us there.

"No, thanks," I said. "We'll be on our way. We also have a few addresses in the next village."

They all relaxed. I asked for water, and Paltyn graciously handed me a glass, and offered to make me tea.

"Are there any Jews around here?" I blurted out.

"No," they all answered at once. "Oh, no!"

"There's one," Mrs. Paltyn said. "There's one roaming around the villages. His name is Konyak."

"Could I see him?" I asked.

"Oh, no, sir! We don't know where he is. He shows up every once in a while and then disappears. They say he's hiding out in the Wiszniew woods."

"Do you know of any other Jews in the area? We want very much to meet up with some Jews!"

"There are absolutely no more Jews around here," Paltyn proclaimed.

"Are you sure? Think hard. I'm ready to pay." I start taking money out of my pocket.

"No. There aren't any. Absolutely not!"

"Really, now, think hard. I'll pay. We'll be very grateful."

Paltyn thought hard. He began rubbing his forehead. "Wait. Wait. Maybe. . ."

"No! Absolutely not!" Mrs. Paltyn stared desperately at her husband.

"That's right, that's right" the Waceks said from the next bed.

"Of course not," Paltyn said. "I just thought. . .No!"

"Too bad!" I said. "Do you happen to know anybody who is hiding Jews, or who hid any, or who is helping them? We want to reward them."

"No, we don't know anybody hiding Jews. But all of us are helping Konyak as much as we can. We often give him bread and hot food."

"That's fine. Go on helping him right to the end! You'll be rewarded. In a few months we'll be back with the Red Army. If

Konyak is still alive, we'll see to it that you're rewarded. You'll get medals and cash from us and the Soviet general staff. The more Jews you save or help to survive, the more you'll be rewarded, you and the whole village."

"Of course we'll help him all we can!" the Paltyns solemnly pledged.

I took a notebook and pencil out of my pocket and asked for the full names of all of them, including the children. "That," I said, "is so we'll know exactly whom to reward when the time comes. But if we find out that anybody in your village turned in a Jew, we'll burn the entire village to the ground. The guilty ones will be hanged, and all the rest will be sent to the camps! Everyone will get whatever reward or punishment he deserves!"

I took 100 zlotys out of my pocket and handed fifty to each of the women, "to buy sweets for the children," I said. Then I put my index finger over my mouth, to say that everything must remain a secret, said goodbye, and quickly left.

* * *

Esther was trembling with fright when I returned. She had wanted to come after me, she said, but she hadn't been able to stand on her feet.

She leaned on me for support, but she couldn't take a step; her legs seemed to be paralyzed. I felt like lying down. My head was pounding and I couldn't stand up any longer. However, I managed to drag myself back to the barn and called Froiman. Together we went to the woods to get Esther and carried her back to the barn. We crept into the cellar and sprawled out on the potato pile. Ephraim and Froiman said prayers on our safe return.

I told them about my failure. Froiman is worried that the tracks we left in the snow will be discovered. But they all agreed that the risk had been worthwhile; we really had nothing to lose anyway.

* * *

Before dawn, someone quietly opened the barn doors and approached the cellar. It was Mrs. Felek. She lifted the cellar door and asked how we had slept. "Very well," we said.

She tells us not to remain here. Everybody knows this cellar. Even the hideaway inside the double wall would be better. Maybe they won't search there. She'll camouflage the opening wall. We can go inside right now. It's still dark outside and nobody will see us.

One by one we stole into the cottage and went behind the partition. Mrs. Felek handed us several thick slices of bread and two bottles of coffee, and carefully concealed the opening.

Soon afterwards Auntie and Janek came along. They were in a good mood. Janek offers us brandy. "Brandy," he says, "is the best medicine. Drink drives away all your cares." He's just had a drink and already he's not afraid of a thing.

Auntie tells us to come out of the hideaway. She starts singing Christmas carols. Mrs. Felek shouts that she's crazy and drunk.

At about 8:30 p.m., in walks our dreaming neighbor, Mrs. Rechniakow. She's flustered, and keeps apologizing that she isn't to blame; she has only the best intentions towards them all. But as a good neighbor, she's come to offer some advice. It's all for their own good, the good of all the neighbors, and the good of the entire village. The headman has asked her to warn them that he will have to call the police if they don't get rid of the Jews in their attic immediately. He hasn't called them yet, because he feels sorry for them. But he's not ready to endanger himself! She advises them to drive the Jews out in her presence, right now.

Janek and Auntie laugh. Mrs. Rechniakow, they say, is a fool if she really believes that there are Jews here. Auntie drags her up to the attic to see for herself.

Overhead in the attic we hear movement and noise. Mrs. Rechniakow turns over the hay and straw in her search. "Well," she says coming down, "I guess there really was some mistake. But everyone still says that there are Jews here. Maczuszak and his daughters proved it."

After she left, Janek opened our little door and said: "Have yourselves a good laugh!"

He offers us a drink. We plead with him to think of something. Maybe a friend or relative who will hide us for just a few days. Auntie says we have nothing to worry about, that nobody will come looking for us. Now they all know that there are no Jews here: Mrs. Rechniakow saw for herself.

She curses Mrs. Felek, who fled from the house right after Mrs. Rechniakow left. That, she says, will only confirm their suspicions. Auntie says that she isn't afraid. But she must leave for town right away. She has an appointment with Frank Kuczak. It's Sunday. And Janek has to go with her. But we shouldn't worry: they'll be back in the evening.

Just then, Mrs. Felek returned from the village bursting with good news: Maczuszak is going from cottage to cottage swearing that there aren't any Jews at Mrs. Felek's, saying that he invented the whole story just to put pressure on her. He went to the Wolka headman to confirm it. The whole village is laughing at him; he was so afraid that the Germans wouldn't find any Jews at Mrs. Felek's, and then punish him for misleading them.

Mrs. Felek just ran into Mrs. Paltyn, Maczuszak's daughter, who apologized to her about the whole thing. She swore in the name of Lord Jesus that she had never said a word about Jews in Mrs. Felek's attic. She knows that there really isn't anyone there. Mrs. Felek can find out for herself that she, Mrs. Paltyn, has been everywhere and denied the false rumor about the Jews.

Mrs. Felek tells us that quite a few people are supporting her. Right now, Wacek and his wife are denying that there are Jews at Mrs. Felek's before a crowd of peasants. Mrs. Wacek was saying that she often visited Auntie and can state as a fact that there are no Jews there. Wacek declared that whoever repeats the slander is out of his mind; such a person can bring disaster down upon the entire village, and he should be torn to bits. Paltyn swears that his father-in-law, Maczuszak, was only joking, trying to bully Mrs. Felek.

Janek and Auntie aren't going to Kaluszyn after all. They're staying. And, they say, we all must drink a few glasses of brandy. Janek was already fiddling with the bottle when we heard footsteps outside. We quickly shut the door to our hideout.

In walked the Wolka village headman and Paltyn. The headman laughed: He knew all the time that no Jews were here. It didn't make sense that they'd be so foolish to hide Jews. Even before Mrs. Rechniakow told him that she had been in the attic and seen for herself, he knew the truth. But he would like to ask them not to bear a grudge against Maczuszak and his daughters. They didn't mean any harm. They only meant to threaten them a little. They asked him to come here to explain. He wanted them to promise not to bear any grudge.

Janek pours a few glasses of brandy. The headman and Paltyn drink.

Paltyn says that Jews are human beings too, and shouldn't be harmed, even if they do roam around—Konyak, for example.

"Here's to good health!

"Here's to Mrs. Felek!

"Here's to the headman!"

Janek pours glass after glass. Everybody begins to sound giddy.

"Long life!"

They start rocking on their stools.

"Here's to Janek, Auntie and Mrs. Felek!" the headman shouts.

Paltyn stands up and sways. "Long live the headman!"

"Long live Konyak!"

* * *

Soon after it became dark Janek rushed into the cottage with bad news: He heard in the village that police will be here first thing in the morning. Some villager may have gone to them with the story about us. He doesn't know what to do. To go into Mrs. Felek's cellar would really be risky. That's no hideout. But we can't stay in this hideaway either; they'll soon discover it at once. Quite a few Jews have been caught behind false walls lately. I say that we ought to hide in the pit in his barn. Impossible, he says. The pit is full of water. Besides he's afraid.

Zippora pleads with him: We'll bale out the water. He has nothing to fear; nobody will discover us, the pit is well hidden. But even if we are caught, no harm will come to him. He doesn't sleep at home anyway, and his wife and children aren't here (they've been staying in Warsaw and don't even know of our existence). Auntie and Mrs. Felek won't stay around, either.

Finally, Janek agreed, and he took us to his barn.

We uncover it, and the pit really is filled with water. Auntie rushes in with several pails. Froiman lets himself down into the pit and starts baling; he hands us the full pails, and we pour the water into holes under the barn walls. Meanwhile Mrs. Felek and Janek keep watch outside.

After several hours of baling, the pit was empty. Froiman spread straw on the floor of the pit and we all lowered ourselves into it. Mrs. Felek brought us bread and water, a candle and some matches; then Janek camouflaged the outside of the pit. We asked him to pile sufficient earth on top of it, and to open it for us the next evening.

Janek placed beams across the opening and filled the 40-inch hole with earth. After flattening the earth to the level of the stable ground, he littered it with garbage and pounded it with his feet. It was quiet after that.

We were completely in the dark. We're glad to be so deep underground. We joke that even Satan can't find us here. The darkness is so thick that we can almost touch it. Ephraim tries to light a match, but it immediately dies out. He lights a second one—it also goes right out. The same with the third one. Froiman finally succeeds in getting the candle lit, but almost at once it dies out. Zippora says that she can't breathe. Neither can Esther.

All of a sudden I feel the straw beneath me turning damp. I poke around and discover a puddle of water. Esther feels pressure in her chest; she needs air. I tell her to breathe in the damp ground. She stretches out on her stomach, clears away some straw, and starts inhaling through both her nose and her mouth. Zippora does the same. Ephraim says that he's drowsy, and he stretches out in a third corner. Froiman and I are sitting in the center. We decide to go to sleep, so that time will pass more quickly. I feel pressure in my chest, and I can hear Froiman's heart pounding. But we were very tired and we fell asleep.

Suddenly I woke up feeling very unwell. A few minutes had passed. I felt a heaviness in my body. I could hardly talk. I ask Froiman how he feels. "Not good!" he says. I ask Esther if she feels any better. No reply. I ask again. Still no reply. Frantic, I start nudging her. Her body is stiff. I shout and pinch and shake her, but there is no sign of life. Froiman says that Zippora and Ephraim have also passed out. He rubs and pokes them, but it doesn't help. We have to open the pit and get some air in! He goes to work. I keep trying to revive the three who have passed out.

I finally get Esther awake, but she's not fully conscious. I rush back and forth from her to Zippora and Ephraim, who are still unconscious. I feel that any minute I'll pass out too. Froiman is trying to break through the sealed pit, but the beams are firmly entrenched in the earth and they won't budge.

I attempt to pull up the boards while Froiman tries to revive the others. He urges me to make it faster, because he, too, is about to pass out. The boards won't budge. "Faster, faster!" he shouts. Froiman stands up and helps me pull. A board gives.

Some earth begins to move. We dig our hands in further and start burrowing upward. Earth pours down upon us. The boards loosen. Froiman quickly pulls one out. Finally the other boards loosen and fall down. All the earth caved into the pit and the hole was open.

Those who had passed out lay there rigid. Froiman hoisted me up and shoved me out through the opening into the barn. He lifted Esther and handed her up to me. I pulled her up by her hands while he pushed from below. I grabbed her under the armpits, lifted her out, and laid her down on the straw. Then Froiman lifted Zippora and Ephraim, and I pulled them out and laid them beside Esther. We spent the next ten minutes reviving them and applying artificial respiration. At last, they came to.

The rest of the night we sat in the barn. We could flee into the forest for a few days, but Esther, Zippora, and Ephraim can't move. They're dozing off in the corners. Froiman and I are also exhausted. I've been feverish since the middle of April. I don't know my temperature, but I'm burning up. We sat there until dawn. When the sky began to brighten, we went back into the pit. Once inside, I pulled the straw over the hole, leaving some room for air to enter; and we all sat there depending upon God's mercy. For several hours we recited Psalms, and then fell asleep.

Mrs. Felek woke us. It was evening. We crawled up into the barn. She gave us the hot food she had brought, and told us that police had searched many places in the village today. There was a report that someone was illicitly milling again. The police had not been looking for us. Thank God that they didn't come searching here.

May 5:

This is our fifth day in the barn. We feel as if we were beaten insensible, and our limbs feel as heavy as lead. Esther, Zippora, and Ephraim remain in the pit, while Froiman and I spend some time in the barn above. Through cracks in the walls, we check for suspicious movements outside. We've established observation points high on two opposite walls, just beneath the straw roof. Through the slits in the walls, we can catch a glimpse of our surroundings. Almost the entire day we're holding on to the rafters, scouting the outside. We strain our eyes and all our senses until each dark spot moving on the horizon assumes a clear form.

It's terribly hot in the barn, and so stifling that we can hardly breathe. Whenever we open our mouths to inhale, we take in the nauseating stench, and start to choke. So from time to time we press our nostrils against the cracks and inhale some fresh air. Then, out of the pit pokes a disheveled head, a pallid face, a pointy nose, or piercing eyes, and grunts something incomprehensible. Two of them in the pit are offering to replace us, since we must be exhausted from leaning so long on the rafters. We're glad that they can get some fresh air too. So we carefully jump off the slats on the wall. Our feet splash around in the damp straw and sink ankle-high into a wet mess.

Ephraim is on all fours staring up at the wall with his nearsighted eyes, about to climb up to replace one of us. Behind him, in an identical posture, is Zippora. Esther is already in Froiman's position up above, the small crack fixed to her eye like a spy-glass, scouting the outdoors. Ephraim struggles to climb up to my former spot, but Zippora pulls him down. No, she'll go up there; he's so near-sighted that he couldn't see a thing. Ephraim resists. She starts climbing. He grabs her foot. But she's already leaning on a rafter, and she kicks her foot free. We can hear Ephraim panting from lack of air. Froiman tells him to lie down with his face to the wall. Air seeps in under the baseboards, spreading across the floor. He revives a bit.

The women are tense at their observation posts. They tremble at every sound, and they lose their balance on the slats. Finally, Froiman makes some more openings under the baseboards, asks the women to lie down and get some air, and the two of us return to our observation posts.

It's quiet outside. Only Auntie is puttering around near the entrance to Mrs. Felek's cottage. She is plucking grass and singing a sad song about Felek "of sainted memory." The crickets chirp and the birds sing along to her tune.

Suddenly, there's a stir in the barn behind us. We turn around, it's empty below. Esther and Zippora are already back in the pit. We see only the bottom of Ephraim's foot jutting out from the pit as he struggles to get back inside. Froiman jumps down, grabs Ephraim by the foot, and asks them to come out to the baseboards and get some air; otherwise they'll pass out again.

They refuse. We might suddenly have to take cover, and the fewer people left in the barn the better. By no means will they come up for air.

* * *

5 p.m. I'm hungry. Our little supper should soon be ready. Auntie is plucking grass for the rabbit couple nesting in a corner of our barn. Janek installed them here three days ago. Thanks to them, it was possible to lock the barn door: now they can say that the door is locked to protect the rabbits, and not the Jews that Janek's supposed to be hiding. The rabbits prick up their long ears at every sound; they're probably upset to be locked up in this strange place. And every time Auntie brings us food, she brings along a heaping basket of grass for them, which also conceals our pot of food. She strides boldly across the yard carrying the basket of grass, and singing merrily. Then she stops in front of the door, looks around, and calls out: "Trush, trush—trush, trush!"

The rabbits crouch, prick up their ears, and leap, perhaps out of fear, or perhaps out of joy at the basketful of fragrant fresh grass. Then Auntie again calls out: "Trush—trush, trush!" This signals to us that she's entering. She turns the lock, the door opens slightly, and the scent of cooked food tickles our nostrils and makes our mouths water. She puts the basket on the floor and leaves, locking the door behind her.

One by one they come out of the pit and seat themselves around the basket. They remove the pot, and throw the grass aside. The rabbits turn friendly; come over, and join them for dinner. Esther, Zippora, and Ephraim gulp down the hot spoonfuls and relieve us at the observation posts so that we too can eat. The rabbits, their ears quivering, also bolt down the grass. Zippora runs her hand over their white angora fur and their long, veined ears; the dumb, crouching creatures gulp down the long blades of grass as they gape at us with red, frightened eyes. They seem to stare at us suspiciously, as if sensing that our living together will bring them no good. We're worried too: some neighbor may yet fulfill an urge to break in one night and steal the rabbits.

Meanwhile, we're grateful to our little protectors, if only for their indifference. Whatever else they may feel toward us, we don't sense that they bear us any hatred.

* * *

We're still kept awake by the fear that someone could break in at night to steal the rabbits. We're always hearing imaginary footsteps, for example, someone slinking through the field to our barn. We would cover the pit and go to sleep inside, but then we couldn't breathe. So three of us sleep in the pit while one of us keeps watch in the dark barn, listening intently to the silence. Each of us does a night of guard duty. We have to fight hard to stay awake. The nights are chilly, but the breeze is refreshing and soothing. Only the same gnawing fear helps us to fight off sleep. Our eyelids stick together and our limbs pull us down, begging to stretch out in the straw. Mice scrape in the straw with their scrawny paws. We hear all kinds of sounds outside too. Many times I grab the edge of the hole with both hands and I'm ready to leap into the pit. Below, the others snore heavily and sigh in their sleep. From time to time they wake up and listen, but soon they're snoring once more.

Gradually the thick darkness dissolves into cold, gray shadows that close in on us. Outside the sky turns blue, the sun rises, the birds are singing. Froiman wakes and crawls out of the pit into the half-darkness. He rubs his eyes and combs his disheveled hair with his fingers. Then he climbs up the wall, mounts the slats with his bare feet, and takes up his guard.

I'm up there already. We both whisper a morning prayer. It's the time for quiet meditation. The day is fresh and radiant; and except for waking nature, everything is still asleep. The world seems so bright, clean, and harmonious. How I'd like to run in the damp grass, wipe my parched face with dew, lie down in the moist earth, and think about absolutely nothing. If only this morning would last forever!

But the morning bustle has already begun. Cottage doors are opening. Peasant women in white kerchiefs scurry to the barns, milk jugs in their hands. It's broad daylight. Mrs. Felek stands sour-faced on her threshold. She's about to let the cow out to pasture. Other cows leave their barns. Everywhere doors open, cows go off to the meadows, peasant men and women to the fields. Hens shove their way into the yard. Birds fly out of their nests. Every creature is out in the open.

We check to make sure the door is locked tight. We seal all but a few cracks in the walls, spread straw around the pit opening, and get ready to leap into the pit at a moment's notice.

* * *

It seems that there was a reason why Ephraim had been fainting during the past few days. He had another fit this morning, similar to the one he had three and a half months ago in Mrs. Felek's attic. It happened at about ten o'clock.

Auntie told us that police were at the other end of the village, searching from cottage to cottage for some villagers who had been taken for forced labor in Germany, but had escaped. So while Froiman and I kept watch from the side walls, Esther took up a position at a crack in the rear wall. Zippora and Ephraim remained in the pit.

We watch, and we listen to the silence in the village, a familiar, terrible stillness. We're even afraid that our hearts are beating too loudly. There's not a living soul outside. As though the ground has swallowed them all up.

Opposite us, at Maczuszak's place, the front door slowly opens and a blonde girlish head pokes out. It's Mariszka, his youngest daughter. She looks around cautiously, whispers into the house, and slinks out. Following behind her is young Woczalak, a neighbor's son, a short, dark, red-cheeked boy. They listen to the silence for a moment, then tiptoe toward the tall grass near the pond by our barn. They sit down, bury their heads in the grass, and, certain that no one is watching, quickly forget about the police in the village. . . .

We all hold our breaths. Froiman slides down from the wall and cautions Ephraim and Zippora to be absolutely still. But a minute later we heard a strange bellowing below us, followed by muffled sounds of suffocation. It was Ephraim. We all leaped into the pit at once. Ephraim lay rigid, his jaws locked, fists clenched, a red froth covering his face. Froiman and Esther tried to revive him as I hurried back to my crack in the wall.

Woczalak and Mariszka were listening now, trying to determine the direction of the sounds. When it became quiet again, they sank back down into the grass. But soon there was more noise—shrill outcries this time. They had managed to wake up Ephraim; but he hadn't recovered consciousness, and was shouting in Yiddish: "I want to go home!" When they tried to shut him up, he resisted and shouted even louder.

Mariszka and Woczalak jumped up. "Germans! Germans!" she screamed, and started to run away. But he insisted that they hide deeper in the grass. Meanwhile, Ephraim continued to shout.

"I hear German voices!" Mariszka screams. "Let's hide quickly!" They bury themselves in the grass.

But the screams keep coming from out pit. They subside for a minute, then start again. I can hear the struggle inside, a life-and-death struggle.

Suddenly Woczalak leaps up and shouts: "Those aren't Germans! Those voices are coming from someplace near here!"

They listen again. Ephraim's Yiddish screams pierce the air.

"You're right," the frightened Mariszka confirms. "It's close by. It sounds like German but not really."

They start creeping toward our barn.

Just then, shots were ringing out everywhere in the village. Green spots appeared in the distance.

"Germans, Germans, hurry up, Mariszka!" Woczalak grabbed her hand and the two of them ran to the oak wood.

A few minutes later the village was swarming with police. They charged into the cottages and barns and dragged out young men and women. They were moving in our direction. We think of covering Ephraim with our clothes and blankets, and shutting the hole tightly; but we know that he wouldn't survive. We drench him with water and massage his hands and temples, but his convulsions continue. The police move from cottage to cottage, from barn to barn. They are just a few houses away. Their big hounds run ahead of them. Two policemen approach us. We pound our heels with our fists: "Oh, God!" Just a few more steps and they'll hear Ephraim screaming.

In the pit, the others are tearing their hair. I am still up by the crack. I want to smash my hands, bang my head against the wall. Ephraim keeps on bellowing. Any second now!

Suddenly a whistle shrieked. Police came running from everywhere, lined up, and, taking a few captives, marched off to the other side of the village.

* * *

Half an hour later we dragged Ephraim up into the stable and laid him down by the cracks at the base of the wall. He felt the breeze, gradually closed his eyes, and fell asleep.

Outside, peasants assembled in clusters to tell each other their miracle. What luck that the Germans quickly caught the ones they were looking for, let everyone else go, and cut short the raid. What a miracle! If they had gone on searching, think of all the contraband they'd have found, the unregistered hogs they would have confiscated. What a miracle!

* * *

We also thank God for today's miracles. We feel puny in the face of these events; we're too weak and tired to grasp their meaning. Yet we sense the Eye of Providence, incomprehensible though it may be. We won't believe that it was only chance. No, not chance! We're swamped with wonders. "*I am with him in his travail.*" We feel it all the time, the mystery of our ordeal. Perhaps the outcome no longer matters.

May 7:

Janek told us that Polish policemen from Minsk Mazowiecki took part in yesterday's raid, and once again the Polish "blue policeman," Brodowicz, distinguished himself. The very sound of his name makes me shudder.

It was the Tuesday after the bloody Friday when the Jews of our town were wiped out. As I've mentioned before, that Saturday night a German dog tracked us down in Kontraktowicz's haystack, where we had been hiding since Friday night. That pile of hay was about fifteen feet high and sixty feet wide. We lay on top, covered only by a thin layer of straw, loosely spread over us so that we could get some air. At every sound we buried ourselves deeper in the straw. During the day we sweltered, pressed up against each other in the straw. We couldn't budge, because Kontraktowicz's sharecroppers were working just a few steps from us. So we lay there and held our sweating breaths.

Suddenly, a few of the workers decided to take a break; they climbed up on the heap and sat down right on top of us. They were talking about the Jew-hunt, enthusiastically reporting the latest news about newly-captured Jews and the mass shooting. Meanwhile, we heard a volley of gunfire; the men counted the shots and calculated how many Jews had fallen. They told about Poles who knew how to exploit the situation: "They were making a living and even getting rich." They prowled the fields and the forests rooting out Jews; after they stripped them naked, they took their clothes and raped the women. The Jews were thankful to be left alive. One man told of a gang of youths in a nearby village who had caught a gorgeous Kike girl. She had fought like a wildcat, clawing at their eyes with her fingernails, kicking and biting. They stabbed her, but nothing helped. What a fool she was! Why was she making such a fuss? It was all over with her anyway! Only after she lay unconscious from their beatings could they rape her.

The other workers enjoyed these stories. One of them even complained that it was too bad that he had so much work and no time to go Jew-hunting himself in the woods. Another man, with a gruff voice, swore by Lord Jesus that he doesn't want any personal profit. He would take those Jew-lice by the neck and drag them to the police. They can keep their stinking money and their females. The rest of the men laugh at him. He's a jerk! The Kikes are going to die anyway, so why should the Germans get all their belongings?

We lay buried in the straw, digging our fingernails into each other. We practically had to keep our hearts from beating so that the men sitting on top of us wouldn't feel the vibrations. One of them was sitting on Esther's face, and she nearly burst from holding her breath. By some miracle, they saw Kontraktowicz approaching in the distance and rushed back to work.

We prayed for death. Esther again said that we should take poison. But we all still believed that our mothers and families were alive somewhere. In any case we had no poison. We didn't even have the courage. All day we lay in the straw gasping for life. Only in the evening, after it became dark and it was quiet all around, did we push away some straw and raise our heads outside. A breeze began to dry our drenched, sweaty bodies. We were coated with straw and filth and all dried up inside. It was two days since we had tasted as much as a drop of water. We started taking deep breaths. We sat up to stretch, when suddenly we heard savage, drunken voices in the distance. German voices.

We understood that a band of drunken Germans had come to the village looking for Jews. Like field mice we burrowed our way deep into the straw, until we touched ground. We were unable to control our tremors. For nearly two hours we lay there that way. Afterwards, when it became very quiet, we were still too terrified to come out. We remained buried in that mass of straw for several more hours. It was only at about midnight that we moved back to the top of the heap. Then we saw a tall shadow approaching us. It was Kontraktowicz. He told us that a company of Germans had been in the village. They had asked about Jews. Because it was dark, they hadn't searched. But they warned that they would be back tomorrow to conduct a thorough search. Kontraktowicz was trembling as he gave us the news, and demanded that we leave the village immediately.

We were stunned. Kontraktowicz suggested that we leave for town now, under cover of darkness. Perhaps we could still sneak into a Jewish labor camp somewhere. There are fewer patrols out now, in the middle of the night. Early in the morning, the streets fill up with corpses. This morning, as soon as the day broke, a few hundred Jews, including women and children, were led to the cemetery, shot, and buried in mass graves.

Suddenly a dog started barking among the cottages. Kontraktowicz winced and said: "When you go, you must be careful to avoid that dog. His master is a German, and with the help of that dog he has tracked down quite a few Jews in the villages and woods around here."

We wanted to leave immediately for the woods, but Kontraktowicz advised us to wait for the dog to quiet down. Then he went off.

We merged into the darkness and waited for the dog to calm down. But his barking grew louder, more furious and ominous. The barking echoed through the air, then began approaching us.

We dug ourselves into the straw again. The dog came closer. He was on the pile of hay.

With a leap he was directly above us, barking and digging in the straw with his paws. Then he just stood there, barking at the cottages, as though calling for help. Soon he started to howl. The howling lasted for some time.

Suddenly he dashed off toward the houses. From the way he was barking now, we knew that he was prancing and jumping at someone. Then we heard a man speaking German. A minute later the German was standing over us. The dog was barking again and pawing at the straw.

"Ja, gut! Fine!" said his master. Then he left, followed by the dog.

We knew that we couldn't stay here a moment longer. But daylight was approaching. The German would catch us immediately. So we leaped down from our haystack and ran over to another big heap nearby.

We had barely managed to dig in when the German was back. It seems he had returned with a gun. Not finding us in that haystack, he searched all around. He searched a long while and left.

Our new haystack was even worse than the other one. The straw was more tightly packed and we were unable to move. Besides, hundreds of field mice were scampering around, squeaking in our ears. Huge rats planted their paws on our faces, and we were afraid that they'd bite us.

We remember the Germans' warning that there would be a thorough search. So it's too dangerous to flee to the woods. The hunt will begin soon. Did they leave a camp of Jewish workers in town? If they did, we ought to sneak in there. But how will we find out, and how will we get in? There isn't much time to think. It's light outside. It's a bad time for all of us to escape: three people together will be too easily noticed.

Esther and Zippora think that we should spend the rest of the day here in the hay. Our German neighbor is sure that we've run away, and they might not even find us in this huge haystack. After dark it won't be so dangerous to flee.

No, I say, it's a pity to waste a whole day. First I have to find out whether we can still get to a work camp. If there is a camp, I'll try and find a way to get us all in safely. Meanwhile, the others must remain in the haystack. There's no time for discussion; I'm leaving!

They start crying and we embrace. They're not letting me go! I'll be caught and shot, God forbid! No, they're not letting me go alone!

156

"No," I say, "I must go! Let's pray that everything goes well. We must try! There's no other way. If we don't try, we'll definitely be caught. I'll have a better chance of getting through alone, and I'll find a way of arranging something. Be strong, my friends! I'll be back in the evening."

I shook myself free of them like a sleepwalker from his trance. I jumped down from the mound of straw and crept over to Kontraktowicz's cottage. Quietly I tapped on the window. He came out in his underwear and opened the door. "What?" he said, opening his drowsy eyes at me, "you haven't left yet?"

"We're about to leave for the woods," I said, "But we'd like to take along some bread and water."

He gave me a chunk of bread. In a daze I took it, shivering all over.

"Make it fast!" he shouted.

I helped myself to a large jug, filled it with water from the well, and went back to the haystack. I found the women huddled together like a single mass, sobbing and hiccoughing. They stared at me. "I've brought you bread and water," I said. They started weeping bitterly. I put down the bread and water, kissed the women, and ran off.

* * *

I'll never forget that morning. I scampered through the fields like a wounded bird. Ahead of me, in town, there was shooting, and I ran toward it. The crying of the women echoed after me. I ran in the middle of the fields, across potato and vegetable beds.

"Oh, God, protect the others!" I murmured as I ran.

It was a little more than two miles to town. But in order to get to the other side of town, where I assumed the work camp ought to be, I had to do an extra two miles through the adjacent woods and fields, cutting through the Jewish cemetery.

The gunfire grew steadily louder. At one point I could hear continuous outbursts of machine-gun fire, as though a mass slaughter were taking place. I thought I also heard screams. The shrieking wind carried strange echoes, apparently from the direction of the cemetery. I was pulled, as if by momentum, in that direction.

Not a living soul to be seen in the fields and woods. It is horribly still. My frenzied footsteps must be echoing for miles. From time to time I hear a rustling in the bushes, as though some startled animal, or a runaway Jew, were drawing deeper into the forest for protection. My heart pounds louder and I'm running faster. I am close to town.

I slow my pace and look around. The brilliant sun is high in the sky, pouring buckets of blood on the town and cemetery. In the distance I make out the German army barracks. I quickly drop to the ground, and crawl on my belly toward the nearest houses. Now I have to cross the main road to get to the fields running through the cemetery to the camp. This road leads from the German barracks into town. Slowly I made my way to the edge of the road. I held my breath and glanced sharply in all directions. Nobody is in sight. The road, paved only a few weeks earlier with the sweat and blood of Jewish boys and girls, stretched out broad and clean, smooth as a table; the surrounding greenery was reflected on the asphalt. Quickly, on all fours, I scurried across the road.

I was nearly across, when someone suddenly appeared in the middle of the road. A husky young man in civilian clothes was riding a bicycle, his hair flying in the wind. With a leap I was in the ditch. He noticed me and stopped the bicycle, dismounted, and walked over to me. I think I lost consciousness for a moment. When I lifted my head and looked at him, he was just a few steps away. He paused, leaned an elbow on the bicycle, and we stared fixedly at each other. My eyes misted over and my heart felt as if it would spring out of my chest. But something told me not to avert my eyes from his penetrating gaze. That went on for a few minutes. Suddenly, he swung around, grabbed the bicycle, mounted it, and sped away.

I lay in the ditch exhausted. But realizing the danger, I pulled myself out of the ditch and started running blindly through the fields bordering on the cemetery. Volleys of gunfire nearby woke me. I quickly sobered up, dropped to the ground among the thorn bushes, and listened. The peril was right here before my eyes: I was not far from the cemetery. From inside the cemetery came a deafening din of German voices, weeping, and moaning. Single shots rang out. I crawled backwards into the nearby woods, came out on the other side, and, running wildly through the fields, bypassed the cemetery, cutting through the grounds of the municipal hospital to the camp area.

The Kopernik school, the site of the camp, was clearly visible. The red-brick building stood out among the others. But suddenly I felt my strength drain; any minute now I would collapse. I crept into a grove of trees in the middle of a field and stretched out on the grass.

It was absolutely quiet. I strained my ears, eager to hear a sound. Wasn't there anyone in the camp? I heard only the sounds of birds. I put my ear to the ground, hoping to catch some echoes. Instead, tiny worms wriggled on the ground, exaggerating the silence. I crawled out of the bushes and gazed toward the camp in the distance. I couldn't see a thing. The compound was enclosed by a wooden fence, and it was impossible to see beyond it.

Just in front of me, something stirred in the trees and bushes. I leaped back into the bushes behind me. I could see a pair of glittering green eyes staring anxiously at me from the opposite bushes; a frightened rabbit sprang out from the lower twigs and scampered off. I followed it with my eyes and saw a bent old peasant standing in the field, whip in hand, watching a cow graze. I looked around again, mustered my courage, straightened up, and walked over to him. The peasant listened to me indifferently. I tried to read something in his glance, but his face wore no expression. He was grazing his cow, as usual, among the stubble of the harvested grain. For a moment I imagined that I had awakened from a bad dream and now everything was back to normal.

There was a commotion in the distance. I shivered. The peasant, who was examining some plant, said slowly: "It's nothing, just the noise of the Jewish workers whom the Germans have brought into the camp."

* * *

It was 5:30 a.m., Sunday, Elul 10, 5702 (August 23, 1942), when I stole into the camp through the broken fence. I seemed to fall into the Vale of Tears. Dozens of people were groveling in the dirt, beating their heads, and wailing.

I was noticed, and the news of my presence spread like lightning. People came running at me from all directions, from every door. In a matter of minutes I was surrounded by dozens of Jews, acquaintances and strangers, embracing and kissing me: "Oh, it's so good that you're alive!" All of them pushed their way through to me, grabbed me, and burst out crying. My mind began to clear, and I started crying too. It was a scene of mass hysteria. Women wrung their hands, tore their hair, beat their heads with their fists, fell into each other's arms, and sobbed wildly. Men were clapping their hands in the air and screaming into space; some gripped the walls and banged their heads against them; others fell to the ground and lay there like corpses, rolling their eyes from time to time as if they had gone mad. Several children huddled in the corners in frightened silence; from time to time they cried "Mama, Mama," wept, and were silent again. Some people controlled themselves and, with tears in their eyes, were telling me what happened to them. Nearly everyone here was alone in the world now; all their families were gone. "Alone, alone, all alone!" they repeated over and over again, beating their heads with their fists.

Friends of mine who found out I was here fell into my arms weeping: "Oh, you're still alive, you're still alive!"

Suddenly, my good friend Moyshe Zisserman elbowed his way through the crowd. He embraced me: "Oh, Leybl! Oh, Leybl! I have final regards from your mother, final regards from your sister, final regards from your whole family!"

I haven't the strength to go on writing. I can't! I want to scream until the whole world is engulfed in tears! Oh, Mama, Mama, Rivke Blume daughter of Yitzhok and Miriam Rokhl. I feel naked, uprooted, like a fallen leaf.

Everything in me wanted to erupt. I bit the ground, groveled in it, reached into space with my hands. At that moment, it was as if they had never been. A chasm opened in front of me. The entire past sank into the pit. They had never existed! I am all alone in the world.

* * *

I had no time to mourn. I wasn't even able to cry.

That morning, more people were gathering in the camp, people who had escaped the slaughter, fugitives from the forests and other hiding places. Somehow they managed to slip through the gunfire and they brought news from the final action against the remaining Jews: how they were dragged out of their hideouts and shot, on the roads, beside walls, in yards and gardens. The camp was filled with mourning.

I didn't know what to do first, talk with the others here, and mourn over the death of my family, or do something to rescue Esther and Zippora. Only now did I realize what I had done.

Why had I left them? I felt that soon I would lose them forever. I imagined how desperate they must be. Again I started wringing my hands. I ran from one person to another explaining the situation and asking for advice. My friend joined me and we wept together. Everyone promised to do something "afterwards." Meanwhile, "we have to wait." Soon German soldiers would be taking people to the various factories and workshops. They take them in sealed trucks. Maybe we could go to the village, pick up the women, and bring them here. The soldiers do that sort of thing in exchange for a piece of jewelry, a golden trinket.

I weep loudly. I don't know if it's because of helplessness over the bitter news that my friend brought me; from imagining the women's desperation back at Kontraktowicz's place; out of fear that it might be too late; or because of the hope that we can still rescue them; or perhaps all of these reasons. "Mama, Mama, Miriam!" I cry with all the others. "My dearest Esther, Zippora!"

The tumult increases. In the middle of the compound stands a sturdy young man, his hair flung wildly over his forehead, in a crowd of people who have just arrived in the camp. He's telling his story:

It was yesterday, Saturday morning, as the soldiers were taking us to work. They led us through the very streets where the Jews had marched to the railroad platform that Friday evening at candle-lighting time. The route was littered with congealed blood and brain matter, and detached limbs. Alongside the rigid corpses, in the blood, were hats, shoes and other garments. The workers marched in formation and their boots stepped in the blood and in the dried-up splotches of brain. Every so often someone recognized a bloodstained garment. One of the men recognized a bald, decapitated head lying on the pavement as that of a neighbor woman; a few steps away lay her matted wig. We kept marching, stepping over the bodies.

* * *

Another boy who had part in yesterday's march relates:

They made us do some work at the railroad station. It was nearly six o'clock when we arrived there. They had just finished loading the Jews into the freight cars. The doors were already locked and the train was moving, car after car, like a dog-catcher's wagon with barred windows. Through the bars we could see only eyes and hands. The only person we were able to recognize was the ghetto mailman, Shmuel Avrom Popovsky. He waved to us. As the train moved past us, the crying inside became louder. The police began to shoot at the barred windows. We felt as if we were the entire town's funeral procession.

* * *

There is a girl in the camp who escaped from the railroad station yesterday morning as people were being loaded onto the train. She doesn't look more than fourteen or fifteen. Her name is Rokhele. She lies huddled in a corner in the straw, in total shock. From time to time she says something, then becomes silent again. People stand around her. She stares over their heads. I ask her if perhaps she saw any of her family at the railroad station. I feel like hugging that blonde, long-braided girl as if she were the rescued sister of us all. I would give my life to protect her. It is hard to get her to talk about that night when she secretly reached maturity.

All night she had sat on the loading platform with her mother and two younger sisters. Her father and four-year-old brother were missing. Nobody knew where they were. From all sides the searchlights focused on the crouching Jews. Machine guns pointed at them, bullets flew, SS men snatched babies from their mothers and tossed them in the air. All around them lay the corpses of babies and adults.

Throughout the night the "blackcoats" kept dragging girls out of the crowd. When their mothers tried to pull them back, the "blacks" hit them over the head with their rifle butts. Then they pushed the girls into the darkness. After a while, they returned, bloody; their dresses were ripped.

Rokhele's mother had hidden her between her two little sisters. From time to time the blackcoats came to search. In the tumult, the children kept crying for water. Near them sat the family of Gross, the tailor, including his mute daughter, Sima. Their small children screamed at Sima: "Water! Water!" Not far from them, the blackcoats seized a girl. Sima's parents quickly hid her. She lay down drowsy. From time to time the noise shook her out of her nap. Her little brother slapped his mother on the cheek demanding water. Sima raised her head. The girl who had been seized a while earlier returned. Sima understood everything. Suddenly she saw a blackcoat scouring the area. She jumped up and ran over to him. It was too late to stop her. With a mute, helpless gesture, she let her parents know that nothing mattered anymore. She just had to get some water! Her parents tore their hair. After a while she emerged from the darkness, her hair disheveled, with a bottle of water.

An hour before sunrise, there was a change of guard. The fresh group of blackcoats weren't drunk. They were still sleepy; one of them shouted that the Jews were to blame for waking them in the middle of the night. Every time he yawned, he cracked his whip angrily at the crouching people. He had a difficult time keeping his eyes open. He kept rubbing them as he cursed and kicked the heads below him. Then, many of the children fell asleep leaning on the parents. Families huddled together. The sharp cold penetrated their bones. Then Rokhele dozed off, leaning on her mother and trembling.

Later she heard the clatter of moving trains. A locomotive whistled and chugged by. Germans shouted. Bedlam. People leaped up and ran across the sleeping bodies. Children cried in their sleep. It was daylight. She ran, too, She was unable to shake off the drowsiness. She heard her mother calling to her. She couldn't see any faces through the crowd and the blows. By the thousands they stampeded into the freight cars. Rokhele tried to get to her mother. But she had lost her. Shoving her way through the mass of people, she kept on running. The sound of gunfire rang in her ears. She continued to run, turned into a yard, and entered a storeroom. She slept there until dusk. After dark, she came to the Kopernik camp. She has a high fever. She lies rigidly in the straw. She has stopped talking. She didn't see any of my family in the railroad station.

* * *

My friend Moyshe, who was also led from the marketplace to the loading platform, escaped from the railroad station in the middle of the night. He described that evening's march through the city streets.

Volleys of gunfire echoed from every direction. Entire battalions of SS men and police ran up and down the flanks of the long procession, pounding away at the heads of the people with their batons, rifle butts, and bayonets. And they kept on shooting. All along the route, in front of the houses where Germans were staying, they placed radios and phonographs playing festive songs. Fat, drunken Germans stood in front of the taverns enjoying the parade. The sidewalks, doorways, balconies, and windows were jammed with Polish men, women, and children jostling each other to see. They all seemed to be looking for Jewish faces. A Polish policeman in a dark-blue uniform hit passing Jews in the head with his rifle butt, and punched them in the face with the clenched fist of his free hand; he was laughing over his shoulder, and saying: "They won't be sucking our blood anymore! They've sucked our blood enough!"

"The Kikes are going to Palestine!" a coarse voice shouted down from an attic.

"Be seeing you, Kikes!" another voice yelled from across the street.

Here and there you could spot a pair of sympathetic eyes, even some fearful ones. But others expressed unbridled joy. Germans placed their cameras on top of cars to film "the comical scenes."

* * *

It is nearly eight o'clock. People are still sneaking into the camp through the fence after fleeing their hideouts in town. Those already here quickly surround them, and they hug and kiss each other, question each other, and tell their tales. Every few minutes there are fresh outcries of weeping and wailing.

"*Gevald*, Jews, we're lost!" a tall, old man in a corner cries out. "The bandits will slaughter us, too!"

My friend Moyshe, who's roaming around the compound with me, tells me whatever he knows:

He sat in the marketplace near my mother, sister, my mother-in-law, and my youngest brother-in-law, sixteen-year-old Shmulik. Shmulik was one of the first to be brought to the marketplace. He had been caught near the bridge early in the morning, given a brutal beating, and chased to the marketplace. My mother, sister, and mother-in-law were brought in at noon with a large group of Jews, including the wealthy Yankev Rosenberg. They had been hiding at Bartnicki's place on the outskirts of town. He let them into the house in the morning, and locked them in a room. First he took the bundles they carried. A few hours later he demanded their money and jewelry. He said he needed to bribe the Germans, who kept coming to search his house. They gave him everything, and then he reported them to the police.

Several blackcoats led them to the marketplace. My mother ran, as if impelled by some supernatural force, holding on to my sister and mother-in-law. She was afraid that she would be shot on the spot if she didn't move. In the marketplace, among the thousands of people, she lay half-dead, her mouth parched, watching my sister. My mother-in-law begged the Jewish orderlies for water, and gave my mother the single swallow of water they allowed her, even though she herself was burning up from fever and thirst. In silence, she hugged her son Shmulik to her bosom.

My friend Moyshe got a bottle of drinking water. Everyone grabbed a sip. Nearby sat old Pinye the shoemaker. "Moyshe," Pinye said, "for forty years I was a member of the burial society doing charity for the dead. Now give me some charity and let me have a sip of water."

Moyshe also saw Froiman's father. At dawn, as soon as it had all begun, he gathered together his seven children and ordered them to run away: each one in a different direction to increase the chances of at least a few of them surviving. Then he took his prayer-shawl and went to the marketplace. He sat there murmuring chapters of Psalms. Near him sat Moyshe Tuvye with the velvety black beard, a Hasid of the Porisow Rabbi. He kept his eyes covered with the palm of his hand, and told a young Hasid sitting next to him that he had only one wish: in his last moments he wanted to see the face of his rabbi of blessed memory. He hoped that his suffering wouldn't make him lose the vision of that face, God forbid.

Not far from them sat my family. My sister Miriam, sweating heavily from terror and helplessness, seemed to be struggling against her body. "They kept asking for you all the time," Moyshe said. "They didn't know whether you had been shot or if you were still hiding at Mrs. Szczepanek's. Later, on the way and on the loading platform, I could still see your mother-in-law and Shmulik. I didn't see your mother and sister again. Maybe they were shot along the way because your mother wasn't able to walk. I don't know."

My friend's voice rose to a shout: "Remember! Remember! We mustn't forget Bartnicki! You're their only avenger!"

* * *

At eight o'clock the camp was nearly empty. A squad of German soldiers led the Jews off to work. Everyone was pushing to go along, hoping to get on the work roster. Only a small group of Jews remained in the camp, including me. The sudden stillness became oppressive. I couldn't remain calm, and tried to think of ways to bring Esther and Zippora here from the village. Some of my acquaintances who had gone off to work promised to do everything possible to get a German soldier to drive them to Kontraktowicz's place and then bring them over. I promised to give the soldier Esther's only piece of jewelry, the only one that Breker didn't take: her golden ring.

Meanwhile I pace around the camp like a caged beast. Let it only not be too late. I shudder at the thought. I would try and catch up with my friends at work, but to leave the camp now means certain death. In any event, they advised me to stay here. During the day, when the Jews in the camp are out working, soldiers often come here to deliver people caught hiding. If that happens today, they said, I should talk to the soldiers myself about delivering Esther and Zippora in exchange for the ring. The hours pass and there's nobody in sight but SS men and policemen who patrol the perimeter of the camp with loaded weapons. The only others now inside the camp are some old men, a few women, sick people, and some children whom we just hid in a garret to be safe from the SS. These people remained here because they feared being declared unfit for work, and then handed over to the police. So they roam the compound sweeping, cleaning, washing the walls, and cooking lunch for the workers. I join in the various chores, but I'm frantic.

Outside, the sound of gunfire doesn't cease. The manhunts and raids continue. I shudder every time I hear a shot; Who is it this time?

The hours fly past. The day is nearly over and they aren't here yet. What if they couldn't find a soldier to go to Kontraktowicz's to pick up the women?

Meanwhile, the few Jews in the compound pour out their woes. But there's hardly any strength left to mourn and to wail.

Mama, Mama, Miriam!

I have an urge to rush outside and get shot by the soldiers.

The tall old Jew lies in a corner of the yard holding his knobbed cane. He chews his tip of his gray beard as he speaks. "This," he says, pointing to the cane, "is all I have left. My wife, children, grandchildren, sisters, brothers, all my relatives, they're all gone, all gone! I've had a long life, and now I have nothing to show for it. There's nobody to mourn for me. They're better off already," he adds, pointing with his cane to a corner of the yard where a few corpses have been buried.

I kept on running back and forth like a madman. I felt like running away. But the SS men and policemen continued their patrol like wild beasts in search of prey. The ground was burning under my feet. I rushed into a barrack, flung myself down on the straw, but couldn't lie still; then I ran into the yard and clung to the fence. There was nobody in sight.

Suddenly a shot rang out, and someone bounded across the fence into the camp. He looked like an acrobat in red costume; his face, hair, and clothes were all red. It was Mikhl, Sapir's fifteen-year-old son. He had fled from the cemetery where the mass execution took place. After the Germans left, he climbed out of the pit where the dead bodies had fallen. He hadn't been touched by a bullet, only drenched by blood of the dead falling on top of him. He had been conscious the whole time; he only pretended to be dead until the murderers left and it was quiet again. Then he crawled out and hid in a field. A farmer pointed out the Kopernik camp to him. Because he was all red with blood, the guards noticed him and shot at him. But they were afraid to approach him. He fled like a blazing torch.

The bloodsoaked boy shivered from cold. He addressed each of us by name, which gave us an eerie feeling. We recoiled from his touch. We didn't believe that he was alive. Some people asked if he had seen their relatives shot in the cemetery. He didn't hear us. He looked for a pit to hide in. Then he uttered some names as if in a trance. Many people were still alive in that pit in the cemetery, groaning and writhing, he said. A dying bearded Jew had bitten his arm when he tried to push him away. The blood streamed across the bodies crowded together, and flowed into his mouth and throat.

Now he began to vomit the blood he had swallowed, while his hand gripped the spot where the dying man had bitten. Somebody brought him a change of clothes and underwear, and a bucket of water for washing. He looked like a corpse rinsing himself before burial. The sun stained the window red. It was a garish scene.

Then he told us about the cemetery. When they were brought there to be shot early in the morning, the place was already piled high with the corpses of those who were shot yesterday. There were hundreds of them, piled up in a pyramid. At the apex lay old Saul, "the Giant," who had been the town's "Samson." The

Germans had placed him there stark naked, on his back, his legs stretched out, his circumcised penis jutting upward.

"God's covenant with the Jews has been abrogated!" the old man with the knobbed cane shouted. We all went outside and paced the yard behind the buildings. I wanted to run away from here. Hours had passed and there was no word.

After dark, we could see figures approaching in the distance. Soon we heard a rumble of marching footsteps. The gates were opened, and hundreds of laborers, ringed by soldiers, entered the camp.

Within a few minutes, the compound was once more a tumult of speaking and sobbing voices. I found my friends: they couldn't do anything about Esther and Zippora. Everyone came into the barracks. I remained outside, collapsed to the ground. In the barracks, they were weeping.

May 8:

Nearly two years have passed, and I still cannot shake the horror of those nightmarish days of August, 1942, the days of the death agonies of an entire people.

I vividly remember my frenzy those two-and-a-half days in the Kopernik camp, separated from Esther and Zippora. My friends tried to comfort me and told me to be patient. But I didn't know whether I would still find them in that haystack, whether they were still alive there at all. Like a wounded beast I raced back and forth in that cage, pressing up against the barbed wire, against the fence, wanting to run out of there back to the village. I hoped to make it in the dark. "Esther, Zippora!" I moaned.

Two soldiers promised to drive me to the village, but they kept putting it off. I felt that everything was lost. In this way, two nights and two-and-a-half days dragged by; it seemed like an eternity to me.

On the third day, I was already resigned. I didn't believe I would ever see them again. I tortured myself for having left them there, remembering how, in the haystack at dawn, they had begged me not to go alone.

The camp is empty again. It's nearly noon. Almost everyone is away at work. What should I do? No, I'm not waiting anymore! Right after dark I'm sneaking out of the camp. I must get to them. If I don't, I'll kill myself!

It's nearly noon. Some women are busy in the kitchen. They're preparing lunch for the workers: watery beet soup. They're in a hurry: at any moment a German soldier should drive up in a truck to take the soup to the work places. That same soldier comes every day. He seems to be a nasty fellow. He shouts at the women. Yesterday he roamed the empty barracks and searched the workers' crates, helping himself to things which he stuffed into his pockets. I winced at the dirty look he gave me.

Twelve noon. I can hear a car honking in the distance. It's that army truck. Probably the same driver. He'll murder us; lunch isn't ready! Dishes drop from the women's hands. The truck is parked outside. Yes, it's the same soldier! He tells us to hurry up and heads for the empty barracks.

I follow him into the corridor. He stops and glares at me: "What do you want?"

"Nothing, I want to give you a golden ring!"

His eyes search my fingers greedily.

No, I tell him, it isn't on me. My wife has it. She's not far from here. About two miles. In the village. If he likes, we can ride over there. I'll show him the way. We'll give him the ring. It won't take long. Just a couple of minutes. Meanwhile, the women will finish preparing lunch. He'll have to bring us back here to the camp!

His steely gaze makes me avert my eyes.

"You're not screwing me?" he suddenly asked. "She's really got a ring?"

"Absolutely. A beautiful ring. Gold!" I hardly knew what I was saying.

"Then make it fast!" he barked.

Sitting inside the truck, under the tarpaulin, I thought I was dreaming. "My precious children," I murmured.

As we approached the village, my fears mounted. I was afraid of the moment when I would call them to come out of the hay. I clutched the frame supporting the tarpaulin. I decided that if, God forbid, anything happened to them, I wouldn't return to the camp. I would ask the soldier to shoot me. Or I'd shut my eyes and run into town, right into the guards.

I was about to close my eyes, when the truck stopped.

"Make it fast, dammit!" the soldier shouted.

I crawled down from the truck. My feet barely obeyed me.

"Faster!"

"Esther, Zippora!" I called out hoarsely.

Silence.

"Esther, Zippora!"

My heart stood still. I scoured the haystack.

"Esther, Zippora! Children!"

Suddenly I could see the mound move. The hay seemed to be lifting itself.

"Children!" I shouted at the top of my lungs.

"Yes," came a faint voice. Two heads poked out.

"Esther, Zippora, don't be afraid."

I ran to them. They lay there helpless, stunned. They stared at me, unable to speak.

"Make it fast!" the soldier shouted.

"Don't be afraid, children! Come, we're riding to the camp."
They couldn't get out of the hay. Their feet were numb.
"Make it fast!" the soldier shouted, grabbing them, each in turn, by the hands, fairly ripping the ring off Esther's finger; he pulled them out of the hay, and carried them to the truck.

* * *

The events of that day happened so quickly that I had no time to catch my breath. It was a short trip from Kontraktowicz's haystack to the camp. The soldier drove wildly over the roads and through the streets between the armed, green-helmeted patrols. We sat in the van, hidden by the tarpaulin, as the speeding truck bounced from corner to corner. The women stared at me in shock, not believing that they had really gotten out of the haystack. From the moment I left them, they were certain that I was no longer alive. Right after I took off before dawn, they heard gunfire in the field and assumed that I had been spotted. During the following two days they pictured me riddled with bullets in the field.

I told them what had happened in those two days. They clung to me.

They wanted to know about the rest of our family.

"Don't ask, children," I said. "Let's just pray that we stay alive."

The guards were shooting everywhere. As we passed through the ghetto, the three of us peeked outside: empty streets, deadly silence. Hollow doorways, smashed windows. Furniture and belongings scattered in front of the plundered houses; tables, chairs, sewing machines, beds, ripped bedding, feathers, shattered crystal on the sidewalks and roads. Guards in the patrol squads were digging in the piles. The presence of death was everywhere. A municipal wagon crawled through the empty streets; two street-cleaners walk beside it picking up the corpses and piling them on the wagon. The wretched horse trudges along, and trickles of blood drip down from the wagon and stain the pavements. The entire street is splattered with blood. We speed along. Patrols on our route salute our driver, and he speeds up. We pass the synagogue yard, where children were playing only a few days ago. It's absolutely empty now. Now we're outside the ghetto. We're at the camp. The soldier drives the truck through the gate.

"Children, we're in the camp!"

Ten minutes, that's how long the ride lasted. The women rush up to tell us that lunch is ready. They want to help me get Esther and Zippora off the truck. The soldier gnashes his teeth. "Dammit!" he shouts, chasing the women away; then he lifts Esther and Zippora off the truck one by one, and wipes his eyes with his sleeves.

We stare at him. Something stirs inside us. Finally, we all burst into tears.

* * *

At about 1:30, the soldier drove his truck into the camp again. Before he had left, Garfinkel, a young man working in the barracks, had promised him a golden watch if he would deliver his family from their hideout in the ghetto. It was very risky, because the ghetto area was swarming with SS men and police. It had to be accomplished quickly. Garfinkel asked to go along, so that he could help carry his old father and mother from the attic into the truck. A few neighbors were also hiding in that attic.

The soldier works speedily now. He seems to have taken to us, and tells us not to be afraid. Esther and Zippora remain in the barracks with a few Jews and we ride off. We pass the ghetto again. We hear German voices in the courtyards. They're calling the Jews out of their hiding places. Nothing will happen to them. They will only be taken to the nearby ghetto, in Kaluszyn where there are more Jews.

We drive past quickly. But the voices pursue us. Accompanied by Polish policemen, the Germans go from courtyard to courtyard shouting the same message in German and Polish. Here a German and some Polish police lead a group of Jews who've come out of a chimney. There are two men and several women; one of them is nursing a baby while holding two children by the hand. They're all covered with soot from head to foot. Their clothes, faces, and hair are black; all you can see are their eyes. The children hold on to their mothers. The women look around. They stare at the gun barrels aimed at them and draw their children closer. They're being led along the street where Gestapo are quartered.

Our truck turns into a side street behind the church at the border of the ghetto, and stops in the courtyard. Garfinkel jumps down and I follow him. The soldier draws his gun, gets it ready, and waits. We run upstairs, through the dark lofts.

"Papa!" Garfinkel shouts. "Papa! Mama! Open up! It's me!"

Beams rustle in the darkness. Hoarse voices emerge from a hole.

"Hurry!" Garfinkel whispers.

Shadowy figures crawl out of the hole, men, women, children.

"Quickly!"

We ran back down the stairs.

Out in the yard the soldier was surrounded by a band of Polish laborers whom the SS had brought in to loot the Jewish houses. They quickly surrounded us: "Stop. You're not going any further. Wait!" Some of them ran to call the police. The others held us down. The soldier got frightened and drew his bayonet; he hit a few on the head, and fired a few shots from his gun. The Poles fled.

"Get in, fast!" the soldier shouted at us. He hurried into the truck, started the motor, and began to turn the steering wheel. Garfinkel and I were helping the others into the truck. The motor roared. The men were already inside. We shoved the women and children into the truck. About ten people altogether. They were all inside. Garfinkel climbed in. The truck started to move. I ran after it. It was almost within reach.

I'm already surrounded by Poles. They grab hold of me. The truck moves off, speeding like the devil. Several Poles and SS men run after it, shooting at the tires. But the soldier turns the corner and the truck is gone.

I'm in the grip of strong paws. They're laughing and cackling in my ears: "Ha, ha, ha! Just wait a minute, only one minute more!"

Several SS men pass by. They're hauling valises stuffed with valuables, and they don't even notice us. A few minutes later the black-uniformed Polish policeman Brodowicz entered the courtyard.

In the camp, I had heard about the murders that Brodowicz had committed in recent days. The workers had told each other.

He eyed me and said: "Let's go, you bastard!"

The Poles laughed and released me.

"Come on you bastard!" Brodowicz said, holding his gun to my head.

I shut my eyes and started walking.

Suddenly, I was stricken with blows to my head, neck, shoulders, sides.

"Faster!" he roared.

I wanted to run. But he grabbed on to my arm, and beat me fiercely, as hard as he could, all over the body. After a while he released me and ordered me to run. I started running. He ran after me, striking me with his rifle on the head, arms, and legs. I fell down, but he drew his gun and fired over my head, shouting, "Hurry up!"

I got up, and under a fresh deluge of blows ran until I fell again, got up again, fell down once more, and ran again. By this time I hardly felt the blows, only flashes of light bursting in front of my eyes and weird noises echoing in my ears. I tore my eyes open and saw the SS men standing around me; they were laughing, applauding, and shouting: "Bravo! Bravo!"

Then they came after me and kicked me from behind. Brodowicz enjoyed that one, laughing loudly, waving, and shouting the only German word he knew: "Jude! Jew!"

We emerged from the ghetto into the Polish streets. Curious onlookers stopped to stare. On street corners and in doorways stood groups of people, many of whom had been acquaintances and neighbors. They whispered to each other, and mentioned my name. Brodowicz gave me a kick in the rear and shouted:

"Get a move on! Faster!"

"It's all over with you!"

"You sucked our blood long enough!"

Harsh blows hacked into my neck and my arm muscles. My head spun, I saw circles, laughter echoed in my ears.

Brodowicz pulled my hair and ran ahead with me. I was drenched with sweat. I couldn't catch my breath. My mind was foggy, and I couldn't see. I was about to collapse. But fresh blows revived me; I felt as if sharp pins were digging into my body.

Suddenly I turned around and looked right at him.

"Sir, you're a Pole!"

"That's right," he said, "a Pole!" And with his fists he started furiously pounding me in the face, under the eyes, on my forehead, in my chest.

Then he pointed his rifle at me and ordered me to run. I ran. Gunfire was breaking out behind me, bullets flew over my head and past my ears. I shut my eyes and drew my head down between my shoulders.

"My dearest! *Shma Yisroel!*....!"

The gunpowder made me cough and chafed my eyes. I couldn't tell if I was still alive.

"*Shma Yisroel!...*" Amidst the sparks and flashes I saw Esther's face.

Then I opened my eyes wide; we were in front of Gestapo headquarters.

A moment later I stood in the main office of the Gestapo. At the desk sat Skoblinsky, chief of the Expropriation Bureau, a German civilian of about fifty who was in charge of the confiscation of Jewish property. On that black Friday in the marketplace, he went directly through the mob of Jews with an open satchel, whipping people and ordering them to toss in all their jewelry; whoever possessed any valuables afterwards would be shot on the spot. In this way, he filled several satchels with gold and jewelry.

He wore a white silk shirt, and his beady green eyes peered at documents through gold-framed spectacles. On the desk before him lay a shiny revolver.

Brodowicz stood up tall, clicked the heels of his boots, and saluted.

Skoblinsky tore his eyes away from the documents and took us in.

"*Jude, ghetto,*" Brodowicz blurted out in German, and told him in Polish that he had caught me prowling in the ghetto, looting the abandoned houses. He shoved me into a corner and ordered me to stand there with my hands up.

"I did not loot," I said in Polish.

"Shut up, you swine, you Kike gold-sack," Skoblinsky barked at me, banging his fists on the desk. "Soon I'll shoot you down like a dog, you criminal!"

He grabbed his revolver, rushed over to me, and ran the cold barrel of the gun over my forehead and temples, waving it in my eyes. "You see?" he said, grabbing me by the shoulder and dragging me to the window. "Look!" In the yard lay several corpses. Nearby, sat a group of Jews who had just been dragged from their hiding places. They were guarded by police.

"See?" he said, pointing to the corpses. "Soon *you* will lie there!" I shivered.

"Scared?" he roared and again pointed a menacing finger at me. Then he suddenly dashed outside.

In the yard, he stepped over the dead bodies to the spot where the Jews were gathered. He ordered them to line up by the wall with their hands up, and searched them, the men, the women, even the children.

"Hand it all over," he shrieked, "all of it!" They stood there petrified. All at once he snatched a gun from a policeman and started shooting. I moved away from the window.

"Don't worry," said Brodowicz, "you'll soon be lying there!"

I hear moans in the yard. Footsteps in the corridor. The door flies open. Skoblinsky shouts: "Did you see?"

In the yard, the Jews are huddled in a corner. Several fresh corpses are piled up on the ground.

"*Donnerwetter!* Children of Satan!"

The telephone rings. Skoblinsky picks up the receiver. "Hello! Yes. Yes, I'll be right there!"

He slams down the receiver, snatches his jacket, and barks at Brodowicz in German: "Take him out and shoot him!" Then he rushes out, slamming the door behind him.

"*Jawohl!*" Brodowicz shouts after him.

"What did he say?" Brodowicz asks me.

I shiver.

"What did he say?" he asks again.

My teeth chatter. I shake my head. "I don't know."

Brodowicz runs out and promptly returns with a German civilian. "*Jude!*", Brodowicz tells the German, pointing at me, and talking in Polish.

The German looks from Brodowicz to me. "*Jude?*" he asks.

"*Jude, Jude!*" Brodowicz vigorously nods.

"Damn you!" the German shouts at me. "What are you up to?"

I lower my eyes.

"Speak up!" he shrieks. "Answer right now! What are you doing here?"

"I'm a worker," I answer feebly.

"A worker? Where do you work, you swine?"

"For the *Wehrmacht.*"

He gives me an astonished look and lowers his voice. "In that case, what are you doing here?"

"I got lost on the way."

"*Jude, Jude!*" Brodowicz shouts, not understanding what we're saying.

The German sits down and asks me to explain what's happening.

I tell him that I would like to get back to my work.

"*Raus!*" he shrieks. "Get the hell out of here! Fast! I don't want any Jew workers! I won't have anything to do with the likes of you. The *Wehrmacht* can keep you! *Donnerwetter!* Scram!"

"*Jawohl!*" Brodowicz clicks his heels and snaps to attention. "*Jawohl!*"

"To the *Wehrmacht*, fast!" the German shouts, looking at Brodowicz.

Brodowicz nods, then asks me what the German said.

"That I'm to go back to work, to the *Wehrmacht*," I say in Polish.

Brodowicz steels his eyes.

"Fast!" The German bangs a fist on the desk. "Fast!"

A black-uniformed policeman comes dashing in from the next room.

"Fast!" the German shouts at him. "Tell him to get that swine out of my sight. Let him go to the *Wehrmacht*!"

"To the *Wehrmacht*!" the blackcoat says to Brodowicz, pointing at me.

Brodowicz shouts "*Jawohl!*" and orders me to walk ahead of him.

"Dammit!" he shouts when we're outside the office, "the inspector told *me* to take you there?"

"I think so"

"Then get a move on. I've got no time. On the double!"

Half an hour later Brodowicz led me into the Kopernik compound.

* * *

Our joy did not last long. Things kept happening.

Inside the camp, I found my sister-in-law, Chaya, and her husband, Sholem, who was older than I. On Friday night, when Mrs. Szczepanek chased us out of her place, the two of them couldn't get to Kontraktowicz's barn, because Chaya was in her ninth month of pregnancy. So when we parted, they ran to other acquaintances. Those people wouldn't keep them either, so they spent a few days in a pigpen and in a garbage dump. A group of Jewish workers who passed by in a wagon found them and brought them to the Kopernik camp. They had been having a hard time keeping Esther and Zippora from looking for me in the ghetto. They reassured them that I would return, recounting the miracles of the past few days.

Suddenly, I appeared in the doorway. "Children!" I cried out. Esther and Zippora jumped on me. Sholem and Chaya tore them away and embraced me. They had been sure that I was no longer among the living. People came from the other barracks to see me with their own eyes. One woman told us to all say the prayer of thanksgiving. It's pointless to go on tormenting ourselves, said the old man with the cane; those bandits won't let us survive anyway.

I got my people together and we went out to the well. We washed ourselves for the first time in several days and had a drink, and then we sat down in a corner of the compound; we started talking about the events of the last few days. I'm the only one of my family who's still here. Luckily, I have Esther. My brother-in-law is worried about his wife. Esther keeps hugging her sisters, Chaya and Zippora, and she strokes my hand. Chaya's having a hard time with her first pregnancy, and she's breathing with difficulty. If only she had a bed to lie down in and her mother to comfort her.

My heart is bursting. We're exhausted. We can hardly keep our eyes open. If only we could have a few hours of sleep.

"What's that?" It sounds like an approaching army. Everybody runs out of the barracks to peek through the slots in the fence. The Jewish workers are returning from their labor.

It's only five o'clock—still daylight. Why are they coming back so soon?

We hurry to the gate to greet them. We can also hear the sound of another group returning from a different work place.

The first group of workers are inside the compound. They don't know why they've been brought back so soon. The other groups don't know either. Neither do the soldiers, except that an order came from the police to bring the Jews back to the camp.

The camp is full. Everyone is confused. In addition to the 200 registered workers, several hundred people made their way here from different hiding places during the last few days. Only one thing is clear: something terrible is brewing. We don't know whether to try and make a run for it.

We look for some place to hide. But there are no hiding places in the camp. We climb up into the attic of the red-brick building.

Suddenly, there's a commotion outside. I rush to the window. Dozens of vehicles are lined up outside the fence, their motors running. Companies of armed Germans, police, SS, blackcoats, Polish police, and plainclothesmen converge on the camp from all directions. We can hear the gunfire. The Jews in the yard stampede into the barracks. All the rooms are packed. Babies cry. Women are hysterical.

"Out! Everybody outside!" They're shouting at us.

"Outside! Fast!"

The doors tear open. The mob pushes its way out, jumping out of windows, crushing and leaping over each other, charging through the doors.

I'm pressed against a mass of women and babies. I've lost sight of my family. I'm shoved toward a door. Whips lash our heads. The outcries are deafening. I'm caught between some Germans, I can feel their blows. I've passed through the door. The Germans are shouting at us. My head swirls. I step over some people, dead bodies, I think.

We run out to the yard. Polish policemen order us to sit down in rows. From every direction people run to us. I sit in my row and look around. My brother-in-law Sholem is not far from me, he's searching for his wife. Zippora pushes her way to my side. She doesn't know where to find Chaya and Esther. People keep charging through the doors. I recognize Skoblinsky. He stands in his white shirt facing the mob. He's cracking his whip in one hand and firing a gun in the other. People are falling. Others jump over the dead bodies and run toward us.

Suddenly I see Esther come tumbling out of the doorway. The person beside her falls down. She doubles over, and leaps over the fallen bodies; then a German shoves her in our direction.

"Esther!"

She runs toward me, and drops into the next row.

"What happened?"

The German hit her in the chest with his revolver. She leans her head on me, and twitches in pain.

"Is there anything you want me to do?" I ask.

"I'm all right," she replies. "But they shot Chaya. She's lying there. I think she's still alive!"

She clutches me.

Sholem shouts at us: "Where's Chaya?"

Esther writhes from the pain in her chest. It's quiet around the barracks. No more people are charging through the doorways. The SS men are searching the rooms and attics. They toss some children out of the windows. Nine wounded people lie in front of the brick building. There's a boy of about ten who was shot, and beside him his fourteen-year-old sister. She tosses and turns, digging her fingers into the grass. Six seventeen-year-old girls lie dead in a row. Chaya is lying among them. She's still alive. She kicks her bare legs into the earth, and her pregnant belly is heaving.

Bullets fly over our heads. Skoblinsky runs around cracking his whip at us. We hug each other and crouch as close to the ground as possible. Several bodies are stacked on the fence, shot while trying to escape. The Germans order us to stand up. The men and women are to line up separately. Zippora leads Esther away to the women's section. Sholem grabs me and asks: "Where's Chaya?"

"Shut up, you assholes!"

The police chief, Gutbelein, reads off the names of the two hundred registered workers. They're to remain in the camp. They are separated from us by a cordon of SS men.

Everyone whose name is called is led through the row of SS. In the turmoil even some who haven't been called pass through. Whips are cracking, heads are split; people cry out in pain. Some people don't answer to their names. Others rush forward in their place. They're hurled back. But some get through. I'm standing in the first row, pushed back and forth by the throbbing crowd, swallowed up in the mass.

I hear them call out the name of my friend Froiman. I know that he isn't here. "Esther!"—an idea flashes in the back of my mind. I can barely hold my own against the people shoving from behind.

"Froiman!" the German with the list shouts again.

I stand there, shut my eyes, move back. Several people charge forward together. I'm trembling. But I'm staying with Esther! She isn't going alone! I felt good.

Then I saw soldiers lead them off to the work places. Some of the women, whose names were on a list, were also led off.

A few hundred of us sat there and waited. It started to rain. The SS men and the police commanders entered their vehicles and drove off. We were surrounded by a heavy chain of German policemen, green-helmeted SS men, and Polish police. The silence is deadly. Gun barrels aim at us from all sides. The rain pours down upon us. An SS man with a pad and a pencil moves among us counting heads.

"Five hundred . . . Six hundred . . . Seven . . ."

A Polish policeman whispers that they're digging pits for us now in the Jewish cemetery. But another one says that we're going to the Kaluszyn ghetto.

Then a car arrives. Several SS officers led by the Gestapo chief, Schmidt, get out of the car. The SS man with the pad hurries over to Schmidt, salutes, and reports on our numbers. Schmidt, tall, husky, carrying a white handkerchief, dashes about checking the count.

"Stand up!" someone orders. "Line up, men and women together!"

The rain is heavy now. It was already dark when we marched out, four abreast, through the camp gate.

May 9:

I wrote for two days. I lay on the floor of the barn next to a crack in the baseboard, writing, while Esther kept watch up above, by the wall. She's very tired. At five o'clock this morning, I went up to relieve her. I look outside, and I can still see the images of those days before my eyes.

God in Heaven, it's nearly two years since then, and we're still caught up in the nightmare of those days. We haven't had five peaceful minutes in which to take stock. Who would ever believe that it would go on so long and that we could endure so much?

Oh, God, it's unbearable! We don't have any strength left. We just want ot stretch out on the ground, shut our eyes, and lie still. We often feel like people who've been shot and are running around on momentum alone. Just a bit more and we'll collapse. But momentum can no longer sustain us. This is what frightens me. Our bodies are unresponsive, our senses dulled.

This morning I saw Ephraim crawl out of the pit. It was at dawn, when I was alone in the barn peering out through a crack, Ephraim crawled out like a mole. I didn't recognize him. On all fours he dragged himself across the floor of the barn, breathing heavily. He seemed to be covered with dead hair, his eyes were dull and glazed. He looked like a huge wrinkled beast that had just crawled out of a swamp. There was a gentle smile in his eyes. He hadn't fully recovered from his last attack. I looked at him, and began to cry. He huddled in a corner, clinging to the ground. At the slightest sound, he would crawl toward the pit.

God in Heaven, how much longer must we go on suffering? We've been locked up in this barn tomb for nine days. We're quietly fading away.

We're well into the month of May, and the front lines are still quiet. All winter long we looked forward to a spring offensive. There were rumors that big things would happen on the Eastern front in early April, and that a second front would be opened in the west. We can't stand the quiet. Maybe one of these days we'll hear the cannons, and next thing you know they'll be here? They're only 125 miles away. Or maybe the front will advance in our direction and then stay put. Who knows what's in store for us? I just hope disaster doesn't overwhelm us at the last minute. God in Heaven: If You want to do any saving, do it quickly! Another moment and it may be too late.

May 9, 6 p.m.:

I spent nearly twelve hours up on the wall today looking out, thinking all kinds of thoughts. Grotesque images of the past few years keep swirling through my mind. I can't believe it has all really happened.

I remember that evening when they led several hundred of us, men, women, and children, out of the Kopernik camp. It was after eight o'clock. We marched in rows, in the dark, stepping on each other's feet. We were thrashed by the driving rain.

We were soaked to the marrow. Esther walked on my right side and Zippora and Sholem on my left. There were frequent explosions overhead, thunder, gunfire, or both; but the most deafening noise was the barking of the Germans. We sloshed through the mud. Sholem wanted to know where he could find Chaya. SS men and police rode back and forth on bicycles, motorcycles, and in cars. Volleys of gunfire tore holes in the darkness.

Esther clung to me. She said nothing. Later, she told me that she had had a number of opportunities to join the women who were to be kept on as workers. The crowd had been pushing her in that direction, when they were calling out the names of the workers. But she had held her ground. She had known that I, too, would stay put. "It's good that we're going together! Let's always stay together." She hugged me and squeezed my hand. I could feel her body shiver and her teeth chatter. We walked on in silence. We heard only our own footsteps on the wet road.

None of us knew where we were going. We seemed to be heading for the cemetery. These little streets lead to the cemetery, we whispered to each other. All at once, Schmidt cracked his whip and ordered: "Sing!"

Spontaneously, we burst out into the same song—"*Kol od balevav penima, nefesh Yehudi homia!*"

The song pierced the air, and inflamed our last hopes: "*Od lo avdoh tikvosenu,*" "We still have not lost our hope. . ."

I squeezed Esther's warm hand. I was glad that she wasn't alone, that I was going with her, that we were together to the end. I squeezed her hand as hard as I could.

Our song rang out: ". . . that ancient hope. . ."

The SS men held their breaths. They ordered us to slow our march. But we were beyond all that, beyond all danger. Our footsteps marched along to the melody: "... *L'aretz, l'aretz avosenu!*" "To return to the land of our fathers!"

We were already in the street leading to the cemetery. "Halt!" voices shouted.

"...that ancient hope..." the song went on.

We heard Schmidt's order: "We cannot carry out the operation because of the storm and the darkness. It will have to wait until morning. Meanwhile, they can spend the night in Jurczak's empty house."

Then, another command, to us: "March to Jurczak's house and keep singing!"

Our voices rose: "To return to our fatherland, to the city where David camped!"

We forgot where we were. Our spirits had risen above our murderers. Our death trek had become a kind of macabre triumphal march.

* * *

Ten minutes later we were in Jurczak's house. It was surrounded by an unfinished four-story wall. Sentries were posted all around the building. They had stationed machine-gun positions everywhere, as though around a besieged fortress. It felt as if we were locked in a cage. We scattered throughout the building, looking for a corner to hide in.

"Jews, let's save ourselves!" people called out. It was pandemonium. People ran around looking for their dear ones, for their closest remaining kin. Desperate cries filled the air: "Jews, let's flee for our lives!"

A Pole has passed the word that freight cars are waiting in the railroad station to take us to Treblinka in the morning. Women sob hysterically. Young men hope that it's true about the train: they might try to jump off and escape. Hundreds of people with parched throats and lips run about begging for water.

Somebody discovers a filthy hole filled with liquid. Some people drop to the ground and take a few licks before they realize that it's sewage. All at once there's an outburst of wailing: "Water! Water!"

Babies, women, men, everyone sucked his parched lips, licked the window panes and walls. The Polish policemen opened the windows, placed a few buckets of water outside, and started to hand out some bottles. A gold piece or a 100-*zloty* note got one a drink of water. People paid, guzzled down the water, and came rushing back for more. SS men shot at the windows. The Polish policemen left. Several Jews tried to escape through the windows and were shot dead beside the house. Others envied them, and they did the same. I caught sight of Yona "Good-for-Nothing," with the blond little beard and sidecurls and blue eyes, whose constant talk about becoming a rabbi had been the laugh of the town; when he passed me in the dark, his eyes glared defiantly.

I sensed danger. I gripped him by the arm and said: "Yona, don't. Don't!" He tore himself from my grip and shoved his elbow in my chest. As he jumped out of the window, a gun barrel smashed into his skull. When I looked outside, Yona's corpse lay on the ground among all the others.

Inside, we fled from the windows. But not before I glimpsed some SS men dancing on the bleeding corpses, Yona's included, and singing bawdy songs.

Later, we spread out on the floor. Some people fell asleep and snored, and others discussed ways of escaping. I lay in a dark corner close to Esther and Zippora. They wanted us to stay awake on our last night together.

Two figures were crawling through the darkness toward me. They were the ten-year-old twin daughters of my former neighbor, the refugee Piennik. I could never tell them apart. Now they were alone in the world. They laid their heads on my chest. Four long dark braids, tied with red ribbons and uncombed for several days, fell into my arms. I hugged them. Their dark eyes glowed sadly.

"We're afraid," they said, hugging me. They asked me if dying was horrible.

All night long I held the four of them and tried to give them courage. I think the two little girls believed me. They fell asleep shortly before dawn. Outside, the sky began to turn blue. Inside the house, people were stirring.

My friends were shocked by my appearance. My hair was too long. The Germans might shoot me on sight. One of our friends had scissors, and Esther trimmed my hair.

Apparently, it worked. When the SS officers came at about 8 a.m. and took us all out into the yard, I still looked suspicious; so they took me aside, looked me over, and questioned me. In the end, they told me to go and sit with the others. We sat in front of the house and waited. Just before ten, Germans from various factories came in to select workers. The old, the feeble, and the children were taken away. The rest of us, the young men and women, were sent to various labor camps.

May 10:

Today is sort of a holiday for us.

Last night I made Konyak's acquaintance. I met him in Janek's stable. We hope to bring him over this week. It's been so long since we were in such a good mood. We feel like singing. We wish he were already with us.

Yesterday, well after dark, I peeked through the crack and noticed a suspicious movement in the oak wood. Soon I saw someone sneaking among the trees. A few minutes later he came out of the woods, and I recognized Konyak, He looked around carefully and went into Janek's stable opposite our barn. I hurried down from my perch and told the others. We realized that he had come to spend the night, and we were excited.

We decided that I would go to him after midnight. We didn't know whether to ask him to join us here immediately, or whether to just reveal ourselves and show him our hideout later. I decided to first talk to him and then do as I saw fit under the circumstances. I would be cautious. First I would find out his connections and his acquaintances. If everything seemed in order, I would ask him to join us right away. Nobody else, not even Auntie, was to know about it. They didn't come into our pit, and couldn't tell, from the barn, that he was with us. We would share the food.

I put on my boots and shirts, combed my disheveled hair with my hands, and brought along a chunk of bread and the revolver.

I'm very nervous. It's almost two years since we last spoke to a Jew. The others encourage me. They want me to bring Konyak here.

Time seemed to drag for several hours. We couldn't begin before midnight. I get up. My knees are shaking. I muster up some courage, climb the wall to the straw roof, remove some of the straw, and poke my head outside. The others hoist me up from below. In a few minutes I'm outside on the barn roof.

I sat down to catch my breath and listened carefully: midnight hush, the whole world is asleep. I couldn't see anything in the pitch darkness. I climbed down to the ground, looked around, and started crawling toward the stable. It was only about ten yards from the barn. One of the planks in the stable wall was missing, and I crawled in through the gap. The darkness was palpable. But all I could hear was my own breathing. I sat up and called out:

"Konyak! Konyak!"

Somebody stirred in the straw, like a mouse, and it was quiet again.

"Konyak!"

Not a sound.

"Konyak, I'm a Jew, a Jew, where are you?" I whispered in Yiddish. The whisper spread in the dark silence.

"Konyak, don't be afraid. This is a Jew calling you." My throat was dry.

"Konyak! Konyak!"

No reply. I was startled by the resonance of my own voice. It seemed to carry far into the darkness.

"Konyak, Konyak!" I called out desperately. "Answer me! I'm a brother, a Jew! Don't be afraid!"

Another silent pause, and then I heard a sound, as if the straw in the corner had moved.

"Konyak! Come! I'm a Jew!"

Something rustled in the straw; and someone crawled over to me.

"Who is it?" a thin, childish voice squeaked.

"It's me, a Jew!"

I felt someone beside me.

"Konyak!" I grabbed hold of him and hugged him. "Konyak, my friend, don't be afraid!"

"Who are you?" He tore himself from my embrace.

"A Jew, a Jew! I'm hiding out not far from here."

"Konyak!" I hugged and kissed him. I didn't know what else to say, He sat there trembling with fear.

"I'm a Jew. Don't be afraid!"

Suddenly he became firm. "How did you get here?" He wanted to know who I was, where I was staying, and how I knew about him.

I told him that I was with a group of Jews in the woods not far from here. We were living in a hole, I said. We were armed. I showed him the revolver.

"Would you like to join us?"

"No!" He wanted only to know how I knew about him.

"Why don't you want to be with us?"

He was too frightened to answer.

I gave him the bread, and said: "Konyak, I'm a Jew. We've been looking for you for a long time. We would like you to remain with us."

I told him how we found out about him and how we had been observing him. Unfortunately, I said, we couldn't reveal ourselves to him before, but now we could take him with us. And I told him everything that we knew about him, even things that had happened to him.

"But how do you know all that?" he insisted.

"Because you're our brother, and we took an interest in you. We know who's been helping you and who's been trying to harm you. From now on you won't be at everyone's mercy. I've been following your movements for some time, and I was waiting for the chance to speak to you. You'll be with us. You don't need to roam around on your own anymore."

I asked what had happened to him lately.

At last, he opened up.

"How long is it since you heard Yiddish spoken?" I asked.

"Oh, I hear it and speak it often." He told me that he had been meeting a Jewish family that lived in the forest.

"Well," I asked, "are you joining us?"

First he wanted to know where. In any case, not today. First he had to meet a peasant he knows. Perhaps he'll join us in a few days. We'll meet again.

I asked him about that Jewish family. No, he'll tell me the next time we meet. We'll discuss everything then.

We agreed to meet here tomorrow at midnight.

* * *

All day we've been discussing the events of last night. It's clear that Konyak doesn't trust me very much. Our encounter took him too much by surprise. Besides, he must think that everyone's out to get him. A pity that we couldn't look each other in the eyes.

We feel less lonely. Maybe we'll meet that Jewish family through Konyak. And if he joins us, he'll no longer be so exposed, like a defenseless animal.

But nothing bad must happen! He can't risk his life in joining us. How could we face him in the end?

May 11:

Since we moved into Janek's barn, there's been a kind of truce between Auntie and Mrs. Felek. They're still angry at each other, but they've stopped most of their quarreling. Auntie spends most of her time visiting people in the village. Now that we're no longer in the house, Auntie is afraid that if they quarrel, Mrs. Felek will reveal everything to the Germans.

Auntie is angry, but Mrs. Felek is in high spirits. She's cheered up since we left her attic. She sings hymns as she putters around the house, thanking Lord Jesus for delivering her from evil. Auntie can't bear it. She charges out of the house, slamming doors behind her. She doesn't even visit us much any more. For some reason, she can't look us in the eyes.

But Mrs. Felek comes to see us more often than she used to. She sits at the edge of our pit and gives us the latest news. She looks content as she curses "that old whore" who doesn't give a damn about us. She doesn't even care about feeding us. Why, we might get sick!

Mrs. Felek brings us a bite to eat almost every day, coffee, a few potatoes, a radish, and sometimes even some milk, or a pat of butter on the bread. "Don't you worry about food. I'll see to it that you don't starve!"

This sudden show of concern worried us at first, but we know that she has no bad intentions. Summer is almost here, prices are rising, and her own income doesn't provide her enough to get by. So she may as well get along with us, especially as she isn't risking anything. If the Germans find out about us, well, we're in Janek's barn.

We're satisfied with the situation, too. We only hope that Auntie doesn't find out about Mrs. Felek's visits and her bringing us food.

May 12:

Konyak has joined us.

When we met in Janek's stable last night, I convinced him to come to our hideout.

He's sitting in the pit, and the others deluge him with questions about his life, the village, the peasants, the Jews he knows in the forest.

Froiman and I, keeping watch by the cracks, were also eager to talk to him. Esther and Zippora relieved us several times while we went down into the pit. Now he regards me as his savior. Until we came down here, he didn't fully trust me. But after we were down in the pit, and the others embraced and kissed him, he seemed dazed and happy.

Now he apologizes for being so suspicious. He knows that Gestapo agents often used the trick of speaking Yiddish to draw Jews out of their hideouts. During the forty-eight hours between our two meetings he was afraid, he confesses. He had even decided to run away, but something drew him to me and compelled him to keep our appointment. Although at the last minute, when he was already in the oak wood not far from Janek's stable, he still had to resist an urge to run away. I had even noticed this myself.

At midnight, while I waited for him in the stable, I peered through a crack at the woods. I saw the trees rustling, and finally I made out Konyak. I didn't know why he hesitated before coming to the stable. Then I realized that he was afraid, and I crawled out to the wood and hid behind a tree. When I saw that it was really him, I sneaked up behind him, took him by the hand, and whispered his name.

He turned around, and followed me into the stable. We sat down in a corner, and I asked him if he was ready to come to our hideaway. He asked me all sorts of questions about us, how we were sustaining ourselves, what kind of hideout we had, and who were our contacts. At first I said that we were hiding on a nearby farm, and I described our life. From time to time I stood up to ask if he were coming along. But I warned him to make up his mind once and for all; once he was with us, we wouldn't let him go.

He came out of the stable and crawled after me. He was stunned when I told him to climb up on the roof of that same Janek's barn. "Here?" he said, turning two astonished eyes upon me.

I told him to climb, and I climbed after him. From time to time he looked at me questioningly. I shoved him upward. We crawled through the hole in the straw of the roof and went down into the barn. I showed him how to get to the pit. Whispers came from the pit. I told them to get some light.

"Here it is, Konyak! Crawl in!"

I followed him in. We covered the opening. For a few moments there was a tense silence.

"Konyak!" I cried.

"Konyak!" came a muffled chorus. "Konyak!" And they all engulfed him with their hugs and kisses.

May 12, evening:

Konyak told us that his real name is Yitzhok and people call him Itche. He's the youngest child of the Kaluszyn tailor Khone Rosenberg, who was nicknamed *"Oval — "the Oval One";* all the members of the family are referred to as the "The Ovals." Not only the Jews of Kaluszyn, but also the peasants of the surrounding villages, knew his father; he used to make their clothes. Thanks to that, Konyak has a few acquaintances among the peasants, and he secretly does some sewing in exchange for food. But he has to watch out for most of them. In a few villages some peasants give him a piece of bread and some soup. But he can visit a home only once in two weeks. So every night he goes to a different village. In some villages he can't show himself at all; he would face certain death. All the villagers, without exception, are on the hunt for Jews. As for food, he really can't complain. He had a whole storehouse of food stashed away in his forest hideout, and he can pick it up tomorrow, if we'd like.

At noon today, when Konyak saw the small pot of food that Auntie brought us, he couldn't understand how we lived on so little. When we told him that was our typical food ration, he looked morose.

An hour ago he asked me to let him leave the pit every evening, after dark, so that he can eat at some familiar farms. He's very hungry, and the little food we can share with him, is not enough. He doesn't understand how we can live this way. We can't even breathe in here.

Then he sat quietly in a corner of the barn. I think he wants to leave us, but is ashamed to mention it. He tells me that he must go out for at least two or three hours. He wants to visit a certain farmer. A few days ago the man told him to come over, and he would clip his long, lice-infested hair. He'll eat something there, and then come back. At first I tried to tell him that I'd cut his hair myself, but he wouldn't hear of it. He wants to visit the farmer. Finally, I said that he could go, but we were sorry: we won't know what to think if he doesn't come back.

Right now I hear him chatting away in the pit. He is talking about Auntie, Mrs. Felek, Janek, and all the neighbors. Now, he understands why Auntie has always been so kind to him. Still, he doesn't want her to see him here. When she brought our lunch, he tucked himself as far back into the pit as he could. He says that the villagers look at her as some kind of witch. Oh yes,

191

he just remembered, he had heard from a few people that Auntie was protecting some Jews.

I jumped into the pit and asked him where he had heard this.

It may have been, he said, from Maczuszak or Paltyn, and once even from a peasant girl who gave him a piece of bread, little Tereza, Jaszko Odrobinszczak's daughter, that's who it was, Tereza! She told him that Jews were hiding in the attic of the Felek home, and that Auntie was always calling us, banging on the ceiling with a rod. He asks us if we really were in that attic. He never believed that Jews were really hiding here.

We ask him whether the peasants will send the police here. Konyak doesn't think so. They don't have any facts, and they're afraid of making false reports. If the report turns out to be untrue, the Germans will punish them and Auntie and Mrs. Felek's family will take revenge.

"Of course," Konyak adds, "it isn't absolutely safe here. But where is it perfectly these days?"

May 13:

We had wrongly suspected Konyak. He returned later last night, after only a few hours in the village. He is a changed person. His skull is mirror-smooth. Paltyn shaved it.

We ask him questions, and he tells us about the two families living in a nearby house: the Waceks and the Paltyns. They've been treating him well lately, feeding him soup and plenty of bread. They urge him to take good care of himself and survive, for the war will soon be over and the "Russkies" will be here. They know it for a fact, but he mustn't tell a soul.

Konyak reports that they have many such secrets. They told him that on April 10, the "Reds," or "Bolsheviks," drove the Germans out of Odessa, and they'll probably be here soon. In the village they're already preparing themselves for the Russians. All of them are treating Konyak somewhat better. Although nobody has shown such a turn for the better as have Wacek and Paltyn.

Last night Paltyn, after shaving Konyak's head, told him that if the "Reds" ask him how he survived, he should say that he, Paltyn, and his neighbor, Wacek, had helped him. Mrs. Paltyn asked him to say that her father, Maczuszak, had also done him many favors; after all, her father is a very decent person, but unfortunately a very nervous type, which is why it's better not to go to him.

Konyak brought back half a sack of bread, dozens of pieces, dry, hard, moldy. After his haircut, he hurried to his hideout in the forest, grabbed the sack, and rushed back here. Now he's feasting on the bread.

May 13, evening:
I'm sick. I've had a fever for three weeks, and a very bad cough. I've been trying to hide it, but the others have noticed. My eyes have a feverish glow and my pale cheeks are flushed.

They're especially worried about my cough. I'm not coughing loudly. So, whenever I feel a cough coming on, I get down from my perch and cough into the pit. But it's just this muffled cough that frightens them. What's more, I've lost my appetite. I don't have a taste for food, not even for a sip of milk. Konyak sits in a corner of the barn feasting on the bread in his sack, slice after slice. I feel like vomiting. I don't understand how anyone can eat. He may be reading my mind. He's staring at me. I say to him: "Hearty appetite!"

May 14:
Last night Zippora stood guard up in the barn. The other five of us slept in the pit. Suddenly Zippora woke us and in a frightened voice said that were strange sounds inside the barn. We sat up and listened. Sure enough, we heard scrambling noises up there, as if someone were crawling across the floor. Then, we heard someone banging on the boards on top of our pit. Silence, and then more knocking.

Zippora crawled into the pit, and I crawled out and listened. Soon I could hear someone creeping around practically under my nose. Whoever it was kept banging on the boards next to me. I stretched out my hands and groped in the dark, but I didn't feel a thing. The noise continued. Again I stretched out on the ground and waved my hands about; and again I felt nothing. The knocking became louder. It was right beside me. I poked my head into the hole and could hear teeth chattering.

Inside, the noise was even louder. I began to crawl all over the barn, groping about with my hands. I measured the length and breadth of the barn floor, tapped all the four walls, and listened at all the cracks; except for the noise coming from the middle of the barn I couln't hear a thing. Finally I let myself back down into the pit.

The others were also trembling from fear. We didn't know what to think. Suddenly we realized that the rabbit couple was missing: neither Froiman nor I had encountered them during our searches. The two of us crawled out again. The rabbits were gone! We guessed that a thief had stolen them. In that case, he knew about us. But why did we still hear the crawling and banging?

We closed the pit opening, and spent the rest of the night in fear. The noise over head didn't stop. Finally, early in the morning, it became quiet. Now there was not a sound. But we kept on sitting, afraid to budge. Several hours later I climbed up, and, strangely enough, the rabbits were back!

Froiman came out too, and we began to search for an answer to the riddle. Is it possible that the rabbits also have a hideout somewhere? We searched until we found a narrow hole in the barn floor. Froiman stuck his hand in: it was very deep. We started digging, until we hit upon a narrow channel. We dug through to the end. The channel led right to the boards on top of us, a full yard under the surface. Right above the roof of the pit we found a nest of soft hay containing eight little bunnies, eight darling white angoras.

We called the others out of the pit. We all looked at the newborn little creatures. Their parents stood some distance away, fearfully observing our assault on their haven. But Froiman ruled that we must banish them from their home right over our heads; if there is a search, the channel they dug could mean disaster for us. We prepared a new little nest in a corner of the barn, carried the bunnies over there, and filled up the channels that we and their father had dug.

May 15:

Yesterday afternoon, while Zippora was on guard at the crack on the wall, she saw a girl sneak away from the front door of Mrs. Felek's cottage. Pinned to the door Zippora saw a sheet of white paper with writing on it. One by one we climbed up to loook at it. We were worried. Later, when Froiman was on guard, he saw Mrs. Felek look angrily at the sheet, rip it off, and put it into her pocket. A few minutes later she opened the barn door. She asked us to read the notice she carried. Printed on it in big block letters was:

"MRS. FELEK, GET THOSE FILTHY JEWS OUT OF HERE FAST! IF YOU DON'T, YOU'LL COME TO A BAD END!"

Mrs. Felek started wringing her hands; then she ran out and paced in the farmyard. Zippora thinks that the girl who pinned up the notice is Maczuszak's daughter, Mariszka.

Auntie brought us our supper. We showed her the notice, and she was frightened. She said she would go to the village to see what was going on. We didn't sleep all that night either.

Early this morning, Auntie and Janek came into the barn. It's nothing, they assured us. They spoke to most of the neighbors, and there's no sign that they really suspect anything. It was probably only a girlish prank.

An hour ago, just before 10 a.m., I saw two silhouettes approaching. It was two women: young Mrs. Staszko and Mariszka. They passed our barn and stopped opposite the wall. Gesturing and whispering, they pointed to the barn. I saw Mariszka point at the barn wall.

Janek approached from the distance. Mrs. Staszko tugged at Mariszka's sleeve. They both turned around and ran toward Janek. Mariszka gestured to Mrs. Staszko and laughed aloud when Janek started fondling her.

When Janek came into the barn, we told him everything. He shrugged and said he would discuss it with Auntie.

May 15, evening:

We had visitors today: Mariszka, Maczuszak's daughter, and Mrs. Staszko's baby girl. Auntie brought them in so that they could see for themselves that nobody was in the barn.

At noon, Janek sent Auntie to us. She suggested that we all get into the pit and seal the opening; she would find some excuse to show Mariszka that not a living soul was in the barn. We tightly covered the opening, leaving only a bit of the straw loose for air. Meanwhile, Auntie placed a large wire basket over the opening so that Mariszka wouldn't step on it and cause it to cave in. Then Auntie invited Mariszka to come and see the newborn bunnies. Soon we could hear girlish laughter and they were at the barn door.

We heard Auntie call out: "Trush, trush, trush!" Soon she was showing Mariszka the little creatures. Mariszka stroked them and talked to them. She didn't want to leave them and she begged Auntie to sell her at least two bunnies. Auntie said she could have a pair for nothing; she wouldn't think of taking money from a neighbor.

Mariszka grabbed the two bunnies and ran off. Auntie bolted the door, cleared the pit opening, and told us to come out. Esther, Froiman, and I climbed out. They went up to the watch-posts. Auntie told us how Mariszka had scoured the whole barn with her eyes and seen nothing but bare walls.

Then Auntie left, locking the door from the outside. A few minutes later we heard her voice again. She was running around outside, laughing and talking to herself. As she approached the barn door, she called out: "Tursh, trush, trush!"

She unlocked the door and entered, holding a baby in one arm. "Trush, trush, trush!" she called out. She said the baby was Mrs. Staszko's. She had snatched her from her mother's arms to show her the newborn bunnies. Now Mrs. Staszko could see that Auntie wasn't afraid to take people into the barn. But she asked us to be on guard in case Mrs. Staszko should come running after her baby.

Froiman stood watch, while Esther and I begged Auntie to get the baby out of here. The baby was staring hard at us. Auntie laughed: Why, the baby can't talk, and she doesn't understand anything yet; she isn't even half a year old! Esther is afraid that later the baby will pull her mother toward the barn. The child frightened me, too. Auntie laughed at us. She wanted to stay here with the baby for a while, to dispel suspicion. But, since we were so afraid, she would leave immediately. "Trush, trush, trush!" she called out. She locked the door and disappeared with the baby.

May 16:

Today, there was a nasty scene involving Mrs. Felek, Auntie, and Janek. Nearly half the village had gathered here. The shouting continues, and as usual we're the scapegoats.

Janek decided today that he was entitled to some of his sister-in-law's land. The field belongs to Mrs. Felek, and she's been planting it for years. It borders on Janek's property. This morning, while he was plowing his field, his plow crossed into Mrs. Felek's furrows, which, he claims, really belong to him. So long as Felek was alive, he didn't object if his brother used a few of his furrows. But he wasn't about to let that bitch of a sister-in-law work them.

Mrs. Felek screamed that it was her field. Felek had bought it from the previous owner with the dowry she had brought him. But Janek plowed a few more of her furrows. Her outcries brought peasants running from their fields. She protested that she was a desolate widow with no one to stand up for her. Now that Janek had seen Maczuszak steal a piece of her land, he had decided to rob her, too. Then Auntie started shrieking curses at Mrs. Felek. The peasants joined in the mocking laughter and whistling. Their shrieks penetrated our hideout. We can't stand it any more.

Mrs. Felek threatened and Janek went on plowing. Maczuszak stood in front of this cottage inciting Janek.

Mrs. Felek ran into her house crying, and the crowd finally dispersed. When she came into the barn, she was still crying. She called me down from the watchpost crying: "Juzek, Juzek! If Janek doesn't stop tormenting me, I'm going right to the Germans!"

At first we didn't say anything. But she raised her voice to such a high pitch that we were afraid her shouting would be heard outside. I tried to calm her down: Janek will surely return her land. I'll talk to him. If necessary, I'll even pay him to give it back. If he refuses, I'll pay her the value of the land, so she can buy another tract. She went on crying, and then Janek ran in: he had seen her enter his barn, and now he would throw her out. She repeated her threat to go to the Germans and reports us all. Janek wanted to hit her, but we stopped him. Still screaming, the two of them left the barn.

Afterwards Auntie came to see us. I asked her to settle the matter at my expense. But she was so furious at my suggestion that I quickly dropped it. I also tried to talk to Janek. Mrs. Felek remained outside, wanting to join us. But Janek had taken away her key. Now the three of them are in the yard shouting at each other.

May 16, evening:
Itche-Konyak is very frightened by the quarrel. When we tell him that they often carry on this way, he can't understand how we remain here. He's also afraid of the notice that was tacked to Mrs. Felek's door. We must get away from here, he says, the sooner the better. It's more dangerous here than in the forests, although he admits that we would probably have been dead in the forest long ago.

He tells us how local Poles murdered Jews caught roaming in the neighborhood. Except for us and that family he told us about, there isn't a single Jew left in the Dobre and Wiszniewo woods. Either the Poles captured them or reported them to the Germans. Whenever Itche meets with Motl, the head of the Dobre family hiding in the forest, Motl tells him what miracles happened to him, his wife, and his brother-in-law. Itche himself has been stopped dozens of times but always, at the last minute, he managed to get away. Right here, in our village, he's been stopped by old peasants, young men, and even children. Once they bound his hands and feets, and tied him by the neck to a fence. He was kept in their cellars while some went to get the police. We tremble as he tells us how he escaped each time. We listen to dozens of stories about Jews who were caught in this neighborhood.

He thinks that we're in mortal danger here. Besides, he's sure that I have tuberculosis. No wonder, living in a hole like this! Not only is the hole dank and moldy, but it smells from the animals that used to be here. "It's impossible to breathe here!" We'll get sick. We must get out of here!

May 17:

There's turmoil in our district. Yesterday evening, the Germans burned down a house in the village of Zimno-Woda. During a manhunt, they came upon a band of partisans in a stable. Gunfire was exchanged and several partisans were killed. The owner, a peasant woman, her daughter, and a few partisans managed to escape. The police set fire to the cottage and stable. Now, there's a rumor that they'll search the whole region. The peasants are furious that the woman kept a nest of suspicious characters. She deserves to be burned alive for all her trouble-making, they say. Who knows if others aren't hiding suspicious characters too? Let's go root them all out and call the Germans, and they'll know that we don't tolerate secret hideouts. Besides, they're not even partisans. They're Jews, Jewish bandits who rob the peasants. Let's root out every Jew and tear him to shreds. Isn't it enough that they're skinning us? Must we suffer at the hands of the Germans because of them?

Janek and Auntie know that the villagers are watching them. They advise us to go into the forest for a few days. We'll find Konyak there and he'll show us where to hide. When things quiet down, we can come back.

Right now, groups of peasants huddle in the farmyards discussing the disastrous events in Zimno-Woda.

Konyak-Itche says it's too risky to run for the forest; we'll be caught on the way. Besides, we might not be let in our hideout afterwards. No, going to the forest means suicide now.

But maybe Itche knows a farmer who will hide us, for money? Itche laughs. He lists all the neighbors, individually. He knows them all well. Not one of them will let us in. Not one of them will agree to hide a Jew, not for all the money in the world. There's nobody in any of the nearby villages either. Most of them are nasty people, and the very few decent ones are cowards. We have to stay put.

But this place isn't very safe either, he says. And if there's no alternative, we'll have to go to his forest bunker, even though it couldn't hold us all. After they found the hideout where he had stayed with the Moszko woman, he dug a new pit and camouflaged it. It holds only one person. A bigger pit would be too hard to camouflage.

I ask him about the peasants he knows, the "few decent ones." He counts them on his fingers, but he's sure that they all would refuse.

Felek had once told Esther about the wife of a village thug, who's living alone since her husband has been sent on forced labor in Germany. Felek said she was a strong woman, stronger than most men, and liked conspiracies. We could try her. Her name is Malczewski.

Konyak smiles. He knows the Malczewski woman well. She often gave him bread. But it's no good. The police are always searching her place. Besides, she has too many underworld connections, including a few boyfriends. They could murder us just for our possessions.

* * *

Konyak can't stay put. I'm willing to let him go until things quiet down. He says that it all happened because of his bad luck; he isn't destined to have even a few peaceful days. With us, he has a family feeling, and he's glad that he doesn't have to face the peasants, even the few good ones.

Maybe that's why he won't come along and try to work something out with any of them. He's afraid that they won't take the risk, and that he'll lose whatever help he had before.

But I beg him to think of at least one peasant who can be trusted. We can go together, and it will be good for him, too, if we succeed. We could fix up a fine hiding place that no one would suspect. We would get good food and live in peace.

Konyak stares at me in shock; I don't know the peasants, so I can believe that we'll find such a place. Still, he tells me the names of the few "decent" peasants, and describes their personalities, their families, their cottages, rooms, barns, villages, farmyards, and neighbors.

It's bad. Now I also feel that we couldn't possibly arrange something with them. Each place has its drawbacks. Most of all, the neighbors are so crowded together that our presence could never be kept secret.

Finally Konyak mentions a good peasant, Szube, who lives in an isolated spot between the two villages with his wife and eight-year-old son. Szube often allowed him to sleep in his granary, and Konyak helped with the chores in exchange; he threshed the grain inside the locked granary. Even though nobody comes to visit, they'd have to watch out for Szube's neighbor, who lives about sixty yards away.

Szube and his wife are the most decent peasants that Konyak knows. When he works for them, they feed him well. But he's sure that they won't agree to hide us there. They'll even resent our asking them. Szube's wife is very frightened. And they're not at all poor, so the offer of money won't entice them.

Itche thinks there's no point in going to them. Besides, it's five miles to their place. But I insist, and he agrees to take me there tonight.

May 18:

I went with Konyak to see Szube last night. We discussed the matter, and Szube agreed to let us fix up a hideout in his granary!

At about 11 p.m. Konyak and I sneaked out of the barn to the oak wood. For a few hours he led me through the woods, avoiding the villages, and we arrived at Szube's farm just before 2 a.m.

I was hardly able to walk. After about half an hour of walking I had to stop and rest. My feet simply refused to obey me. It was only fear and the sense of danger that kept me going in the dark. Itche would rush ahead and then stop to wait for me. On a few occasions I nearly fainted. But some force sustained me. When we finally arrived, we were greeted by a barking dog. I was afraid that the barking would wake a neighbor or even some hidden "ghosts." Itche spoke to the dog: "Quiet, Morwa, it's me, Konyak!"

He went up to the dog and petted it. The dog started to growl softly, wagged its tail, and licked Konyak's boots and hands. Slowly we approached the window. I hid behind the wall and Konyak tapped on the window.

"Who's there?" came a woman's voice. "Who's there?"

"It's me, Konyak."

A moment later a half-naked peasant came to the window. "What the devil! In the middle of the night?"

"Please open up," Konyak pleaded. "It's important. I'll tell you right away."

"Dammit!" the peasant grunted. "What's so important?"

"Please open up, it's very important."

A moment later the door opened. Itche took me by the hand and pulled me inside.

"Who's that?" the startled peasant asked.

"One of ours," Itche said.

"I have to discuss something with you," I said, extending my hand.

We went into a dark room, and bumped into some empty milk cans that started rattling.

"What happened?" said the woman, who rushed over in her underwear.

"Some fellow wants to discuss something with us," the peasant shrugged.

"I don't know a thing!" the woman snapped at her husband. "Leave me out of it!"

"Please cover the windows and give us some light," I asked them. "I have something very important to discuss with you. Don't be afraid."

The peasant and his wife grumbled and covered the windows with blankets. Then they lit a kerosene lamp.

It's a big room, with whitewashed walls and a few pieces of rustic furniture. An icon of the Mother and Child with rosy cheeks and a crucifix are prominently displayed. Our hosts stood in the middle of the room, half naked, staring fearfully at me. The farmer is short and stocky, pale-faced, with long, gray whiskers, and a pair of small piercing eyes. His wife is a round woman, with full, rosy cheeks, and deepset catlike eyes. They stood there half asleep in their baggy underwear, staring at me.

I smiled at them. They were unable to shake off their sleep. They both got back into bed and continued to stare fearfully at me, as if I were part of some bad dream.

"What's wrong, Konyak?" they said, rubbing their eyes.

I told them that we were a few Jews hiding in the Wengrow woods. We have some money and valuables. The war will soon be over, and we want to survive. We are decent, innocent people, and we don't deserve to die. We know that they are good, God-fearing people. We'll give them everything we have, and God will reward them too. I see that their red blankets are uncovered. I'll give them sheets and slipcovers. I also have good things for the little boy in that other bed. Won't they please hide us? No harm will come to them. Nobody will know. They won't search this place. Won't they please have mercy on us? I'll pay well, and Lord God will reward them also.

They were stunned by this unexpected visit. What a thing to happen in the middle of the night! The woman crossed herself, shook herself out of her daze, and screamed at her husband; under no circumstances would she agree. He rubbed his forehead, blinked his eyes, and growled at his wife. He was bewildered. He sat up. "Impossible!" he said, lowering his eyes. "But where did you get it all?" he blurted out. "You must be bandits!"

I swore that we weren't bandits. Let him see our women, how gentle they are. We owned those goods before, and some people in town are guarding them for us, wealthy, good people. We'll give it all to him. First of all, we'll give him the sheets and slipcovers.

The peasant shook his head. "Impossible," he said. "It's too risky. What do you say, wife?"

She turns angry eyes on us and starts yawning. "You have new sheets and slipcovers?" she asked suddenly. "What kind of prints? What's their color? I'd like to buy them from you."

I raved about their beauty. Their flower prints. But I don't want to sell them. They can have them as a gift.

Konyak confirms that we're decent people, not bandits. Then I told them how we'd fix up the hideout. Not a living soul would know about it. And they'd have a good life, with plenty to eat and drink. The war won't last much longer.

The two of them discussed the matter in bed. I resumed my pleading. Tears came to my eyes. For the first time they looked at me without suspicion.

The Szubes spoke tenderly now. He asked me about the hideout, and who would fix it up. I outlined my plan. We would construct it ourselves, if he would provide some wooden poles and planks. We'd pay for everything.

No, he said. It's not that simple. He has plenty of wood on his land. But—

I handed him some money. His palm was limp. "No, " he said, "I can't." I pressed his fingers around the money, and wished him good luck. The man and his wife looked at each other in amazement. I kissed them both and shook their hands. "Everything is going to be all right!" I said. "God will help us. You'll see!"

She asked when we were thinking coming. "Tomorrow," I said.

They considered it again, and asked us to postpone the move one more day. Meanwhile, Konyak would come to discuss it tomorrow night.

We spoke a little while longer. They asked about us and our forest bunker. I told them how the end of the war was approaching, and how good things would be then for all of us. We'll be grateful to them forever.

They began to plan how we'd live in the hideaway. We helped them along.

"That's settled then?"

"We'll see. Let Konyak come tomorrow night."

Outside, I kissed Itche. He's completely bewildered. He can't understand how they agreed. Only please let them not change their minds.

We hurried back to the barn in the dark. I breathed freely. The fresh air seemed to banish my fever. I'm walking so briskly! I've regained my strength, thanks to the fresh, fragrant May air and the good news I'm carrying back to the others.

We made good time. Still, day was beginning to break when we got back to the barn. They were all outside the pit. They had begun to worry. "Tell us what happened," they shouted as they embraced us.

We went back into the pit, concealed the opening, and told them the good news.

* * *

Konyak is more excited than all of us. Who could have thought that the lonely vagrant living on garbage, whom we had tried to help, would bring about such a change in our circumstances?

We've been with Auntie for eighteen months, fully a year and a half. Every day has been an eternity. Who can count the hundreds of miracles that happened during that time? And who knows what the future will bring? Oh, how we need some strong and firm support. God in Heaven, don't forsake us now!

May 19:

Auntie has been in a rage since yesterday. Whenever she brought us food, she gave us hell. She screams that she's fed up with us. This morning, when she brought up a pot of soup, she started to attack me. When I defended myself, she kicked the pot and overturned it; the soup spilled all over the filthy floor. Then she cursed us and ran out.

She's a strange person; she doesn't know what she wants. Just as she liked us and fussed over us at the outset, so she's anxious to get rid of us now. She can't stand the sight of us. Yet I know that after we're gone, she'll miss us desperately. I'm angry at her, but I also feel sorry for her. I know very well that if not for her, we would have been long ago dead. Now she's cursing us bitterly, but I can still hear her encouraging words. Still, we have to get out! The noose is tightening around our necks. We'll have to slip out in the middle of the night, when they're all fast asleep; that's how we left Auntie's place in Minsk that dark winter night.

May 19, evening:

Some mysterious gray veil seems to cover our hiding place. It's getting denser all the time, obstructing our view. This morning, Mrs. Staszko called Auntie out of the house. They walked around in back of the cottage, and whispered together. I could see Mrs. Staszko's threatening gestures; Auntie looked stunned and said nothing. Mrs. Staszko kept staring angrily at our barn, but Auntie avoided looking this way. She didn't look Mrs. Staszko directly in the eyes either. Finally, Mrs. Staszko became quiet. They paced back and forth without speaking. Then I heard Mrs. Staszko mentioning searches, police, danger, shooting, and Jews. Finally, they went away to the oak wood.

I haven't said anything to the others. They sense that something bad is imminent. But our hope of escaping encourages us. I pray that we make it. In the mysterious race we are running, either evil will overtake us, or we'll be saved, at the very last moment.

If only Szube would agree to take us in. When Konyak went to see him last night, he put the whole thing off for a few days. Tonight I'll ask him myself to take us in tomorrow. God help us if he refuses. He must take us in, at least for a few days. Tonight I must persuade him. I must!

Auntie comes in. She's very nervous. This time she speaks very softly: there's a rumor in the village that five Jews from Minsk are hiding in the barn, and Mrs. Staszko wants to refute it. She'll bring the police here; if there really are no Jews in the barn, she'll put all the gossips in the village in their places. There's no color in Auntie's face as she tells me all this.

After she left, I went down into the pit. I sat in the dark, and I was in Joseph's snake pit, in Daniel's lions' den.

May 20:

Last night I went to see Szube with Konyak and we came back empty-handed. We left the barn after ten and headed towards Szube's village. Itche again led me throught the dark fields and woods. I didn't recognize the way; it looked more menacing than the first time. Soon I stepped into a ditch full of water, and my entire body was chilled after that. I saw suspicious shadows lurking behind every tree. We walked rapidly, not saying a word. I had a difficult time keeping up with Konyak. My mouth and throat were dry from fear and effort. The chilly air dried my sweat. We detoured around villages and houses, roads and paths. After a few hours we came to a potato field. It was opposite a village, less than a mile from Szube's place. As we walked across the furrows, we heard gunfire in the village.

"They're shooting at us!" Konyak said. We threw ourselves on the ground and crawled into a ditch between two furrows. We hid in the tall stalks. The shooting continued, bullets whistling. We lowered our heads and held our breaths. Suddenly it was quiet. It was probably Germans or partisans. "We must beware of both," Konyak said.

Then we heard heavy footsteps nearby. He pinched my leg to warn me to stop breathing so heavily. Silence again. We lay there a long while unable to decide whether to continue to Szube or to return to the barn. They might be searching at Szube's. Besides, it would be too late to get back to our barn before dawn. We decided to return now. We crawled back toward the forest. Then we started to run. I almost stumbled and fell. I thought I heard footsteps, and we hid behind some trees. We kept hiding, crouching, and walking. Soon the darkness began to fade and birds were singing. "We'd better hurry," Itche said. "We have a long way to go, and it'll soon be dawn."

We ran. We entered an oak wood. "That's our woods." Itche

said. "It's a mile and a half to the barn." We were deep inside the woods when we heard gunfire again. "Tonight is a dangerous night," Itche murmured. I stepped into that same deep ditch.

The sky was turning blue when we entered the barn.

* * *

I'm exhausted. I've just written a letter to Auntie. I beg her to forgive us and to understand our plight. There was nothing else we could do. We're going to the forest to join the partisans. I ask her to take it calmly; let there be peace in the house. We will always remember her. We're leaving her some of the cloth we kept in the pit, the cloth we left with Janek, and some cash. We hope to see her soon, as free people.

We'll leave the letter, the cash, and the cloth beside the pit opening. She'll find it in the morning, when she brings us our food.

I've had a high fever all day. This evening we have to see Szube again. I hope he wasn't frightened by the shooting last night. I pray things will go well.

This morning I asked Janek to dig up the earthen jar containing my notebooks. I told him that I wanted to look them over. There are several notebooks in that jar. Each time I finished one, I asked Janek to place it with the others. I always told him I would reward him for it.

He brought me the jar a little while ago. We'll take them along to our new shelter.

May 20, evening:
It has been a week since our battle with the rabbits began. They don't care for the new house we made for them in a corner, and they keep digging toward the tunnel directly on top of us. Day and night they try to hollow out the tunnel that we filled up. We chase them away and stuff the fresh holes they've dug, and a few minutes later they begin again. Their digging and burrowing keep us awake nights. We only hope that nobody outside hears the noise. Today they burrowed more than a yard downward. We've only just discovered it. We don't know whether to let it remain or to fill up the hole once more.

May 23:
We've been at Szube's since the night of the 21st.

What a strange feeling. Our fears have calmed down some-what, but we feel sad and empty. A new life has begun for us, but we're so tired. We need some fresh courage and energy! And what we'd really like is to dig ourselves deep into our new hide-out, into the ground, and sink into a long, deep sleep. I feel espe-cially weary. My mind is tired, and I feel like curling up and sleeping.

But I have to stay awake and keep an eye on the Szubes, spend time with them, entertain them with my conversation; I can't give them much time to think, can't let them think too much about this whole affair. From time to time they come in-to the granary, and I must always have a story ready to keep their minds off the fact that we have brought them mortal danger.

The Szubes are still in a daze. As though it were all only a plan and we weren't really settled here yet. That may be why they keep visiting us, to see whether we're really here. They still haven't reconciled themselves to the idea. In their minds, they're still deciding whether or not to take us in.

Or are we the ones who are dreaming? Sometimes it seems that way. Ever since the night I first came to Szube. I guess that we're all dreaming.

When Konyak and I went to see Szube three nights after our first visit, he scratched his head, shrugged, and told us that he didn't want to die. At first, I couldn't look him in the eyes. Then I summoned up my courage and asked him how many hogs and calves he had. He thought for a few seconds and told me.

"Have they all had an earlobe punctured and been registered?"

"No. Only two of them."

"Do you ever slaughter a hog yourself?"

"Of course."

"Do you know the penalty for that?"

"Yes," he smiled. "Death. Just the other day the Germans in Kaluszyn shot two pig breeders who were slaughtering unregis-tered hogs."

"What about people who don't deliver their full quota of grain to the Germans?"

Szube laughed: "Camp!"

"Do you know that camp means almost certain death?"

"Of course!"

"Do you deliver your full quota?"

"No!"

"Do you grind flour and sell it?"

"Yes!"

"What's the penalty for that?"

"Also camp."

"In other words, also death?"

Szube laughed: "Right!"

"And for what crime don't the Germans pass a death sentence?"

"Of course, the penalty is death for almost everything!"

"So let's see: You don't make any secret about keeping unregistered hogs in your sty, unregistered calves in your barn, and undelivered grain in your granary. And you've never been caught. So why should anyone discover us, hidden deep inside a camouflaged pit? And it will bring you much more money than a few runt pigs and some miserable grain, not to mention the reward from Lord God for doing a good deed, and the reward you'll get when the war is over!"

Szube opened his eyes wide and gazed at his wife. She called me "a very clever Yid," and perhaps I'm right; only, did we happen to have material for a dress? She'd like to buy some from us.

"Of course we do! And what do you mean, 'buy'? When we come tomorrow night, I'll bring it along. It's a very nice print. It will be our present to you."

No, she doesn't want any presents. But, by the way: Do we also happen to have material to make a pair of pants for the boy?

Of course! We have just the thing for him. And my wife can sew anything. She'll personally make Mrs. Szube's dress, according to the latest high fashion. What a beautiful dress it will be! And she'll also personally sew by hand the boy's pants. And she can also knit beautiful woolens. Would Mr. Szube like a sweater?

Szube indicated that in fact he had no sweater. His wife stroked his woven work shirt and said: "This is all he's got. Where would he get a sweater?"

"He'll get one! Don't you worry!"

We started discussing our plan to come here. They wanted us to put it off for a few more days. I said that we're ready to move now and really can't wait any longer; the day after tomorrow we have to pick up some material from a gentleman we know in the city. Either of them could go to the city and bring back sheets, slipcovers, underwear, and material for the dress and pants, as well as some goods to be sold for ready cash. We have to hurry, because that gentleman may leave any day.

Szube asked us why the gentleman wasn't hiding us. We don't want to stay there, I replied. He's very rich and kind-hearted, and he wants to keep us free of charge. But we don't want to take advantage of anyone. We want to pay our way.

Szube liked my answer. He told us to come the following night.

* * *

The following day was hectic. In the pit we packed our underwear, a few odds and ends, and a small bundle of goods for the Szubes. Then we fixed up the barn, removing every trace of our presence there, and waited impatiently for nightfall. All day Auntie paid no attention to us. Mrs. Felek hung around outside our wall, and murmured to herself about going to the Germans if Janek didn't return her parcel of land. We prayed that night would soon come and that nothing would happen in the meantime. We looked out to see where the sun was on the horizon. We noticed the window open in Staszko's cottage. Mariszka Maczuszak came running by. Janek appeared for a moment, then disappeared. We were ready. The rabbits huddled in the corners, their ears cocked and their frightened eyes averted, as if they sensed some trouble brewing.

When the shadows had lengthened, Auntie brought us lunch. She put down the basket and hurried out. It was getting dark. We dressed, stuffed some bread into our pockets, sealed the pit opening, and left the letter for Auntie, the money, and cloth. When it was dark, we followed Itche out of the barn. Carefully we crawled to the oak wood. When we got there, we started walking.

We could hardly feel our warm, swollen feet touch the cold ground. But we tried to encourage each other. Ephraim said the fresh air was good medicine; he kept inhaling deeply. As we moved through the trees, we imagined that Auntie, Janek, and other peasants were chasing us. Soon we emerged from the woods into an open field. A shadow approached us; it was an old peasant woman. But Konyak assured us that she probably thinks we're partisans. It wouldn't occur to her that any Jews were still living. Boldly we headed straight for the nearby woods.

Esther and Zippora asked if we were anywhere near Szube's place. Their strength was giving out. They breathed heavily and leaned on us for support. We sat down to rest in the woods. A falling star streaked down from the sky. We thought we heard shots and even human voices. We huddled together and said nothing. There was some noise in the trees. Itche said it was probably a small animal. We got up, and started to drag ourselves through the woods and fields. Esther and Zippora couldn't take another step. Froiman helped them along. Itche hurried on. He crossed a dense wood and came into a field. He waited for us, then pointed to a dark speck in the distance: Szube's cottage and granary.

We entered Szube's farmyard at 2:30 a.m. Again Morwa greeted us by barking, and once more Itche petted her. The others hid behind the wall and I tapped on the window. Szube looked out and quickly opened the door. I went inside, asked him to cover the windows, and to light a lamp. One by one shadows crawled into the house. I handed over the bundle of cloth and introduced the others to the Szubes, who were lying in bed. Mrs. Szube examined the small bundle. Esther and Zippora struck up a conversation with her. The rest of us got busy with Szube. He was frightened and shocked.

I searched my pockets for things to give them, but I had none. I started telling jokes. Szube smiled. We decided to dig our pit in the granary first thing in the morning. It would be best to gather the wood now. The women and Ephraim went up to the attic, and the rest of us went with Szube to his nearby woodpile. We picked several long young trees that had already been sawed and brought them to the granary. There we found some planks and spades. Szube went back to the house to sleep. I went with him. His wife was sitting in bed in a state of shock. The boy was asleep. I promised to buy him some nice things, but he mustn't know that we're here; they mustn't let little Maniek into the granary. We also agreed that in a day or two Mrs. Szube would go to Kontraktowicz to collect a big bundle of cloth. Then I returned to the granary.

We sat in a corner waiting for daybreak. Itche began to snore. Out in the yard, Morwa howled at the dawn. Froiman yawned and poked Itche to get up. I felt magnetized to the ground. I couldn't move, my eyelids stuck together, my legs felt like logs. We were prodding each other to get to work. My hands were limp, and I couldn't lift the spade. Meanwhile, the other two were digging. The pit would be ten feet long, six and a half feet wide, and eight feet deep. From time to time I picked up a spade

and tried to dig, but I was helpless. Gradually the pit deepe.
They dug quickly, bringing up shovel after shovel of earu.
Froiman asked me to spread the mounds of earth evenly over the
granary floor. But my feet buckled. Soon it was daylight. The
Szubes were at their chores in the farmyard. She came in to wish
a good morning. She watched us work and sighed. Little Maniek
ran out of the house and headed for the granary. His mother
dashed after him and shouted: "Get away from here!"

But Maniek persisted. He peeked in through the cracks. We invited him in, but he ran away. Mrs. Szube said he's a clever boy
and won't say a thing. She took him by the hand and pulled him
into the granary. He stamped his feet and struggled to get free.
With his free hand he covered his eyes. We pinched his cheeks
and promised him a bicycle. Maniek opened his eyes, and when
his mother left he grabbed a shovel and helped with the digging.
I repeated the promise of a bicycle and asked him if he loved
Papa and Mama.

"Yes!"

"Then you mustn't tell anyone about us. Because if you do, the
Germans will kill Papa and Mama. You're not to say anything to
anyone, not even to your friends!" Maniek nodded vigorously,
and asked me when he'd get his bicycle.

Froiman and Itche were drenched in sweat. The pit was
almost ready. We prayed for the day to be over and all of us safely inside the pit.

The Szubes were busy outside, and were keeping a careful
watch. Whenever a stranger passed by on the dirt trail near the
granary, Morwa, chained to her kennel near the granary door,
started to bark. Now I got to work. Our bodies steamed with
sweat. Our shirts were drenched.

We finished digging in the afternoon. We used the sawed trees
for roof beams, and we fortified the walls with poles and boards,
filling the spaces between them with straw and slats. We
covered the beams with branches, piled on newspapers, and
covered it all with more than a yard of earth. Then we piled on
hay and garbage, made a cover for the narrow opening, and
spread more hay, straw and garbage on top. It fit the opening
perfectly. We could remove the cover by pushing up with both
hands. From above, nothing was noticeable. If the granary is
ever searched, we could hold on to the cover from inside the
dugout to prevent it from moving.

oked in and admired our work. Neither of them
gh the narrow opening. Little Maniek jumped in
it a few times.

, Szube went to the village for a bottle of brandy.
brought Esther, Zippora and Ephraim down from
wa stood guard outside, and we all drank a toast.

* * *

When everything was set up, we asked the Szubes for a tub
and a few buckets of water. Esther trimmed our hair. We
washed and put on fresh underwear. The others climbed into
the dugout and Itche and I remained above. Then I told him to
throw away his filthy rags and get into the tub of hot water. I
soaped and scrubbed him, and gave him fresh underwear and
clothing. (Here, and before at Auntie's, our hosts did our wash
for us, often running a great risk.) We buried his rags in a pit
behind the granary.

Then we locked ourselves into the dugout, lit a candle, and
looked around. We felt as though we had moved to a spacious
new apartment. We were all hungry. Mrs. Szube soon brought
us a pot of potatoes boiled in milk. We ate heartily. Considering
how things were at the other place, it seemed that the liberation
had already come.

I wonder what Auntie's thinking now? What are they all saying? I hope things calm down there. We're a bit more relaxed.
It's almost too quiet here. Are we entitled to this much peace?

May 24:
This morning Mrs. Szube went to Kontraktowicz to collect
some goods. She brought him our note, and told him that she
was from a village near Warsaw. We were with a band of partisans, and sometimes passed her village. We wrote that the war
would soon end, and then we'd show him our gratitude. He
wrote us that only a little bit of material was left. We have some
goods stored with two other families. But very little. I hope it
lasts till the end.

Mrs. Szube brought back the bundle and asked us if we really
had partisan connections. Szube also wanted to know. We said
that we had, and that our comrades knew where we were. If
we're killed, they will take revenge quickly. And those who help
us will be rewarded.

We opened the bundle, and the colorful slipcovers dazzled them. They passed them back and forth, and couldn't take their eyes off them. A pity to sell any of it, they said. They could use it themselves. They decided to sell only the small items, for some cash. They'd keep the rest, and share their food with us. We shook hands on that, and they took most of the goods.

Today Esther is sewing the slipcovers and the pants for Maniek. Mrs. Szube is as pleased as a fancy city lady when she drops in to see how the work is progressing. She stands and stares, first at us and then at the sewing. The sight of us makes her sad, but the slipcovers bring fresh bloom to her cheeks.

* * *

How time flies! We're in a new hideaway, with a new family, and our spirits are a little better. This hideout seems relatively safe. We even have Morwa for a guard, barking at every stranger's approach. Morwa is a medium-sized bitch with white-spotted tan fur. When Szube unchains her each evening, she comes dashing into the granary and sniffs around. But before she's unleashed, we all climb into the dugout. We're afraid of Morwa. We don't want to get too close to her; she might yet betray us.

In the new hideout, two of us still stand guard up on the wall of the granary, peering through the cracks. People often pass by on the grassy trail behind the granary. They often pause by the well in the yard on their way to the next village. Szube offers them a drink of cold water. He has many friends. He used to know many Jewish people. He visits the granary every day, and tells us stories about Jews that he knew. They were storekeepers, who lived in the surrounding villages. Some of them were honest people, and others were swindlers, who cheated the farmers. His nostalgic stories depress us; all those village Jews are gone, with their flour-dusted tunics and boots and little beards sprinkled with straw. Those Jews with the floury caps and faces brought trade to the village, and the bond between them and the villagers had lasted for generations. They had been part of the village. The farmer spoke of them in the same warm tone as he spoke of the harvest of ten or fifteen years ago. In my mind's eye I saw those good, familiar faces, solid plain Jews who were here not long ago, it seems like only yesterday, and now are gone. Szube's stories make me feel like an orphan.

May 26:

We had a visitor today: Szube's married daughter who lives in a nearby village. Szube came into the granary first. He told us that his daughter is a very fine woman. They had to tell her about us, because his wife is very frightened and needs somebody to talk to. Manka, their daughter, is a brave girl, and she'll be able to help out, in selling the cloth, for example. Every Wednesday she'll sell a little in the Dobre market. She'll also buy us some things that we need.

Mrs. Szube soon followed with Manke. Manke, in her twenties, is blond and skinny, with bleary red eyes. She looked bewildered as she stood by the door of the granary, just stood there staring at us. In her arms she held a baby wrapped in a blanket. Manjek held on to the side of her dress, sucking a finger. He quietly told her about our promise of a bicycle. Mrs. Szube shut the granary door. I greeted them, offered Manke a hand, and asked her to come in. She followed me timidly. We sat around the dugout and talked about the high price of textiles. Manke talked about "Yids" captured in the vicinity, and said that her father and mother will get themselves killed yet. Mrs. Szube glared at us. I let them in on a secret: thousands of Jews are in hiding and they haven't been caught yet, because the "gentry" that hide them are clever. Nobody knows about those who are not caught; people only hear about the ones captured in the houses of silly farmers who don't know how to be careful. They can't imagine how many of their neighbors and friends are hiding Jews; nobody suspects, because they're so careful.

Szube jumped at the idea and began to list villagers who "were hiding Jews for sure." He felt certain about it; nobody suspected them because they're so clever.

But Mrs. Szube groans: "But what did we need it for? God, what for?"

Manke thinks that we have to be careful. Come to think of it, there are probably Jews hiding in her village, too. (She lives in the same village as Mrs. Felek.) They say that the widow of the bandit Felek is hiding some Jews from Minsk. They've searched her place quite a few times without finding anything. At any rate, Felek's sister, tall Auntie, is under heavy suspicion.

We give Manke a glass of brandy, and Szube tells her what a clever "Yid" I am. But I say that I'm not clever at all. Lord God taught me how to talk and Lord God didn't let her father and mother refuse us. It's all part of the Lord's plan!

Manke says that the "Yids" are also God's children. Once we were even the chosen people, but we're being punished for rejecting God's Son. Her husband can't stand the sight of "Yids." She won't tell him about us.

Manke's baby started to cry. They all stood up and left at once.

* * *

After Manke returned to her village, Szube explained to us that he didn't want to tell his daughter, but his wife needed someone to talk to. He's not at all worried about Manke; she knows how to keep a secret. As a little girl she knew all the secrets of their bandit neighbors, the Cegelszczaks. She had often played with their daughter. The police even questioned her once, but they got nothing out of her. But he's worried about her husband, Maczek. Even before the war he would beat up Jews. If he were to catch a Jew now, he would beat him to death himself or hand him right over to the Germans. At any rate, Manke's a clever one. She won't tell her husband. She wouldn't endanger her parents' lives.

Szube says he can't stand killing; he has too soft a heart, just the opposite of his son-in-law, Maczek.

Once they were traveling together from Mrozy to Kaluszyn. It was last winter, in December. The Jews who were rounded up in Kaluszyn were being marched to Mrozy; there, they were loaded on the train to Treblinka. It was freezing. He and Maczek traveled by sleigh, and they saw the Jews on the road, perhaps a few thousand of them: men, women, and many children and babies. The roads were littered with corpses, with punctured heads and bellies. Szube couldn't stand the sight. He looked the other way. But Maczek whipped the horse and yelled: "*Psia krew!*"—Dog's blood! The plague take them! They should rip all their bellies open, not just shoot them. That's what I like to see."

As they approached Kaluszyn, they saw police chase some Jews to the cemetery to be shot. In a nearby street they saw a wagon carrying a pile of corpses to the cemetery. Szube shut his eyes, crossed himself, and said a prayer. But Maczek laughed and said he was too soft-hearted, like a woman or worse. All those stinking Jews should be wiped out.

Szube tells me not to get upset. Maczek is still young: no older than me. When Maczek is as old as Szube (past fifty), he'll probably be wiser. Meanwhile, we have to watch out for him.

When Szube left the granary, I went into the dugout. We shut ourselves in, and I told them about Maczek. Konyak knows him. He's had to flee from him more than once. One time, Maczek got hold of him, dragged him to his cellar, and tied him with a strap to the wall. He left, probably to get the police. Meanwhile, his wife Manke came along and let Konyak go.

May 30:
The days go by slowly at Szube's place. We've been here only a week, and our stay with Auntie, Mrs. Felek, and Janek seems like a bad dream. The weather is lovely, mild and gentle. We look outside and our eyes don't get tired. Except for our neighbor Kowalczyk's farm and a few scattered huts in the distance, all we see for miles around are fields and woods. The Szubes' farmyard is a gray island in a sea of green. Szube's cottage stands right beside the road, like a hostel, with windows on three sides. If not for the roof of wet, decaying straw, which seems to press the cottage to the ground, the house would look like a summer verandah. The farmer and his wife go about their chores in the yard. They're carrying buckets, baskets, and pots from place to place. Szube has a mild manner. He does everything slowly, smiling into his graying whiskers. Mrs. Szube waddles about, from time to time casting nervous glances at the road and the granary. If not for that path behind the granary connecting the villages of Zimna-Woda and Dobre, they would be completely cut off from their surroundings. But now the sight of an occasional traveler on the path is frightening. Every passing cart is a reminder of the city, the world, people, and the everlasting terror. Peasants work in the nearby fields, but they seem to be far away. They're absorbed in their work, and we don't even exist for them. We keep switching observation posts, and time drags. It's quiet on the front lines, even though we're well into spring. The weather is dry and mild; what are those generals and marshals waiting for? Why are they delaying? There were rumors about the English opening a new front. But meanwhile the old front, the Russian one, is going nowhere. Who knows, maybe they're starting to move now, at the very moment that I'm writing this!

Meanwhile, time moves too slowly, and we all seem to be asleep. The sun doesn't enter our dugout. For us it's always night, the pitch dark "night of the long knives." Outside it's spring, blue and green at play between sky and ground. In here it's gloomy, black.

Every so often a passer-by drops in on the Szubes, acquaintances from the nearby villages. Among other things, they talk about Jews. This week an old peasant told Szube that the Polish partisans in our area were killing Jews: Free Poland had to be rid of both enemies, the Germans and the Jews.

I told Szube that the old man was a fool. The new Polish government will reward people who hid Jews and will punish those who killed them. As he knows, we have connections with the partisans. Szube left pleased. Afterwards, Konyak told us that the Polish partisans really were killing Jews. They search for them in all the villages. He even had some narrow escapes from them.

June 1:
When all is said and done, we have to appreciate the miracle that brought us to Szube's place. The tension has lifted a bit, and we're calmer. The Szubes don't know how we'd been living, close to starvation. They treat us like human beings. Twice a day Mrs. Szube cooks a big pot of soup with fat or milk. Because I'm ill, she fries me an egg twice a day. We wash up and change underwear regularly. The granary is well ventilated, and fresh breezes blow in from the nearby fields. Ephraim is getting better; he says that the fresh air is healing him. Froiman has stopped coughing. Zippora is feeling well. And Itche is no longer the Konyak we knew: he's almost glowing. But Esther still has trouble breathing, and the pains in her side are still there. I'm also feeling better. I gulp down the fresh air like water. In the evening I lie down on a pile of hay near the wall and inhale the fresh air that seeps in through the cracks. Two of us keep an eye on what's happening outside. Morwa is also at her post. A few days ago we began watching at night. The granary isn't locked and it's close to the road. Some traveler could sneak in to sleep here, and he would find our hideout exposed. So each night one of us stands guard by our dugout.

June 2:
I saw Maczek today. He came riding up to his father-in-law's place on horseback. He had been in the cottage only a few minutes when he came out and started prowling in the farmyard. He kept turning his head to glance at the granary. Maczek had a nasty look; his beady eyes were set deep in their huge sockets. He seemed nervous, and his hands dangled at his sides. Szube and his wife went outside and began to argue with him. Little Maniek scampered around his brother-in-law, and Maczek felt the boy's new trousers. Then, with his hands tucked into his pockets, he strolled back and forth by the granary walls, whistling, and tossing back his long chestnut hair. I alerted the others in the dugout, and got ready to jump into the pit at a mo-

ment's notice. But he examined only the outside of the building; then he resumed whistling; jumped on his horse, tickled its belly, and raced off.

After Maczek had gone, Mrs. Szube came in. When I questioned her, she blushed, and stammered that he didn't know a thing. She went out sheepishly, and Szube entered. He said that even if Maczek knew about us, he wouldn't talk. Manke has her way with him, and he does what she says.

June 5:

Szube warned us to be very careful about his neighbor Kowalczyk. He's a sworn enemy and is only looking for a chance to harm him. They've been quarreling for many years over a field and the pond opposite the granary.

The pond belongs to Szube, but it borders on the Kowalczyks' farm; so they're always helping themselves to Szube's fish. Kowalczyk is rich. He owns a large tract of land and abundant cattle, and yet he steals fish. Mrs. Szube waits in ambush for him and often catches him in the act. Each time there's a big fight. There are also fights over the hens and geese. Kowalczyk's fowl sometimes wander into Szube's furrows, where they peck at his seeds, and sometimes Szube's fowl stray into Kowalczyk's fields and garden. When the two wives attack the marauding fowl, the rumpus begins. The battles last for weeks on end.

They've often sent robbers to Szube's place. On dark winter nights they throw stones at his cottage; they want him to think it's the work of demons. They've even told the Germans that he's harboring partisans. That was a few days before we arrived, when the Germans killed those partisans in Zimna-Woda. A wounded partisan had fled, barefoot and his legs bleeding. He came running up our path, held his rifle to Szube, and demanded his boots. Kowalczyk told the Germans that he had seen a partisan enter Szube's house. When they found the trail of blood, Szube took quite a beating before he persuaded them that he was the victim, that he'd been robbed of his boots.

Szube again urged us to be very careful. But he doesn't know if it can help, because Kowalczyk's wife is a witch. She finds many things out by her witchcraft. Once she almost cast a spell on him. She lured him to her house and told him to sit on a stool. He did as she asked. Suddenly he saw her circling the stool, and he realized that she was casting a spell upon him. He wanted to escape, but she spoke to him cordially, calling him "friend" and "dear neighbor." He felt drained of his will, unable to budge. But he managed to free himself and run away.

That witch inherited her power from her father, who was a sorcerer. Once he cast a spell on some visitors and horses returning from a wedding. Two horses unharnessed themselves, and almost killed the passengers in the wagon they were drawing. Let's hope she doesn't cast some spells on us. We must beware of the whole family, even the son and two daughters. The older daughter is a moron. Her mother must have bewitched her. We have to be very careful, and pray for good luck.

* * *

Manke was here again today. She took a few pieces of cloth to sell in the Dobre market. She admitted that Maczek knows about us. She herself had told him. But there's nothing to worry about, he won't tell a soul. She made him swear. "I told him I'll be killed if he tells!"

I told her that I saw him that day he rode over in his horse, and I took a liking to him. I'd like to meet him, drink a toast with him, and shake his hand. She'll bring him over, she said. He has a fine jacket and pants, but he can use two shirts. Won't I sell her some of my cloth? Maczek said he would pay for it. I will? That's nice. No, she doesn't want it as a gift. Besides, I can discuss it with Maczek. He'll pay. But there's something else. Isn't that material with the flower print just perfect for a little dress for her baby? And maybe even for a dress and kerchief for herself? "Of course!" All right, then, she'll take it. She'll pay with milk and sour cream. She'll bring it the next time she comes; she insists. We won't have to worry about Maczek. We'll see for ourselves when we meet him. First she'll make him the shirts, so he'll have some good clothes. Then he'll come and have a drink with me. She'll sell some more cloth in the market and give us the money later. And she'll use some of the money to buy brandy and goodies. We'll drink a toast with Maczek.

June 7:
Today we had a long talk with the Szubes. I bought several eggs from her. Mrs. Szube boiled them, and she and her husband served them to us with bread and salt. We ate together and had a pleasant conversation.

220

Szube wondered why the Jews were being punished this way. His wife said it is because they were dishonest. Once, the Jewish bakers kneaded their dough with poison and sold the baked goods to Polish children. But Szube maintains that there were many honest Jews who even helped the peasants. The Jewish shopkeepers in town treated the peasants better than the Polish shopkeepers who took over their stores. You could bargain with a Jewish shopkeeper; and you didn't have to stand there humbly with your hat in your hand, the way you must now with the Polish merchants. Mrs. Szube admits that she can't shop in town nowadays because of the high prices. They charge twice as much as the Jewish shopkeepers used to charge and they don't let you bargain. They're high and mighty with the peasants. The Jewish shopkeepers always allowed you to charge it. They even peddled their goods in the village, and let you buy on the installment plan.

In the nearby villages there had been Jews who lived just like the peasants, working the fields, keeping cows, and producing dairy products. There were Leybke in Wola, Pesakh in Gorcyn, Itzik in Wolka, and others. They're not alive anymore. The Germans wiped them out. What did the Jews do to deserve such treatment? It must be because they killed Lord God!

Szube asks how we lived before coming to him. I whisper to him that we hid out at Felek's and Janek's, in the village where his daughter lives. He grabs himself by the forehead: "You don't say! That bandit? Felek was a bandit!"

He tells us how Felek used to operate at the Dobre and Kaluszyn fairs. He had been the "master" of all the thieves and robbers. Szube can't understand how Felek didn't murder us, and he makes the sign of the Cross.

I tell them about Auntie. Mrs. Szube knows her well. She meets her at church in Wiszniew. Now she understands why Auntie, who is usually cheerful, looked so gloomy at Mass last Sunday. Auntie didn't speak to anyone and hardly even prayed. She left early and hurried home.

June 9:

Today Szube came running in with a newspaper, and pointed to the good news that a second front has been opened in the west, in France. On June 6 the Allied sent an expeditionary force through the English Channel into northern France.

We can't restrain our joy. It's begun at last, and the Russian offensive in Poland must soon get under way. Oh, God, is it possible that soon we'll be free?

We exchanged good wishes with the Szubes and I promised them a bottle of brandy. But we put off the toasts until Maczek's visit, tomorrow.

June 11:

Maczek called on us yesterday. Again he came on horseback. Only this time he was dressed like a city slicker. His hair was neatly combed, and he wore a suit and the new shirt that his wife had made him. He came into the granary frowning. The others remained in the pit, but I had come out. Maczek looked frightened, and I shook his hand warmly. I congratulated him on the opening of the second front and launched right into an analysis of the progress of the war. Maczek listened wide-eyed. I called Esther out of the dugout and asked her to pour drinks. We sent for Szube, and then we drank a toast. Maczek's eyes started to gleam, and I slapped him on the back. He drank a few glasses, his face flushed, and he began to talk.

"I don't care for Yids," he said. "In fact, I can't stomach them!" He burst out laughing. "But don't worry," he continued, "I don't mean you. You're one of the boys! And you're a smart Kike!"

I say that he probably doesn't really know any Jews. We're all alike. If he knew a few others . . .

"No, no, no!" he shouted. He doesn't want to know any. Not even those down in the dugout. They can stay there. He doesn't want to talk to anyone but me.

Szube smiles and says that Maczek isn't really as bad as he pretends. "But when it comes to Jews, I'm real nasty!" Maczek yells.

I start telling him about the war again. It will soon be over, and then he'll see that the rest of the world likes the Jews. Only the Poles hate them, but really wise nations like them. All people are equal in their eyes.

Maczek smiled, and asked if the Jews abroad were really so rich; how much would they pay for a head, that is, for every live Jew delivered after the war.

"A mint!" I said.

"How much, more or less? How much!"

"Oh, around a hundred thousand dollars."

"Really? Not bad! It might be worth it. So," he said, turning to his father-in-law, "how much will that bring us? Let's see now, how many head do we have?" He started counting on his fingers: "One, two, three. And Konyak makes four. How many more are there?"

"Two," Szube said.

"So how many is that? Four, and two more, that makes six. Six head. How much money does that come to?" Maczek looked at his father-in-law. "Not really very much!" he added.

My forced geniality vanished. I felt the bottom drop out from under me.

Szube rose and pulled at his son-in-law. "Come on, Maczek!"

Maczek stood up. "Dog's blood! Let's go!"

He started wiping the straw off his jacket. Suddenly, I noticed a Jew's kapote, a Hasid's blackcoat! He was wearing a hacked hasidic kapote, shortened and made over into a jacket by a village tailor.

Cheerfully he gave me his hand and told me I had nothing to worry about. He'll come to see me again. But he doesn't want to lay eyes on those Kikes in the dugout. "Bloody Kikes!" he spat, and left.

Maczek was a little drunk, and he wobbled and skipped in the yard. It seemed to me that he was dancing on the body of the dead Jew who had owned that kapote. He was tearing it off his body, and shouting: "How much, how much would I get for a head?"

June 15:

The day before yesterday, when Froiman was peering outside at the pond, he noticed Kowalczyk's son sneak behind a tree, lie down, and look in our direction. Froiman called me over, and sure enough I saw Kowalczyk's son, a blond fellow of about twenty, lying at the far edge of the pond surveying our farmyard. Whenever Szube or his wife came out of their cottage, he would hide behind his father's stable and watch from there. After they went back inside, he sneaked behind the tree again, and resumed his watch over our granary. Many times it seemed that his glance had met mine through the crack.

We told the others in the dugout, and one by one they came out, peered through the crack, and confirmed that he was looking our way. We were terrified. They must have sneaked over to the granary while Morwa was asleep on night and eaves-dropped; or they could have seen Mrs. Szube bringing baskets of food into the granary and concluded that people were staying in here. He kept his watch for several hours. A few times I saw him crawl over to the edge of the pond and hide in the grass.

Later, Mrs. Szube came inside. She also saw them through the crack. But he was only waiting for a chance to steal some fish, she assured me. She went out of the granary, and Kowalczyk's son ran off. After a while he returned and hid in the grass. No, he wasn't waiting around to steal fish. It was almost dark, and he kept crawling back and forth between the tree and the pond. We didn't see him steal any fish. We slept very badly that night.

The scene was repeated all day yesterday. Again Kowalczyk's son lay in the grass staring our way. That couldn't be about fish! We had another sleepless night. This morning he reappeared at the crack of dawn.

At about twelve noon, his sister sneaked up beside him, carry-ing something. I looked hard: it was a little fishnet. She handed it to him. He dropped it into the water, hauled out some fish, and tossed them into her open apron. Then he dropped the net into the water again, hauled up some more fish, ran off for a while, and came back. This scene was repeated many times before evening.

* * *

I've been meaning to write about our bitch, Morwa. Szube warned us to beware of Morwa: "If she catches you inside the granary, she'll tear you to pieces." Almost every evening, after dark, they unchain her, and she runs with the neighboring dogs. Our first few days here, she would come into the granary and sniff around. She barked furiously, as if to let us know that she was on to us. She clawed at the ground and sniffed all around the place.

Early one evening, Mrs. Szube asked us to come out of the dugout to eat the food she had brought. She and her husband would keep watch outside. We were spooning food out of the pot in the dark when someone crawled in under the granary door; it was Morwa. She ran up to us, and glared. Then she got down on her belly, started whining, and crawled closer. For a few minutes she crouched on her knees, then leaped up and licked Esther on the cheek. Then she was nuzzling our laps, moving from person to person, licking our hands with her tongue. We offered her food, but she refused. We stroked her fur and she looked up at us lovingly. After a while the Szubes came in and couldn't believe their eyes. They pulled Morwa outside by the collar but she refused to budge, reaching toward us with her belly and paws.

The Szubes say that dumb animals sense everything. When they tried to lead her out again, she refused to budge. Only after we all returned to the dugout would she let herself be led back to her kennel.

Since then, she visits us every evening after dark, as soon as she is unchained. She cuddles up to us, licks our hands and faces, and can't take her eyes off us. Her gaze seems to tell us that she understands our plight.

June 20:

We've very worried about little Maniek. He has too many playmates. He spends whole days playing in the fields and woods with them, and we're afraid he'll tell them something. Whenever we see him with them, we watch the expressions on their faces. Afterwards, we call him over and ask him what he tells them and what games they play. We caution him about the Germans and repeat our promise of a bicycle. He has shrewd black eyes, and he doesn't look like a peasant. He often gives us a bad scare. With a perfectly straight face he confesses that he told his friends about us, then admits later that he was "only fooling." I can't tell which is the truth. Only after his parents question and threaten him do we find out that he hasn't said a word.

Once, he climbed up to the straw roof of our granary, and suddenly whispered down to me and Froiman: "Quick, hide! Germans! I see them!" We stampeded into the dugout. He leaped down from the roof, followed us, and again whispered: "Get in, fast! Germans!" After we'd dragged the cover across the opening, he burst out laughing and said: "I fooled you, I fooled you!" It took us a few hours to recover. But the child just laughed away. We told his parents, and Szube gave him a few slaps on the cheek.

We're also worried that he's playing too much with shepherd boys from the neighborhood. Esther gives him daily lessons in reading, writing, and arithmetic by candlelight in the dugout. She tells him that we'll get him all sorts of nice things if he stays away from his friends. But it doesn't help. He always manages to disappear to the grain fields or the woods, to be with his mischievous friends.

June 22:

We had quite a fright last night. Froiman was keeping watch by the dugout opening, while the rest of us slept in the pit. Close to midnight I awoke, gasping for breath, and my head throbbing from fever. I decided to sleep above ground beside the opening. I fell asleep quickly, but I slept badly, tossing and turning, waking up and falling asleep again.

At about 3 a.m. I woke up and couldn't go back to sleep. I could hear Froiman snoring and wheezing. I poked him, and he stopped. Suddenly, I heard human voices and footsteps. I grabbed hold of Froiman. People were walking and talking adjacent to the granary. I pushed Froiman into the pit and jumped in after him. Before I went underground, I could see flashlight beams light up the farmyard and penetrate the cracks in the granary. I heard them knocking on Szube's window. Someone called out: "Open up!"

I quickly covered the pit opening and sealed it tight. The others woke up. We were afraid to breathe. At daybreak, Szube came inside. He told us that some partisans had passed by, asked for a few loaves of bread, and continued on their way.

June 25:

There's a problem with our hideout. The ground is flooded with water. It seeps through the straw on the floor. Perhaps there's a spring underground. Every day we bale out a few dozen pailfuls. But it didn't help, and we're sitting in a puddle. We even tried to dig canals that would carry the water to the little reservoir we dug in a corner. But that didn't help either. Szube says that the granary stands in a valley and collects water from the surrounding terrain. "Now," he said, "it's tolerable. The worst times are spring and fall. In the fall the pit will be filled up with water." Szube laughed as he went on:

"In the fall, you'll have to leave anyway. After the harvest I'll need the granary for storing my crops. There won't be any room left for a needle then. I'll fill the place up with corn and wheat."

"We've got a bumper crop this year," his wife added. "What did we need all this trouble for? Look at the fields! Look at all that wheat and corn out there."

We looked around and sure enough the fields are bursting with a rich harvest. The long stalks are bent almost to the ground, heavy with produce. During the last few years the earth has been fed a surfeit of blood, and now it's rewarding the world for its generosity; there'll be enough food to last for years.

Only, beneath the earth's surface, the blood cannot congeal. One day, in a mighty volcanic explosion, it might yet erupt.

* * *

The Szubes often talk to us about their bumper crop. If they had known in May that they'd have such a good harvest, they'd have never agreed to shelter us. Last year, they didn't have such a good crop. They had barely enough. They don't have the best soil, and they thought this year would be like the last.

Once I told them that they were having a good year because Lord God was rewarding them for helping us. We had peace for a few days afterwards. But yesterday Szube told us once more that we'd have to find a new place soon after the harvest, even before autumn.

The two of them came in together early this morning. They looked sadly at us. I went into the dugout, and Esther came up to talk to them. Again they spoke about their bumper crops. After they left, I went up and looked outside. The tall golden stalks pierced my eyes like gleaming bayonets.

June 27:
The Szubes have it in for Itche. Suddenly they can't stand him. Even though he sews them trousers and repairs their old clothes, they always grumble about him, especially Mrs. Szube: "Look how he's fattened up here! See how his cheeks have filled up and how his buttocks have spread!"

Itche really has improved in the last few weeks. Before, the lice were sucking his blood, and his life as a scavenger had turned him into a skeleton. Now, he's gained weight and the color has returned to his face. As long as he was a wretched stray, Mrs. Szube felt sorry for him. but now that he's "thriving," she's angry at him. "Why, he looks like a baron!" she says.

So Itche stays in a corner of the dugout with Esther, where they've set up a kind of workshop. By candlelight, he sews for our hosts and she knits. They make things to cover them from head to toe, working away for Szube, for Mrs. Szube, for little Manjek, for their daughter Manke, for their son-in-law Maczek, for their granddaughter, and even for some relatives who don't know about us.

* * *

June is nearly over and it's quiet. Nothing is stirring in the east. What's taking them so long? The western front is also quiet. The Allies set one foot inside France and stopped. What will happen to us after the harvest? The Szubes really mean for us to leave. Meanwhile, the days drag on. Outside, it is high summer, heat and vegetation abound. The world is wide open, and we're rotting underground. Our bodies reek of moisture and mildew. We've turned into subterranean creatures, swamp beasts. Not human, but dreamers nonetheless. We dream, and long for the day when the world will wake up from its nightmare. We wait for the new day, for the rise of "Him Who each day renews His Creation." Meanwhile, the world is ruled by a powerful devil, playing his game, mocking us, laughing at us.

June 29:
Every morning peasant boys from the neighboring villages gather in Kowalczyk's farmyard to pass the time with his daughters. The younger one is a real beauty. The boys bring their bicycles and take her for rides up and down the road by our granary. They sing together, laugh, make noise, and disappear into the bushes. Meanwhile, the others have their way with the older girl, the moron. Sometimes, they take her right behind our granary wall. We can hear them grunting and groaning. Our bodies tense up. We know that those youngsters won't come into the granary. But we make sure that we're on guard, anyway. Kowalczyk's moron daughter is in love with their black-and-white spotted puppy. She runs through the fields with the dog, and hides in the woods and in back of the stable. When her parents catch her they give her a good beating, and we can hear her moaning all day. But she always manages to find a new hiding place. I hope she doesn't wander into the granary one day.

Mrs. Kowalczyk and Mrs. Szube started to quarrel again over the hens and geese, who don't know the meaning of boundaries. Once more they stray into neighboring fields and peck away in a neighbor's furrows. Again the women attack the intruding birds, and their curses ring out across the field.

Kowalczyk's prize cock has fallen in love with Szube's hens. From morning on he struts around with them, leads them from one garbage heap to another—and soon they're pregnant. Kowalczyk's own hens don't have a mate, and they're barren. But Mrs. Szube's hens are followed by clusters of chirping little chicks.

So now Mrs. Kowalczyk is waging war against Mrs. Szube and her hens, and against her own rooster. She chases him with sticks and stones, and he scoots off in mortal terror. But he soon returns to hide in our yard. Then Mrs. Kowalczyk follows him to Mrs. Szube's cottage and to the granary. We're afraid that he'll push his way in through a crack, and Mrs. Kowalczyk will come right in after him.

We're alert to the sights and sounds of summer. The young people wander in the paths every evening. Kowalczyk's moron daughter runs away with her dog. Noise and laughter, grunts and groans. The young people out there are alive, but the blood in our veins seems to have dried up.

June 30:

It's a hot, humid day. We can't stop sweating. The granary is sizzling. We can hardly breathe. The wetness in our dugout is causing the straw, the beams, and our things to rot. The stench makes us sick.

Towards evening it turns cooler. Fresh breezes come in from the fields. The day's tension subsides a bit. We all climb out of the pit and stretch out near the cracks in the wall. The cool air and the dark shadows comfort us.

It's quiet in the fields. There are no travelers on the trail. Even the sky seems to be shutting down for the night; the clouds dart by as if rushing to enter. People are also tired from the day's robbery and slaughter. The farmers are all at home resting. I feel alone, forsaken. Again, I stare at the trees behind Kowalczyk's granary. One massive tree turns into a man with a large head, a black velvet beard, and deep-set dark eyes. Each morning I see this Herzl-like figure gazing into the darkness at me, just like the picture of Herzl looking down dreamily at the Danube. Now, thousands of Jewish corpses are floating on Europe's rivers. I stare at the image. I offer my greetings, from those dying generations who might yet come to life.

* * *

Ever since coming to Szube's we worry that we've lost touch with that Jewish family in the Dobre woods. Itche lost contact with them while we were still in Janek's barn. He used to meet them regularly at an assigned spot in the forest. At each of their midnight meetings deep in the forest, they'd decide on their next meeting place. They were supposed to meet soon after Itche joined us. He wanted to keep the appointment, but we wouldn't let him go. The head of the family, Motl, never gave Itche the location of their hiding place. And Itche never told him where he had his forest dugout. For a short time they lived together in the forest. This was just before the Moszko woman was caught. There were then about ten Jews hiding deep in the Dobre woods. They would steal some potatoes and boil them in a bucket of water in the middle of the night. They built a bonfire of branches and twigs, and stood the bucket on some bricks. They would also roast potatoes for the following day. They couldn't risk lighting a fire in the daytime. In their group there was a young woman from Minsk and her small son. Her husband, Elye Perlman, had been killed. Later, the child ate poisonous mushrooms and died. They buried him among the trees. The group lived together for only a short time. During a raid, they were scattered. Only Itche, Mrs. Moszko, Motl and his family found each other once more. The others weren't heard from again. The group had included a religious young man from Dobre, a tailor, and his fiancee. He used to put on *Tefillin* (Phylacteries) and say his prayers each morning among the trees.

Itche also says his daily prayers. He moves to a corner and looks down at the prayerbook. A narrow strip of light penetrates the dugout through the opening. He prays silently. We made ourselves a prayerbook in Mrs. Felek's attic. Froiman and I recited prayers by heart and Ephraim printed them in a notebook. Froiman and I pray by heart and Ephraim and Itche read from the prayerbook. Ephraim, who attended a Zionist "Tarbut" school, pronounces the words with the Sephardi accent. In pious fashion, he sometimes rolls his eyes as he prays and covers them with his hand. Daily the women say the *Modeh ani* prayer, "*Modeh ani*," thanking God for mercifully restoring their souls every morning.

We thank and praise God for every day and every moment. We're trying to lift our spirits, to cling to a Higher Power. We feel the special spirit of the Sabbath in our whole being. We love the Sabbath. From it we draw our strength for the entire week. As the Sabbath comes to an end, we softly sing "zmires," the Sabbath table songs. *"Bnei hekhala"*—"The children of the palace yearning for the sight of the Divine Presence," ". . . longing for this assembly with the angels"; and "I, God, am with him in his travail." The Divine Presence is also in exile; we are not alone. We cling to the departing Sabbath, for we're alone for the rest of the long week. We anxiously count the days from Sunday to Friday. Then, as Sabbath approaches, I see beautiful tablecloths spread out on the fields to honor the Sabbath queen. The lights flickering in the distant windows look like Sabbath candles. Our mothers who kindled them hover overhead in white aprons. They cover their faces with their hands, and place them on our heads to bless us. A Sabbath melody floats in from somewhere beyond the woods.

On the Shavuos (Pentecost) holiday, "when Heaven opens wide," we sat up nearly all night by the granary door. We had worked out a Jewish calendar, to know when the Jewish holidays occur. We look forward to each of them as a sign of redemption, even if that redemption is only spiritual. Our beings are lifted. How we would like to lift our bodies and just soar away. "Arise from your ruins and your despair. You have dwelt long enough in distress. Shake off the dust of defeat. Rise and don your garb of glory, My people, tidings of the Redemption, Wake, wake, break forth in song: God's glory is about to shine on you." You, too, Heavenly Father—wake up, and reveal Yourself, and redeem us already!

June 30, evening:

That little scamp Maniek! This afternoon I peered out through the crack and saw him playing with some shepherd boys in the pasture opposite our granary. Suddenly, I heard them shout: "Kikes, Kikes, Yids!"

They were playing Jew-hunt. Some of them were "Jews," some "peasants" who had to capture the Jews, and the rest "Germans" who came when called by the "peasants." The "Germans" interrogated the captured "Jews" and beat them, while the peasants stood by yelling: "Lousy Yids, stinking Kikes, shoot them!"

Maniek was a German. He drew a stick, aimed it at the "Jews," and cried out: "Pe-ew! Pe-ew! You're shot!"

My head was spinning. Then Szube came along, and dragged Maniek into the house, where he gave him a good beating. He also questioned the shepherds, to make sure that they didn't know anything. They were only playing the most popular children's "educational" game in the village these days, hunting and shooting Jews.

Maniek laughs at us for being so afraid. We promise him an especially beautiful gift for his Communion; we'll see to it that he goes to church that day dressed up like a high-class city boy. And he assures us again that he won't say a word to anyone, not even to his best friend Jozef, Kowalczyk's shepherd.

We are particularly worried about Jozef. He is older than Maniek. He always questions him about everything that goes on in his parents' house. He often plays in our yard, climbing trees with Maniek. They tell secrets and laugh together.

Maniek swears that Jozef doesn't know a thing. In any case, he'll never tell him. But we'd better buy him a tandem bicycle with two bells as a precautionary measure!

July 1:

A new month, thank God. Every first of the month we start a fresh count of the days. Perhaps the new month will bring some decisive events. Could the eastern front stand still for the whole summer? Szube thinks our cause is lost. "Nobody is going to help you. Not even the Russians care about you!" He reports that two Soviet soldiers who escaped from the Germans are hiding in a bunker in the Wengrow woods. Peasants bring them bread, milk, and cooked food. They weave rustic baskets, which they sell in the neighboring villages.

Those two Russians have already killed a few Jews who wandered into their part of the forest. "We don't tolerate Yids," they say. A Jewish boy and girl were hiding out in that vicinity. When they heard about the two Russians, they abandoned their hideout to join them. Well, the Russians tore off their clothes and murdered them. The villagers say that the Russian people also hate the Jews. They brought about the war.

So Szube thinks we have no prospects of surviving. "It's all the same for you whether the Germans stay or the Russians come!" I don't know what to answer, except that the Soviets punish those who persecute Jews. Also, the Red army has hundreds of thousands of Jewish soldiers who are hurrying to liberate us.

No, Szube says, we won't survive; that's clear. "And whatever I say always comes true!" He had a similar conversation with some Jews a year and a half ago, he reports. He told them they wouldn't survive. "Wasn't I right?"

It was in the winter, early in 1943. Late one night, he heard some tapping on his window. He opened the door and three Jews came in, two brothers and a sister. They asked him to put them up for the night. It was freezing outside. Szube spread some straw on the floor of the warm room and let them sleep there until just before daybreak. "I felt so sorry for them. They were trying to escape from the Germans. Every peasant had chased them away. They looked like animals. I gave them hot tea and something to eat, and told them to leave before dawn, so that scoundrel Kowalczyk wouldn't catch sight of them. As they were about to leave, I told them they wouldn't survive. Well, are they alive? They got lost like autumn leaves in a snowstorm. Probably froze to death somewhere, or were murdered in some camp. I saw immediately that Yids aren't destined to be saved. The people won't allow it, and Lord God won't help them either."

I didn't answer, except to say that we put our full trust in Lord God. His will be done. As for us, we are innocent, and Abel's blood will always be on Cain's head. Szube sighed.

He was depressed all day. We remembered that it was the first of the month. Possibly the fronts could start moving, and the situation here could become tense. We ought to have some goods. Szube got the cart ready and went to Kontraktowicz to bring back the last of our cloth.

July 3:

At about seven o'clock yesterday evening, as night began to descend, I looked out through the crack and saw a suspicious shadow approaching on the trail. I saw Mrs. Szube hurry into the cottage, snatch Maniek by the hand, and run off to the field with him. There was nobody in the house, Szube had gone to the village earlier in the day. When the figure was close to the granary, I saw that it was a man in a green uniform! I jumped into the pit and sealed it. We were holed up, holding our breaths, for nearly two hours. We couldn't hear a thing. When Szube came home and found the house empty, he came into the granary, told us to open up, and asked what had happened. We told him about the German. Szube went outside to look, but nobody was there, it was very quiet. Maybe the German had only been passing by. I climbed out of the dugout and sat down with Szube by the granary door. We looked out through a crack. It was dark in the yard.

Suddenly, in came Mrs. Szube and Maniek, along with her sister from Zimna-Woda, Szwal's wife. They went into the cottage. Szube followed them inside. After her sister left, Mrs. Szube came to see us, still frightened out of her mind. She had fled to her sister with Maniek because she was sure that the German had brought the police.

We asked her if she had told them why she had fled. Why had her sister come along now? She couldn't give me a good answer, just mumbled something and left. None of them came to see us again that night. We sensed that something was wrong, that they were hiding something.

234

This morning, when Maniek came to Esther for his lesson, we questioned him. He told us how his mother had charged into his aunt's house in a fright and blurted out about us and the German. His uncle had been there, too, and heard everything.

The boy went to call his father. Szube was embarrassed. He admitted that his wife had told her sister and brother-in-law about us. She had been very frightened and couldn't control herself. When she realized what had happened, it was already too late.

What a dilemma! They had been so careful about Szwal. Twice a week he came in to thresh hay in the granary. We had always hid in the dugout. Szube made sure to pile lots of straw on top of the pit, so that Szwal wouldn't notice anything.

Szube stood there shrugging awkwardly. Mrs. Szube came in and started making apologies; she was sure that the Szwals wouldn't tell a soul. The two families get along fine. The Szwals won't betray their own flesh and blood.

Szube keeps on shrugging his shoulders. Well, Szwal, maybe. But the woman? She could tell everything to their other sister and to all the in-laws. It could become serious.

We decided to invite the Szwals and talk things over with them. The Szubes went to Zimna-Woda to see them. They were gone for a few hours, and we were very nervous. They returned just an hour ago. The Szwals don't want to come just now. But they wanted to assure us that they wouldn't tell anyone, not even their only daughter. They'd come to see us some other time.

We're very frightened. The farmers around here can't keep a secret. In the pit it's tense, suffocating.

July 6:
The Russian front is moving at last! The Red Army launched a massive offensive in the Byelorussian region; and in the very first days, on July third, Minsk, the capital of Byelorussia, was liberated. They have crossed the Polish border and are approaching Baranowich. The front line at Kowel hasn't moved yet, but rumors have it that action is about to intensify in that section, too. The peasants say that this time the front will reach us.

The village is stirring with excitement. The peasants think that the Russians are already on their way. Some of them are afraid of the "Bolsheviks," while others wait for them eagerly. The Szubes are confused. We listen to the news, and our blood starts racing. I can hardly write!

July 16:

The Russians are advancing rapidly. They've already liberated quite a few towns in eastern Poland, including Vilna, it seems. But the front is still far from here. It's moving now towards Lithuania. In the Kowel region, it's still quiet. But there must be tremendous movement there. All through the night squadrons of German bombers roar past us. We can feel the front lines in the air. We can't sleep at night. But it's quiet in the daytime. In the fields, the harvest is in full swing. The Germans gave the command to quickly clear the grain from the fields. The peasants work at a furious pace. Szube has hired some help: a swarthy girl from his daughter's village. All day long she snoops around in the yard. In the evening she comes into the granary to thresh hay for the cows. We hole up in the dugout. We have to be especially careful now. So many peasants are working in the fields nearby, and they keep coming into our yard to drink some water. Once a peasant girl in a white kerchief almost discovered us. She peeped into the granary through a crack. We disappeared into the corners.

But we must be even more careful. It's only a matter of weeks. We would stay in the pit all the time, but it's impossible. The water keeps seeping in through the floor and the walls, and the rotting straw stinks; we can't breathe inside. The cover must stay open. And we still must keep watch up above. When we do hide in the pit, we can feel the earth quake. Every tremor brings the war a little bit closer.

July 18:

Six days ago Morwa gave birth to five puppies—very pretty ones. Two days later Szube drowned four of them. That seems to have driven the dog out of her mind. She won't let anyone come near her, tries to break her leash, and even barks at her masters.

We can't sleep at night. She howls constantly. She's already hoarse. Her maternal grief saddens us.

Last night Morwa broke loose after chewing up her leather collar. She ran into the granary. I was sitting about ground. She lay down beside me and started wailing. I petted her. She stretched out and nuzzled my lap. She shivered, grunted fiercely, and licked my palms. The others climbed out of the dugout. She came over, nuzzling each of us in turn and imploring us with her eyes. She senses that we feel her sorrow.

We've become very attached to Morwa. She seems to be the

only living creature who is faithful to us. Each morning she would come inside and greet us with a friendly gaze. All day she stood watch outside, keeping strangers away from the granary. When she sensed someone coming, she would bark fiercely and try to pounce on them.

For the last six days, since she gave birth to the puppies and they took them away from her, we didn't have a guard at our door. But today, although she's still mourning, Morwa's at her post again, protecting us.

July 19:

We just survived the first search at the Szubes! Police ransacked our granary today, and we were certain that we would be captured.

It happened at about 10 a.m. The others were in the dugout while Froiman and I kept watch above. He was hanging on to the wall watching the northwest, and I was lying on a haystack by a crack in the opposite wall. Szube had gone off an hour ago to Great Garcyn, about a mile away. Mrs. Szube and little Maniek were working in the fields. Suddenly, Maniek was running towards us. He tumbled into the granary. "Hurry, hide! Germans! Hurry!"

For a few minutes we couldn't move; we couldn't tell whether it was one of Maniek's pranks or if this time it was the truth. Finally we leaped down to the dugout. Froiman jumped inside, but first I questioned Maniek about the Germans.

He said: "Quick, get inside! They're here!"

Szube's face was white as a ghost as he told us that on his way to Great Garcyn he had encountered several truckloads of German and Polish police. They're taking up positions outside the villages. We have to go into hiding. Szube would stand guard outside, and keep us posted. We holed up in the pit, and Szube scattered produce and hay on the floor on top of it. Then he and Maniek left. We remained in the dark pit, silently holding hands.

An hour passed quietly. Szube hadn't brought any news. It's stifling in the pit; we're gasping for breath. But not a sound from outside.

Suddenly, we heard heavy footsteps in the yard. Morwa was barking fiercely. The granary door burst open. The footsteps were directly above us now. They were throwing beams, sheaves of grain, bundles of straw. German voices shouted orders. We huddle together and hold our breaths. They were directly overhead!

They're searching the hay. In a minute, they'd step over the camouflaged pit. One of them turned over a bucket and looked for a hole underneath it. He threw it open. "Nothing! Let's go!" he ordered. Angrily, they went out, leaving open the granary door.

Morwa barked fiercely. I tapped Ephraim to ask how he was. I was afraid he might have one of his screaming fits during the search.

It was quiet in the yard again. Morwa's barking gradually subsided. Not a sound could be heard in the yard. Apparently, the Szubes weren't at home.

Half an hour later we heard footsteps. Morwa barked. Someone entered the granary, prowled around, and left. From the granary doorway a woman's voice cried out: "Mrs. Szube, Mrs. Szube, come home! Where are you, dear friend?"

No reply. The woman left. We sat there for what seemed an eternity with our legs in the water. Our legs fell asleep. Then we heard Mrs. Szube and Maniek return. They shut the granary door. We uncovered the dugout and let some air in. Then Szube arrived. He whispered to his wife in the yard, then came in to tell us that the police had surrounded the village in our vicinity. They were searching for bandits, but left without finding any.

Szube's face was white as chalk. He ran away because he feared that we would be discovered. Mrs. Szube came in, wringing her hands, and cried out repeatedly: "Oh, Jesus, Jesus, what did I need all this for?!" When she had seen the German police approaching, she grabbed Maniek and hid in the wheat field. The police ransacked the entire village.

Szube described the search. It has to do with the advancing eastern front. The Germans expect the war to advance to this region, the front line could be right here. So they want to clear the area of all kinds of suspicious characters, including partisans, thieves, bandits. They're afraid that these people will help the enemy. They searched our villages, because they're swarming with bandits. The Germans have staged many manhunts here and wiped out several gangs, first and foremost his neighbor Cegelszczak's band. They had built a network of tunnels in their fields, and the Germans blew them up. Then the bandits were captured and shot one by one. Now they're looking for new dens of bandits. But Szube isn't afraid. He sees that Lord God is protecting us. But his wife is frightened to death. People say that the Germans will return in a few days to carry out a more thorough search. Only perhaps they won't be here to do it. They say that the Russians are advancing very fast and the Germans are running away in total disarray.

End of July:

We are living through an extraordinary time. Our fate hangs by a hair's breadth. The front line is coming closer, encircling us. The last German newspaper we received tells of a big Russian offensive in the Kowel region. We haven't seen any more recent newspapers. They're not available. The post office in Kaluszyn stopped operating a few days ago. None of the offices are open! The peasants say that the Polish post-office manager and the police have fled to the west. The Germans who ran the army radio transmitter have also vanished.

There's frenzy in the countryside: The farmers are dragging their grain into the storehouses while it's still damp. They're afraid that anything left in the fields will be destroyed when the front advances. For the past few days the villagers are more frightened than ever! The Ukrainian families who served the Germans are fleeing westward with their looted goods, households, and cattle. They're running away to Germany. Along the way they plunder the Poles, beating the peasants and demanding their goods, "because none of it belongs to you Polacks anyway but to the Jews." The peasants here are digging cellars to conceal their belongings. They are actually hiding out in the woods with their cattle and sheep. The Ukrainians steal horses from one peasant and sell them to another. And the Germans grab every animal in sight. A few days ago the Germans drove their trucks into neighboring villages and loaded them up with captured cows, bulls, calves, sheep and hogs. We could hear the shooting clearly in our hideout.

The trail behind our granary is teeming with people. The inhabitants of the towns situated on the main road are fleeing in vehicles and on foot. Hundreds of people from Kaluszyn, Siedlce, and Minsk are running to the countryside, to find cover in the outlying villages until the front line has passed through. They carry stuffed valises and heavy bundles on their shoulders. Through the cracks we notice familiar faces from Minsk, including some fierce anti-Semites. Now they are scurrying for shelter like rats and mice. Their helplessness gives us hope, but they also frighten us. We'd like to crawl even deeper underground to hide for a few days. For the past week the peasants have been pressed into labor, to dig trenches and enlarge the airfield at Janow. Szube also worked there one day. The peasants were ordered to clear the adjacent fields. Szube fears that the Germans will dig in here and put up a strong resistance. This is what they seem to be planning. But the Russians upset their plans. Night after night squadrons of Russian aircraft bomb the area. The earth is quaking under us. Now we sit up in the granary at night. We peer through the cracks at hundreds of colored markers in the sky: dozens of planes dropping flares to light up the area. We notice colorful flames in the sky, red, blue, green, yellow. They mark the German military targets. Later these spots are bombed. The earth is shaking. We clutch the wall beams and feel a strange sense of joy.

They say that the German militia and police have fled. Only the army is here. They're taking up positions. Nobody knows where the front line is right now. We climb down into the dugout to absorb the shock of the earth's tremors, but it's suddenly quiet. Only at night the ground heaves like a volcano. Last night the sky was as bright as day. Flares exploded like bright suns. The sounds were deafening.

God in heaven: Your hand has led us this far. Surely You won't forsake us now!

* * *

For the past two days the Germans have been retreating to Dobre along our trail. Hundreds of units riding and marching past. We haven't left the dugout for days. From time to time soldiers burst into the granary to search for loot. If not for Morwa, we'd have died long ago from the stifling heat and the stench of the water seeping in without letup. We raise the cover a little, and shut it as soon as we hear Morwa barking and straining at her chain. Then the soldiers rush in, conduct a quick search, and run out to catch up with their retreating units. We raise the cover again and inhale some more air, until Morwa once again gives the signal. Szube and his wife visit several times a day. We hand them buckets of water to be emptied outside. It's a veritable flood, every day we have to bale out dozens of buckets. Otherwise, we'd be literally up to our necks in water. All day we choke in the sealed dugout. First thing in the evening we crawl out to refresh ourselves; even then we must be on the alert for even the slightest stir.

It's been quiet in our area since yesterday. The place is empty. The armies have stopped marching. The fleeing townspeople are nowhere to be seen either. A cemetery stillness pervades. The entire region is washed in a soft light. The only sounds we hear are the crickets chirping. It's too quiet. But we're afraid to budge; we can hear our hearts beat. We drag around on the tips of our toes and bale water out of the dugout. Looking through the cracks, we don't see a thing but a sunny stretch of field. At the far edge of the field a few sheaves of grain are still drying. A few suspicious shadows move among the sheaves. We can't make them out. People say that they're Ukrainians who don't want to go west with the Germans. Yesterday evening they crept into our yard for a drink of water. We crawled right into the dugout. Today we don't see them anymore.

The air is tense with anticipation. The peasants are also in hiding. Kowalczyk's yard looks dead. Morwa is stretched out in front of the granary door dozing in the sun. But she looks tense. From time to time she opens her eyes and pricks up her ears. She sniffs, yawns, and plays with her one puppy. This morning she sensed a suspicious visitor. It was at the crack of dawn, a tall fellow who looked like a soldier in civilian disguise. He approached from a side lane, looked around, and sneaked into our yard. Startled by Morwa's barking, he stumbled a bit. Szube tried to talk to him, but didn't understand the man's language. He withdrew in fright and fled. Not a living soul has come into view since.

It was Friday morning, a day very much like the one before. The fields were sunny and peaceful. Not a breeze ruffled the calm stillness. It seemed that the entire scene was waiting for an echo, some kind of repercussion. The farmers didn't dare to step outside. In our dugout, Froiman and I stood guard above ground; the others sat quietly in the pit. We were also waiting anxiously for something to happen. Nobody knew whether the front line was far off or nearby; but there was a feeling that it was coming closer and closer, stealing upon on us like a thief, soon it would explode. Meanwhile, the stillness gnawed at our hearts.

Through the crack I see Szube and his wife steal out of their cottage. They look around and crawl over to the trail. They sit at its edge and stare up the path, as though looking out for an expected guest. Morwa sprawls before the door shooing flies away with her tail. Some specks appear far up on the trail. They grow larger, until I make out several peasant women in brightly colored kerchiefs. When they reached the Szubes, they sat down beside them. They exchanged news. I listened carefully. The women wondered what the silence meant. The Germans have gone and the Russians aren't in sight yet: where is the front?

"Some say it's near Bialystok, and others say it's over by Brest (Brisk)—so why did the Germans run away?"

It was eleven o'clock. Szube stood up and said it will take a long time for the Russkies to get here. Meanwhile, there's work to be done. He still has to bring in the remaining sheaves of wheat from the field and store them in the granary. He went off to the field, and the women kept on with their worried chatter.

I was keeping my eyes and ears open. But I was quivering inside. My lips mumbled a prayer: "Oh, merciful God, merciful God!"

Suddenly, I heard a burst of gunfire. It came from machine guns or light artillery. I froze. The women outside jumped up. They strained their ears.

Another salvo of gunfire, so close by this time! I listen to the light shooting. It stops, and then starts again.

It seems to be coming from the Brest-Warsaw highway, from the direction of Kaluszyn.

"Are they shooting, Leybl?" Heads pop out of the dugout opening.

"Sh-h-h! Yes! Be still!"

"What is it?"

"I don't know. Sh-h!"

"It must be the Russians!" a peasant woman in the yard shouts.

"It may be the Russians," I whisper from the wall toward the dugout.

The peasant woman left. Mrs. Szube came in to ask if we heard the shooting. It's coming from the highway, from the direction of Kaluszyn. It must be the Russians.

The gunfire was drawing nearer. Szube came in with a broad smile on his face: "The Russians, definitely the Russians!"

They left. Froiman and I climbed down into the pit and shut it tight. The staccato sound of gunfire echoed through the pit. To us it was sweet music. But we couldn't utter a sound. We huddled in the dark and listened.

Ra-ta-ta-ta-ta! The gunfire almost knocked me over. I climbed up to the granary.

I hear singing in the distance. I peer out through a crack: off in the distance, on the Dobre road, I see a thick cloud of dust. I hear male voices; they're singing the Polish national anthem. Then along came a man on a white horse, galloping toward the trail by the granary, singing: "Our Poland's not lost yet!"

"Poles, Poles! Poland, our Poland, is free again!"

Szube and his wife came out to their front doorway. The rider turned into our yard. I went over to the other end of the wall to get a closer look at him; a young peasant, unkempt blond hair, pale face, and small green eyes, wearing a rumpled black suit. He looked around. Quickly I climbed back into the pit and sealed it tight.

The others are frightened. "The Polish partisans. He's probably a young partisan commander who's come out of the woods." We hear the horse gallop away. The rider's still singing: "Our Poland—"

"Polish brothers: Poland has come to life again!"

He is gone. The Szubes come into the granary. They tell us to open up, and whisper that a new army is in Kaluszyn. That fellow on horseback told them. Kaluszyn is free. But they don't remember whether he said "Russkies" or "Bolsheviks" or maybe "Soviets." You can't rely on him anyway. He's a well-known bandit from Zimna-Woda who was hiding out from the Germans for the last few months, and has now come out. He's happy that the Germans have left.

We stood there in shock. "The Russians are here!" I called to the others.

Szube and his wife left. *Ra-ta-ta-ta-ta!* came the sound of gunfire. We all climbed out of the dugout.

It was still quiet in the village. In the distance we saw a few people run by.

"The Russkies are here!" a peasant girl shouted to a farmer somewhere.

Another cloud of dust and a horse came galloping in. It was Maczek.

"Hurrah!" he cried, leaping off his horse and dashing right into the granary. "Yids, the Russkies are here! Your people! Bring out the bottle!"

Szube and his wife came in. We all shook hands. The peasants were happy. But our happy feelings were expressed as somewhat odd grimaces. I forced a smile. I felt joy, but also grief.

I took a banknote from my pocket and handed it to Szube for some liquor.

Maczek described how the Russians entered Kaluszyn. It was

quite unexpected; they arrived from the wrong side of town. They had cut through the Lublin highway, through back paths and woods, and arrived by the Brest road. The Germans in Brest and Siedlce are surrounded. The Russians are heavily armed. Now they're resting up and fortifying their positions, and soon they'll advance once more and capture the neighboring villages. They'll be here, too, and from here they'll advance to Dobre.

"Hurrah! Celebrate, Yids!"

"My dear ones, we're free!" I say hoarsely. I have an urge to demolish everything around me.

My people smile. Their eyes turn moist. They wipe them with their hands and smile at the Poles.

Szube hurried back with a bottle of home-made *Bimber* vodka. He asked us to wait for the Szwals: his brother-in-law and sister-in-law would be right over to drink a toast with us. Meanwhile, we discuss our plans, whether to wait for the Russians to get here or run over to meet them in Kaluszyn.

The Szwals arrived. They seemed bewildered. I went up to them and invited them in. I introduced myself and the others by name. They slapped our backs: "*Molodets*—clever Yids, got what you've been waiting for at last! Now you'll live!"

The liquor was poured. We exchanged good wishes and clinked glasses with the peasants: "*Na zdrowie!* To your health!"

I turned to my people. "*Lechayim.*" I kissed them all. We looked at each other. The women burst out crying.

* * *

We sat deep in the sealed pit, introspective and silent. In a corner, Zippora was sobbing. "Mama, Mama, my mama!"

Huge tears ran down Esther's face. She was weeping bitterly. But I blurted out: "Children, we mustn't! Let's go up!"

Zippora sobbed: "Where to? Where can we go? Who's waiting for us? Oh, Mama! Mama!"

Froiman and Itche advised us to go to Kaluszyn, We'll surely find Jews with the Red Army. Esther thought we should wait for the Russians to come here.

The Szubes came in. They think we ought to wait. The paths to Kaluszyn aren't safe yet. The peasants are looking for Germans, to take their revenge. In Wiszniewa, a few peasants caught some German soldiers and sliced them to bits with their scythes. Similar things are happening in other villages. They might kill us, too. Better wait for the Russians to get here.

We decided to wait until tomorrow. The situation should be more stable by then. Meanwhile, under no circumstances would we leave the granary. The neighbors mustn't see us yet.

We baled the water out of the pit, packed the floor with fresh straw, and then spread out alongside each other.

* * *

On Saturday it was quiet in the village again. There was hardly a soul outside. We didn't know whether to go or to stay. We heard no more shooting, and no more news from Kaluszyn. We kept deciding to go, and then putting it off. Finally we agreed to leave after dark, but we were afraid, and decided to wait until Sunday morning. It was a quiet night. We were free, but not really.

July 30:
Early Sunday morning the sun shone brightly into the granary. We climbed out of the dugout. Mrs. Szube brought us water for washing. We shaved, cleaned our clothing, and waited for the news. Maczek's wife Manke arrived to tell us that a Russian advance party had already been seen inside Kaluszyn. She advised us to flee to Kaluszyn. We had a bite to eat and got ready to set out. The Szwals came along and boasted about how well they had guarded our secret. They think we can head for Kaluszyn without fear.

We got dressed and noticed how ragged our clothes were. We looked like beggars. Again we brushed our clothes.

"Yes, we'll be going, right away!"

Meanwhile, the Szubes' nephew, Tadek, came running to their house, his cheeks flushed. He is in his early twenties. He wore a red flower on his lapel and a wide red ribbon tied around his neck like a bowtie. He was waving his hands in the air telling the good news. The peasants all went into the house. He spoke so loudly that we could hear him clearly in the granary. He had been to Kaluszyn to catch a glimpse of the Red Army. They gave him the red ribbon, put him on a tank, and brought him into our village. He had shown them the way. They looked over the village and rode back to Kaluszyn. The entire army will probably be here soon. They had given him bread, meat, preserves. Then he quickly ran off.

We couldn't forgive ourselves: we had missed such a good opportunity! We could have gone to Kaluszyn with them! Now it's

too late. It must be an hour, Szube tells us now, since they returned. He tells us to wait: the entire army will soon be here.

"No, we're not waiting! We'll go and meet them on the way!"

We are about to leave when someone rides up the path on a bicycle from the direction of Dobre. He rides quickly past us and
turns toward Kaluszyn. On his left arm he's wearing a white-
and-red band. He must be a Polish militiaman, a partisan. We're
afraid of those people. So we decide to wait until he's far away.
We're by the granary door, our bundles in our hands, ready to
go. Our feet can barely support us. Finally he's out of sight. We
are about to open the door when suddenly we hear the roars of
motors. The sound of speeding vehicles, cannons, tanks. The
roar of an approaching army! Then, suddenly, that militiaman
comes cycling back toward us on the trail. He nervously looks
over his shoulder, rips off the white-and-red armband, and
races toward Dobre. What's happened. From Zimna-Woda at
the Wengrow-Kaluszyn junction we clearly hear the tumult of
an approaching army. The road fairly bulges from the heavy
rumble of cannons and tanks. And what's that noise overhead?
Planes practically skim the surface of the road and the roofs of
the cottages.

Szube comes running: "The Russkies, it must be the Russkies!"

He calls us to go with him. We ask him to have a look first and
then tell us the news. Somehow we're afraid. He runs a bit with
Maniek, then rushes right back. A crowd of peasants are running wild, waving their hands and screaming. Pale as a ghost
and out of breath, Szube charges into the granary, yelling:

"Hide! Quick! Hide! Germans. Thousands of Germans. The army is here. They're looting everywhere. Quickly, into the pit! In
deeper! Fast!"

We are sealed up in the pitch-black hole. Szube, in one breath,
tosses bundle after bundle of hay on top of the pit.

* * *

The front line is right above us.

SS divisions are pouring in from the direction of Wengrow
and taking up positions everywhere in the villages, woods, and
fields. Kaluszyn and the entire Brest highway are occupied by
the Russians moving north from Lublin; and the area north of
the highway, the Wengrow district and all the side roads, are
held by the German army.

Our granary is right in the middle of the German positions. The trail behind the granary has become the Germans' "main highway"; it moves a constant stream of wagons, heavily loaded trucks, tanks, cannons, the whole range of war transport. From all directions neighbors come running to Szube. His farm is in a valley, so those who can't flee the battleground come here to find shelter. Perhaps so deep in the valley, the shells might miss the cottages. Peasant men, women, and children crowd into our farmyard. These include the nearby villagers. They ask Szube to clear the granary for them. Szube is confused; he looks for excuses. He says that the granary is packed with corn and they'll ruin it. He invites them into his house.

The cannons start roaring. The ground shakes and heaves. Our granary trembles and almost comes tumbling down. The German forces are spread throughout the fields, behind every tree, firing on Kaluszyn. And from that direction, fire and clouds of smoke are pouring down on our neighborhood.

Szube tiptoes over to us. He is shaking all over. He's afraid the German army will station itself here. In neighboring villages, they've already occupied cottages, barns, even stables. If they come here, we're lost. He wrings his hands and rushes out. Then he stops in the doorway and whispers: "We can't bring you any more food because of the neighbors in the house. Matlak, that Jew-hater from Poznan, is also here."

The gunfire continues; the earth shakes. We rock about in the pit.

I climb up into the granary for a quick look outside.

Clouds of smoke are pouring into the sky. Villages are burning. The roar is deafening. Szube's house is filled with neighbors. I can see them at the windows. Vehicles filled with fresh troops come riding up the trail. Morwa barks. I jump into the pit and seal it tight.

They're gone. Morwa is quiet. We can't breathe in the dugout. I go up again and peer outside. Froiman climbs out too and starts emptying the buckets of water that Ephraim hands up to him. Trucks, tanks, and cannons are moving back and forth on the trail. We get back into the dugout.

But it's impossible to remain inside. It's been raining since yesterday and the pit is flooded. We have to raise the cover to let some air in, and we have to keep baling out the water. We're sitting in a puddle. I climb up again and spill out the water that has just collected. Meanwhile, the pit gets an airing. On the trail, motorcycles pass by. Couriers deliver orders. I see Red Cross ambulances, cars carrying soldiers speeding in all directions. We can't afford to go up for air, but we're suffocating.

I climb up again and rush over to a crack. More vehicles. Morwa barks.

This time I don't return to the pit: I'll climb down only when they're right outside in our yard. The traffic doesn't stop. The trenches are in the nearby fields. The peasants stay in the house, too terrified to step into the yard.

Then the shooting stops, and it calms down a little. Szube comes in to tell us about Matlak of Poznan: He's a German agent; he even speaks German. He's turned over many Jews to the Germans after inflicting severe beatings. It would be all over for the Szubes too, if he found us.

Szube reports that all the surrounding villages are in flames from the bombardment. Except for Wiszniew, the Germans set a fire to it themselves, after the peasants had killed some German soldiers with their scythes. The Germans are everywhere, in all the houses and villages. Except Szube's and his neighbor Kowalczyk's.

If our granary should catch fire, we'll be burned alive.

He brings out two white kerchiefs, one each for Esther and Zippora. If the granary starts burning, they could run out and hide in the sheaves of grain. There are still a few left in the fields. If they cover their faces well, perhaps they won't be taken for Jews. "But you men are in trouble!"

The shooting resumes. This time it's the clatter of hundreds of machine guns and rifles. The bullets whistle in the wind.

Szube crosses himself and leaves. It's pouring outside. The machine guns continue to rattle away. A rain of water and of gunfire. Thousands of piercing red flames explode into sparks over the gray houses and fields. I stand by the crack in the wall and hold on tightly to the slats. The sparks swoop down on the granary as though bent on destroying it. With every flashing spark, I curl up and duck my head.

Finally, the shooting lets up. And it stops raining too. For a while, the sun even comes out of the clouds and shines down upon us.

The door of Szube's cottage opens and a tall, burly man of about fifty, with the face of an alcoholic steps out. He looks around with his bleary little eyes. He's followed by a stocky peasant woman, with chubby, flushed cheeks, and two little boys. Then some other peasants come out and stand in front of the door. They look up to the bullish man, who's stroking a thin moustache under his purple nose. The crowd hears German voices in the distance. They rush back into the cottage. That big fellow shoves them inside, orders them to guard his wife and children, and shuts the door. He smoothes his clothes and moustache, and boldly awaits the Germans coming up the road. An armed detail passes. He greets them in German and tells them "to beat the hell out of the Russkies." The soldiers don't answer. They march on. I guessed that this was Matlak. Even he seemed a little worried. He opened the door to the cottage and quickly slid in.

* * *

Evening. It was still quiet. A driving rain splattered the ground, which lay there torn and wounded. The rain seeped into the disheveled fields and cooled off the cannon barrels. Black clouds piled up above the surface of the fields. From the distance came German shouts and peasants wailing. Some soldiers were running our way, accompanied by village boys carrying large buckets. Morwa barked and strained at her chain. We sealed ourselves in. The outcries came closer. They were in our yard. A soldier screeched wildly. There were heavy footsteps, like those of cattle, and loud voices, a medley of German commands and peasant supplications. Loudest of all was the soldier's mad yelling.

Suddenly the granary door was flung open. A few German curses, and they left. The door remained open. The voices were in the yard now. The soldier seemed to be shouting: "Jude! Jude! —Jew! Jew!" In that deafening tumult the cows started to moo. Apparently, the soldiers were taking the cattle.

After about half an hour the commotion was over. We could hear the clatter of the cows' hooves, as if they were returning to Szube's barn. It was quiet in the yard. Soon it got dark. Mrs. Szube came in to see us, wringing her hands. We said nothing. An eerie chill blew in from outside. Szube crawled into the granary, and sent his wife out. He peered through a crack, and told us that they were SS troops. They had checked the papers of every peasant, suspecting them all of being Jews. They're looking for Jews. They wanted to come into the granary, but were afraid of a surprise attack. So they just peeked in. They had brought along buckets and were milking cows everywhere. The milk is for the soldiers in the trenches. "Now it's quiet. Maybe there's no front line action at night. And my neighbors have all gone home."

He wanted to bring us food, only there was no bread left in the house. They were afraid to cook. In any case we were all dried up, and couldn't swallow a thing. Szube sat in the dark with us for quite a while. He sighed: "Oh, why didn't you go to Kaluszyn, to the Reds, yesterday, the day before yesterday?"

We said nothing, but continued to silently berate ourselves for not having gone. We'd have been free already! Why didn't we go?

The farmer stood up, glanced around in the dark, and left.

We heard him unbolt the rear door of the granary. He was removing the bar on purpose, he whispered down to us. If the granary should catch fire, we could leave by the back door and head straight for the fields, the grain sheaves, and for the woods.

We sealed ourselves into the dugout. My head was in a thick fog. I wanted to run out into the rain, hide somewhere, then run some more. We were locked in a cage ringed about by SS divisions.

Why didn't we leave when we could? We were sweating heavily. We were trapped in a dense black swamp of despair and recrimination.

Suddenly, the ground shook, and shook again. The granary quaked. The cannons roared, shells and grenades exploded. We were afraid to remain in the pit. We could be buried alive. With lifeless hands I removed the cover, and dragged myself up. I sat down near the entrance to the dugout.

I lowered my head, and with half-open eyes gazed at the dark walls. Flashes of light pierced the cracks. Giant flames skimmed by outside, flaring up in mighty explosions. The ground shook and heaved. Each flame seemed to head for the granary; soon they would rip us to shreds. I hugged the ground:

Shma Yisroel, Shma Yisroel—

Fingers dug into my flesh. It's Esther. She clung to me. The quaking earth tossed us about. We stretched out on the ground.

It's all over with us.

Somebody called out from the dugout opening: "Let's run for the fields!"

"But it's dark outside!"

A spark flared up somewhere, illuminating the inside of the granary. Esther lay down and curled around me. Ephraim's head stuck out weirdly from the pit.

It was dark again. Occasionally rocket flashes would light up the darkness, peering at us with the eyes of the Angel of Death.

Something exploded nearby, and a fire broke out. All around us it was burning. We heard the screams of drunken soldiers. Quickly we shut ourselves up in the pit.

The dugout shakes. Our heads spin. We lift the cover a little. Voices in the wind. They seem to be approaching the granary. The wind is howling, and we can't make out anything.

It's quiet now. We listen—silence, as though everything has suddenly collapsed. The bombardment seems to have stopped. I open the cover and poke my head out: it's really quiet! Only the flames outside cast beams of light into the granary. The reek of scorched houses and trees assaults our nostrils. Not far from us, the loud screams of women are drowned out by boisterous male laughter, the frightening sounds of bonfire revelry. Women cry out for help, and thick male shouts overcome them. Gradually the flames subside, occasionally flickering to life, then dying out in the wind and the rain. Again it's pitch-dark and silent. I crawl back down into the dugout. We huddle together. We splash around in the puddle beneath our feet. We're afraid to do any baling now, at night, for the noise might carry outside the granary walls. We lean back on the damp straw walls. Some of us begin to snore.

* * *

In the morning, the war tore us out of our weary drowsiness. The sounds of gunfire drummed away in our ears, restoring us to consciousness. I climbed out of the dugout and went over to a crack: the sun cast down a pale, tired light. This morning's shooting sounds like mere chirping compared with yesterday's. Only rifles and machine guns seem to be opening fire now. Nobody was outside. The neighboring peasants were already in Szube's cottage. They crowded at the windows. The yard was empty. Morwa, too, lay back in her kennel licking her only puppy, as if trying to protect him from human malevolence. I told them to hand me some buckets of water to spill out. I poured the dozens of buckets into a side ditch draining rainwater from the yard. Nobody would suspect that some of the water came from the granary. Froiman brought the empty blanket into the pit again. He looked like a shadow. Then he came up to dry his drenched body, and collapsed next to a crack in the wall. He could not longer carry on. I went over to the pit and looked inside. A stench struck my nostrils. They lay there like swamp frogs, snorting. After Froiman dried up a little and returned to the dugout, Ephraim came up. Then, in turn, Zippora, Itche, and Esther. None of them had the strength to say a word. I ran from wall to wall, from crack to crack. No, we won't get out of here!

The shooting continued for several hours, until eleven o'clock. Szube's guests, including Matlak and his family, came out into the yard and sat down on logs by the granary. The sun warmed them. The peasants listened to Matlak.

The Russkies, he said, won't remain here for long. Poland will be strictly for Poles. Polish soil and the Polish citizen will come to life again. The peasants would also be able to stand up straight. Every peasant will have a few serfs, a couple of Germans or Ukrainians or Jews. It will be hell for those three scum peoples. They will be the slaves of our people. They rode the peasants long enough! Enough of their bloodsucking! It will be worst for the Kikes who stay. Those Jews will have to make up for all the years they exploited us. They won't stop working. When there's no work for them, they'll be chained to kennels in the farmyards. Like—he pointed to Morwa—Szube's dog there!

Morwa, who had been growling, started to glare and bark fiercely. Still chained, she leaped up, almost toppling her kennel. The puppy yelped along.

Our group stopped talking. I sensed that Froiman had been the main speaker. He measured me with a look that was at once despairing and triumphant. In the dark I could see the gleam in his eyes:

"Well, why did we torment ourselves so long?" This thought had been haunting him all along, but lately he'd been afraid to mention it in my presence: "Well, of what use was it all? We won't survive anyway!"

I wanted to answer him, to disagree with him. But the words froze on my tongue.

* * *

The battle has been raging for several days with no end in sight. Day and night, endlessly opening and closing up the pit; the perpetual screech of German tanks and vehicles along the trail; the roar of artillery and the clatter of light arms; soldiers raiding the villages, plundering, raping, wounding, killing. Several times a day soldiers come into our yard to milk the cows and hunt for Jews. They all steal into the granary and ransack it. We're afraid they might want to come out of the rain and rest in the dry hay and straw. We wouldn't last inside the stifling, stinking pit. Or else they would soon discover us.

Today Russian aircraft dropped small bombs on the German positions. The German artillery shot down several Russian planes. We jumped up in our pit from the shock. Through a crack I saw two Russian planes burst into flame and plunge down in a trail of smoke.

Our minds are empty. Only the continual volleys of gunfire keep us alert with fright. When there's a lull in the fighting, we turn into zombies again. We're just bundles of dormant fear. The Szubes are no longer bringing us food. We eat grains and drink the water seeping into the dugout. All of us are sick. Fever makes my heart and head pound. There's a heavy load of military traffic on the trail next to the granary. The unending commotion of motors and soldiers drives us out of our minds. They mock us with their Death's Heads, which also adorn the black suede caps, the helmets, and the arms of the officers and troops. These are the robots that will rule the world of tomorrow. I'm getting careless. I jump into the pit only when they approach the granary. And I have to think also of the Szubes' guests who like to snoop around from time to time.

I remember that we had already been free. "This can't be our fate, not after what we've been through." We sit in the waterlogged dugout, and can't forgive ourselves.

* * *

We are a few days into August. Friday. Nearly a week has passed since our moment of freedom, and then disaster descended directly upon us. The battle front is strangling us. The world outside is unrecognizable, torn by the roots. The army is rampaging. They change positions daily. The first-aid vehicles drag wagonloads of corpses, aside from the wounded. This is the first time we are seeing German corpses, and it seems that we don't have any feelings of vengeance. Armaments keep arriving. Titanic instruments of destruction. We never know from which side the bombardment is coming, from the Russians or the Germans. Is the Russian army advancing at all? A Russian advance party had already arrived in a neighboring village, Szube told us last night, but the Germans captured them and shot them behind a stable. After each heavy shelling we expect the Russians. Early in the morning I rush to see whether the Germans are still in sight, or if the roar of motors all through the night had been the Germans fleeing. I press my eyes to the cracks: swastikas and Death's Heads glinting in the daylight! At first we tried to guess the meaning of their deployments: if they moved in the direction of Kaluszyn, that meant they weren't retreating; but toward Dobre in the opposite direction filled us with hope. Now we're completely confused: they're moving in all directions!

Every time Mrs. Szube has a free moment she runs in to us, wringing her hands: "It's no use, we're all going to be killed!"

Yesterday and today she sneaked a few slices of bread to us under her apron. Even some tea. Once she even brought a little potato soup. But we're unable to eat. She pinches her own cheeks and rushes out.

It's unbearable: the Russian line is so close, the Red Army is only three and a half miles away, in Kaluszyn! How many Jews they must have in their ranks, even Polish Jews, the avengers come home after five years hoping to find people like us. What a small patch of ground lies between us! They could be searching high and low for just one surviving Jew, a living witness to the destruction of their families and towns and here we lie completely helpless.

It's Friday, the fateful day. Destiny seems to linger about this day when our mothers would light the candles and bless us, when the Sabbath Queen would visit us. Destiny seems to have marked this gentle day for us. On Friday the Germans rounded up the Jews of our town. At candle-lighting time, our mothers and sisters were driven to the railroad station and their lives, like flickering candles, snuffed out. The Kaluszyn community was destroyed on Friday, on the eve of Sukkos (Tabernacles). Felek was killed early on Friday morning. Every Friday, our hearts and souls flutter like candles in the wind.

Is this our last Friday? We count hours, minutes, seconds. We hold onto each other. Maybe this Sabbath will yet bring our liberation!

It's a sunny day. The puddles are evaporating. For a moment it feels like spring.

There's tumult in the battlefield. The robots are in full motion. Officers dash back and forth, shouting commands. Soldiers shift the telephone and telegraph lines. The gunfire is feeble, only a few bullets flying by. Nobody pays them any attention. Are these truly the final hours before our deliverance?

* * *

A first-aid vehicle drove up to the pond. The soldiers got out, undressed, and bathed. Then they washed the vehicle. Naked they washed the vehicle. Naked they dried themselves in the sun and roamed around the farmyard. They approached the granary. I leaped into the dugout, and Morwa barked her alarm. They entered the granary, but promptly left. There was hatred in Morwa's barking. They teased her. We could hear them yelling by her kennel and Morwa trying in vain to pounce on them. The puppy yelped. The soldiers laughed and threw something, and Morwa called with all her might for help. The soldiers departed. Their distant laughter mingled with the puppy's yelping. Morwa kept on rampaging and howling hoarsely. We understood that they had taken her last baby. She was pulling at her chain for a long time. We didn't know whether she was still mourning, or trying to warn us. Later I quietly lifted the pit cover and listened closely. I tiptoed over to a crack: silence everywhere. The soldiers and their vehicle were gone. Inside Szube's house, the peasants were still crowded by the window looking out fearfully. From the field came German voices. Motors roared. It was noon. The sun was at its zenith. High noon, Friday.

* * *

Suddenly there was a commotion in the distance. A tank camouflaged with green foliage rolled toward us, towing a heavy cannon with a long, thick barrel. In the foliage I could make out ten green helmets. A detail of soldiers marched behind the tank.

All at once the tank turned off the road and headed across the field to Kowalczyk's yard. It halted by Kowalczyk's stable. An officer issued a brief order and, like crows deserting a tree, the soldiers leaped off the foliage one after the other. Another command, and one group of men ran into Kowalczyk's house. Another order, the rest of the men dashed over to our yard.

My head spun. I fell into the dugout and sealed it tight. The day before yesterday Szube helped us set up a tall ladder across the cover of out pit, the side of a wagon used to cart hay from the field to the granary. The head of the ladder leaned on a wall, and the ladder sloped down to the base of the opposite wall. At either end of the ladder, by the walls, we piled logs and iron bars. It's almost impossible to budge it. About ten inches below the ladder is the cover of our pit. Someone coming into the granary couldn't sit down on that spot and feel that a hole was underneath.

We remained sealed in the pit, sensing the sudden danger that threatened us. The worst had come to pass: a German position in our yard.

From the yard came the sound of the Germans shouting, Morwa barking, and trampling on the ground. One of the granary doors opened softly and was promptly locked from within. Somebody crept around on top: it seemed to be Szube. He rustled our cover softly, and tapped: "Open up!"

I raised the cover ever so slightly.

Szube whispered: "Very bad! It's all over! They're taking up a position behind Kowalczyk's stable. Some of the soldiers will be billeted in Kowalczyk's place, and the others will be kept here. They've ordered me to get the house ready for the officers and the granary for the troops. Death! It's the end. We're running away. You're going to be killed!"

He wanted to leave. I could hardly hold him back and ask him a few questions. "They came and chased all the neighbors out of my house. Now they've returned to the cannon behind Kowalczyk's place, and they'll soon be right back here."

I asked him to peer through a crack to find out what they were doing. "They're busy with the cannon."

I went over to the crack. Szube hurried out, quietly shutting the door after him: "We're running away from here!"

I looked outside: the soldiers stood around examining their position.

I wrung my hands: "It's all over, God forbid!"

My eyes fogged up. I went over to the dugout. Inside, the women were quivering: "Leybl, let's pray to God! Pray! Let's pray!"

I went back to the crack in the wall. The tank started up. A few soldiers picked some apples from the trees.

"God in Heaven, save us!"

I felt like tearing myself to shreds. The soldiers kept maneuvering the cannon, moving it around from place to place.

In the pit they cried out: "Leybl, pray for mercy!"

Something inside me exploded. I burst into a fit of sobbing: "God in Heaven, God in Heaven! Help us!" I pounded my head with my fists.

Outside, the soldiers were screaming.

"Children," I whispered into the pit, "pray for mercy!" They were wailing.

I went back to the crack.

"In our despair we cry out to You! From the depths, from the lowest depths! Save us! We are among the last of the Jews!" I was tearing my hair. "If you intend to save us, save us now! This moment! We have no more strength left! *Gevald!*"

I jumped back into the pit, sealed it, and fell into the water. We were shaking with sobs, and tearing clumps of damp mud from the walls.

Outside, the tank roared again. It rolled heavily overhead and the ground nearly caved in upon us.

Suddenly the noise seemed to become fainter. We held our breaths. We could still hear the rumble, but it was farther away. A few minutes later, everything was quiet.

We lay in the pit, nearly unconscious. But our hearts continued to beat.

Esther started to kiss me. Above us it was quiet. We opened our eyes wide and stared into the dark.

Maybe—maybe they're leaving. I was afraid to climb out of the pit.

Once again there was noise in the yard, at the granary door. Somebody was opening it. Morwa wasn't barking: must be one of our people.

The door opened, less carefully than before. Szube tapped: "They're gone! They've left our yard and taken the cannon away. Kowalczyk says that our place is too low for a cannon emplacement."

I climbed out of the dugout. Szube was shuffling toward the foor: "It doesn't matter, we won't survive!" He went out into the yard mumbling to himself.

No one was in sight in the field. Only deep tire tracks from the tank and cannon marked a fresh path. It seemed to be a path to certain oblivion.

* * *

Once more it was raining—drizzling, pouring, letting up, then pouring again. A driving torrent flooded the earth. The waters collected into a deep pool at the bottom of our pit. It took all our strength to bale it out.

It was Sunday. The battle had intensified during the past two days. All day and night tanks, cannon, and other weapons shook up the ground and the air. Everywhere houses were up in smoke. In the skies planes dropped bombs and clouds dropped rain. Deafening thunder, an outpouring of wrath upon the earth. The granary was flooded. The water seemed to be sitting in a straw boat adrift on a raging sea. Or perhaps we were really in Noah's Ark? Was this our generation's deluge? The flood washed the walls of our hideaway. Every hour we baled out dozens of buckets and emptied them by the baseboards. The trail turned into marsh. The trucks carrying cannons sank in the mud; the tow trucks also sank. Soldiers stood outside our walls, cursing. The Russian artillery were bombarding their positions; rockets and flames fell from the skies. Our granary had turned into a living hell, fire above and floods below.

The earth groans and heaves. Soldiers running for cover take shelter in our yard. Just let them keep out of the granary. We're up to our chests in water, and if we don't keep on baling it out, we'll drown. We thought of digging a tunnel, to drain the water and serve as an air vent. But the earth is so soft, it would cave in from digging. And they might spot the opening of the tunnel from outside. So instead we'll rely on miracles!

* * *

The rain didn't let up. From time to time it stopped for a while, and the heavy clouds rolled in the sky like huge tanks refueling. But the artillery fire kept puncturing them.

Szube came in to let us know that the neighbors were back in his house. Near Dobre and Wengrow the Germans had caught some Jews hiding in a stable. They hung them in the woods.

They're still hanging out there. The peasants tore off their clothing and they're hanging naked. A man, a woman, and their daughter. "God is punishing His creatures!" Szube wrung his hands. "It's bad! We're all going to perish! The Germans are strong. They'll drive the Russkies back. You'll see that the Russkies can't stand up to them. My wife is tearing herself to bits. You're lost anyway. Why should we be killed on account of you?"

He left. I climbed up and looked outside.

He's right! God isn't punishing the world or his creatures, but us, the handful of survivors. Perhaps not one Jew is supposed to remain alive? Szube's right. What do we want from them? A world full of murderers is going to survive. Why do the Szubes have to suffer because of us? Perhaps it's because Szube is too decent, too innocent. Szube, that naive farmer, won't fit into the postwar world. He's Felek's sort. They have to perish. The world will belong to Matlak, Odrobinzak, and Kuczak! It may be our duty to perish along with whatever remains of innocence and conscience! But damn such a world! It's cursed forever.

* * *

Perhaps this really is God's punishment raining down on the world, a world up to its neck in blood. It's bound to destroy itself eventually. Is this the beginning of the end? What a privilege to live to see the beginning of the great Judgment Day? What else is there to live for? If only this were really the beginning of the great wrath, the revolt of the blood! Or is it merely, God forbid, a chance little storm preceding the great reign of tyranny.

* * *

I was up in the granary, rushing around from wall to wall, from crack to crack. The shooting and the rain stopped for a while. The soldiers were inside the trenches. No one was in sight. People were talking in Szube's cottage. The window was open, and I could hear them. One peasant said that we were surrounded. The Russians have been in Minsk for a long time, have reached the outskirts of Warsaw, and are closing in on the Germans from all sides. The Germans here are like trapped blind mice. That's why they're scurrying back and forth, trying to open up an escape route. This is why they're so furious, and they'll take it out on the local people here. They'll never surrender. These are the most resilient SS divisions.

It was about 4 p.m. They were sweating and panting in the pit, and I was becoming frightened. I went over to the dugout and told the others: "Take turns coming up to get some air."

I went back to the wall and looked out. When I turned around, Froiman was sitting on the edge of the pit. Only his eyes were alive. He gazed helplessly at the straw roof. I put a hand on his moist hair, and said: "Israel Aaron, we mustn't lose hope!" He stared at me and shook his head.

"We've done everything we could do," I said. There was a cynical smile in his eyes.

"Maybe we ought to try making it to Kaluszyn tonight," I added.

"In the dark we'll crawl right into their laps," he said.

All at once it began to rain heavily again. I peered through the crack and couldn't see anyone outside. Then I returned to Froiman and sat down beside him. "We mustn't despair," I said. "I know you as a person who has faith."

"God isn't paying attention!" he said. None of us said a word.

* * *

A stormy wind started to blow violently, tearing chunks off the cottages. Our granary rocked. Suddenly, the rear door blew open. The light dazzled our eyes.

In the doorway stood a young man staring straight at us.

Our hearts stopped. Froiman grabbed my hand. I averted my eyes.

The man retreated in fright and shut the door after him.

Froiman jumped into the dugout. I could see the fellow slinking along the granary wall. I was suffocating and my eyes were fogging up. My feet felt like lead.

Esther poked her head out of the pit. I signaled to her to get back in the pit. That fellow outside kept creeping alongside the wall, and didn't bother to look into the granary. He finally got to the front door. Morwa saw him and started barking. He quickly ran into Szube's cottage.

I climbed into the pit. "He probably realized that we're Jews," I said. "Now all of them must know, including Matlak."

Again, I came up and looked out: no one is in the yard. It seems to be quiet in Szube's house, too. The window is shut.

The others poke their heads out of the pit and look at me. I returned to the dugout. "I have an idea," I said. "Froiman and I will set out on the trail, then, the people in the house will see us and think that we had only sneaked in here to rest, and now we were leaving."

Esther and Zippora clutched me: "What are you talking about?"

"It's quiet now. We'll go out to the trail, sneak over to the woods, and hide in the underbrush. They'll think we're gone. After dark we'll sneak back in through the rear door."

The women tore their hair. Froiman thought there was nothing to do but follow my suggestion. Even if we failed the others would be saved. But they had to seal the pit tight.

"And we have to wait for Szube."

Esther and Zippora held on to me: "No, you're not going!"

"We must, we must!"

"No, don't go!" they sobbed.

The granary door opened. It was Szube. He wanted to know how it was all going to end. He didn't know what had just happened. We told him. He wrung his hands: "Oh, Lord! That's the end! *He* saw you? That was Czeszlak, the robber and informer!"

He was terrified. He went over to the cottage door, opened it, called his wife out, and told her. When Mrs. Szube came in, she was pounding her head with her fists, sobbing into her hands, and beating her chest. Our tongues were dead. "Say something, murderers, bandits!" she said. "Speak up! How did it happen?"

I told the Szubes that Froiman and I would walk out on the trail, and steal over to the woods where we'd stay until after dark. But they had to help us. They had to tell everyone in the cottage that there were two suspicious characters in the granary, who spoke to them in a foreign language; we wanted them to think that we were Germans or Russians. "You're to ask your guests what to do. Take them to the window. Meanwhile, we'll start walking up the trail. They'll think that we only stopped to rest and that now we're leaving. If we're caught, God forbid, you won't be involved. We'll say that we're living in the forest and came into the granary to escape the rain. That's the only way! If you don't say anything, they'll think you're protecting us."

The Szubes hurried out and I peered through a crack.

In a corner behind the cottage, that fellow who had seen us whispered something to Matlak's chubby wife. On seeing the Szubes, they stole quickly into the cottage. Froiman and I quickly put on our shirts and boots, and drew our caps down over our foreheads, letting some of our hair hang disheveled at the sides. I picked up the revolver and we headed for the back door. In the pit they were all weeping.

We kissed the others; then we looked around outside, noisily opened the back door, went out to the trail and started walking in the direction of Dobre. After a few steps we stopped and looked around again. We saw in a glance dozens of faces were crowded at the window of Szube's cottage watching us.

"Everything is fine!" I said to Froiman. "Let's keep going!"

We were too numb to feel any fear. After about thirty yards we reached the crossroads. There we stopped and looked around. There was no one in sight, except the people watching from Szube's window. I took a sheet of paper out of my pocket, which we spread out and examined as if it were a map. Then I folded it up and put it back in my pocket. We walked on, then turned into a side road.

Szube's cottage was out of sight. We were near the woods. We dropped to the ground and crawled among the trees. Then we started crawling back to Szube's, terrified of stumbling onto a German position. Like forest animals we scurried from tree to tree, until we reached a spot not far from Szube's yard. We crawled into a nearby copse, where we had a view of Szube's cottage and our granary.

"I wonder if the Germans saw us from their bunkers. But if they did, they'll look for us in the direction of Dorbe."

"A good thing they didn't fire at us. Maybe they didn't see us."

We lay in the wet grass. Behind us in the woods it was quiet. In the field in front of us we saw Kowalczyk's son watching. We hid in the grass.

Suddenly there were cries in the distance, coming from Little Garcyn. I could hear women's voices. It was quiet for a moment, and then we saw people running: a group of soldiers chasing peasant men and women across the fields in our direction.

We clung to the ground. They were in Szube's yard. "God in Heaven, protect our dear ones!"

A few German soldiers wielding revolvers charged into Szube's cottage. We heard shouts and screams. The soldiers herded the neighbors out of the cottage, beating them viciously.

We could see Matlak running through the field in mortal terror. All the others scattered like hunted animals. The soldiers flung the granary door open. We stopped breathing. The soldiers peeked into the granary, and then kept on running through the field, shooting. They caught a few peasants, checked their identification papers, and returned to Little Garcyn.

Soaked to the marrow we still dug into the earth. After a while, it became dark. We crawled back to Szube's granary and sneaked in by the back door. We tapped on the dugout. Itche opened, and we dropped into the hole. They were all sitting in water. They hugged and kissed us. Soon the Szubes were here, still out of their wits from the latest German visit. He had been hit on the head by a revolver and was still nursing his forehead. He said they had checked the papers of everyone in the house; they were looking for Jews. Also for women. In Little Garcyn they had dragged some girls off to the woods and raped them. In a nearby wood they had raped and murdered four women, a mother, her daughter, a daughter-in-law and her sister, and they strangled a baby of theirs. They just found one of them with a pig's foot in her vagina.

Well, Szube said, in all the excitement his neighbors forgot all about us. He had done exactly as we had told him and they had believed him. They had been frightened when they saw us marching along with a revolver and a map. Matlak said that we must be Russian parachutists, and Lord help the whole village if the Germans catch us. The Russians might think that the villagers had betrayed us and would take revenge. Or the Germans would kill all the villagers and set fire to the village for sheltering the enemy. The peasants couldn't say a word about it, Matlak had warned.

Outside, the artillery started firing. There were constant explosions. The Szubes hurried out. We got to work baling the water out of the dugout and pouring it out underneath the baseboards of the granary walls.

* * *

Tuesday was a very bad day. The German line seemed to be reinforced with fresh divisions. I climbed up on one of the walls, very close to the straw roof, where I had a commanding view: dozens of tanks, armored vehicles, and all sorts of armaments were moving to the front on all the roads. Fresh sounds of battle filled the air. The artillery fire lasted for hours on end. Then the machine guns attacked, pouring down a hail of bullets. The gunfire wouldn't let up. The battles were fiercer than ever. The troops charged wildly, wrecking everything in their path. They robbed and plundered, savagely beat whomever they encountered, shot down animals and fowl, searched every cottage. Entire battalions rampaged in the woods and fields. Nobody was left in Szube's cottage. The neighbors were afraid to show their faces. They were all tucked away in their hideouts. Szube was hiding in the attic with little Maniek. Only Mrs. Szube sat in a corner of her kitchen trembling with fear. From time to time she took a beating from soldiers who popped in and punished her for not being young. After every beating, she came in to see us; squirming with pain, she blamed us for all of her troubles. She wept, cursed us out, and left.

Then the shooting erupted again. Bullets flew at trees, walls, and roofs; pierced holes in stables, barns, granaries, cottages; even landed in the attics.

Mrs. Szube was afraid that her husband and Maniek would get killed up in the attic. When the shooting let up for a moment, she came to ask us if they could hide with us. But Szube refused to come down. He absolutely refused to sit in all that water and stench. He was also frightened of being caught together with us.

The day seemed to drag on forever. After dark, reconnaissance planes with blinking red stars circled overhead. The German anti-aircraft guns attacked the skies like crazed dogs on a moonlit night. A few planes were shot down.

Toward evening Germans were herding groups of peasants on the back roads. They were sending them to work far behind the lines. In the distance, peasant women were wailing. Mrs. Szube was wringing her hands when she came in to see us. They've taken nearly all the men from Little Garcyn and Zimna-Woda, including the village headmen. They dragged them out of their hiding places. Only her "old man" and several others are still here.

Mrs. Szube and Morwa watch in the yard while I came up to dump the buckets of water we baled out of the dugout. I emptied a few dozen buckets and stared into the dark. Strange sounds came from the villages and bluish sparks crackled in the rain. The clouds were a shade of red. In the nearby field soldiers were laying telephone lines. The Germans seemed to be settling in here. I emptied the last few buckets which the others passed up from the pit. I handed them fresh bundles of straw. They spread out the straw and I climbed back into the pit.

We decided that tonight Itche and I would sleep in a sitting position. We leaned back against the wall. Itche sat by the cover, which was raised slightly to let in air so that he would be able to shut it at a moment's notice. We immediately fell asleep. Itche woke me to say that the others were snoring loudly; shouldn't he wake them up? I was so exhausted I hardly knew what he was saying. "No," I said.

We were awakened by the explosions outside. The cannons roared. We couldn't open our eyes. Itche said that he had also been sleeping. Soon we were fast asleep again.

In the middle of the night, the noise of motors woke us up once again. Soldiers were screaming. We sealed the pit. The dugout walls almost caved in from the commotion outside. Tanks, armored wagons, trucks, cars, motorcycles rode by for hours. German voices shouted commands and curses. Our heads drooped. The water leaked and bubbled beneath us, flooding the pit. We sat in the warm fluid and fell asleep again.

When I woke up, I felt faint in the heart and heavy in the head. I didn't know where I was. We were up to our waists in water. I didn't know what time it was. The others were snoring. I groped in the dark for the pit cover and lifted it. A gray shaft of light entered. I raised the cover a bit more and listened, an eerie silence pervaded everything.

I woke the others. They sniffed some air through the opening. I wanted to stand up and poke my head out, but I couldn't. The soaked rags I was wearing stuck to my body. Froiman told me to wait a minute. He got up and started to climb out.

Just then, we heard a few German soldiers shouting in the yard. Morwa tore at her chain and barked. We promptly sealed the pit again. The soldiers charged into our granary and started throwing things around. They stepped on the roof of our pit, flung the straw about, and cursed wildly. They kept dumping bales of straw on top of us, helping to conceal us while they ransacked the place. Finally, we heard them close the door. Morwa barked again and they were cursing again. They took a few steps, and we could hear Mrs. Szube scream.

We were suffocating in the pit. We could hardly breathe. But we still heard their voices in the yard. The minutes dragged on —ten, fifteen, twenty, half an hour—and they were still shouting. We were breathing with difficulty.

A few minutes pass, and not a sound. Froiman wants to raise the cover a bit. He stands and pushes it up. The cover lifts. It's piled with straw. He's about to push the cover aside when the Germans start shouting again. They're still near the granary. He quickly covers the pit again. The Germans seem to be cursing and threatening among themselves.

Suddenly it's quiet again. It hasn't been so quiet since the front line moved to this region. It's Wednesday, August 9. This is the eleventh day of the battle, the first time it's been this quiet. Not a sound. No vehicles. No shooting. The front seems to have gone to sleep. If we hadn't just heard the soldiers rampaging in the yard, we would have been sure that the Germans had gone. I strain my ears; I hear voices again. The soldiers? SS? Yes, Germans!

We hear them move very close to the granary. As though they were climbing the walls. They seem to be crawling on the straw roof of the granary. Morwa pulls at her chain again and barks fiercely.

"*Donnerwetter!*" someone shouts. "Damn!"

Stones fall on the kennel. Morwa barks even more fiercely. The Germans seem to have come down from the roof and are cursing bitterly.

Suddenly —

Two shots ring out. Morwa's shriek pierces the air, and it's quiet again. We can feel that Morwa is dead. We all jumped at once: *Morwa!* Our last sentry is gone!

Outside it's quiet again. From time to time the Germans let out a curse, and then they're silent. But our hearts are broken, as though we had lost our last hope. Morwa is dead!

Again we heard them crawling on the granary roof. We were quivering all over.

We sat in that pitch-dark pool, and a thick nauseating vapor made our heads ache. We were about to faint. Yet we inhaled the hot, stinking air through our open mouths. Esther, Zippora and Ephraim moaned. We punched them to be silent. Now that Morwa was dead we had no way of knowing whether any strangers had entered the granary. There was no one to alert us. We couldn't hear Mrs. Szube either.

Suddenly, we heard shooting above the granary! We gripped the beams. We couldn't endure anymore! We're finished! I wanted to cry.

Itche and Froiman tried to punch a few holes in our roof with sticks, to let some air in. We put our noses to the vents. Bits of sand and mud fell in our eyes. The clods of earth started to descend from our walls and roof. An overhead beam fell. The dugout seemed to be caving in.

Heavy gunfire burst out all around us. We also heard the roar of motors. The shooting and the motors came closer. The ground shook. Machine guns opened fire. We heard dozens of vehicles ride up the path shooting—at the granary roof, it seemed. The danger was here!

Now they were in our yard. We could hear hundreds of voices. The motors died down. Soldiers were shouting. We froze!

Suddenly, the granary doors were smashed off their hinges and hurled aside. With the last of our strength we held on to each other.

Dozens of soldiers charged into the granary. They began ransacking and trampling everything. They tramped on our dugout roof. We panted, unable to hold our breaths any longer. We couldn't last! They were shouting overhead, but we couldn't make out any words. Esther caressed my hands and feet in the water. We could hear footsteps on top of us.

"My dear ones, let's say *Shma Yisroel!*"

"*Shma Yisroel . . . ,*" our lips murmured. "Hear, O Israel . . . "

I kissed Esther on the forehead. And Zippora and Ephraim. I exchanged kisses with Israel Aaron and Itche. It's all over! I said to myself.

"Germans," someone said. "I hear Germans."

I thought I also heard Russian. Perhaps they were the traitors of General Vlasov's army who had gone over to the Germans, or Russian prisoners who were being locked up here.

In the commotion I can hear Russian spoken, Russian names called. "Naumov!" someone shouts.

"Maybe it's the Russians!" I say. I listen carefully. "No, now I hear German. Oh, God, it's all over! They're sure to find us now!"

Suddenly, the people overhead went out to the yard. The granary was empty.

There's an uproar in the yard. Hundreds of voices. We couldn't endure it any longer. We were suffocating. Our heads were bursting. Our hearts would soon stop beating. I was going to open up.

"I want to go out," Esther burst out crying. "I want to go out! I can't stand it any more! I can't stand it!"

Outside, someone replaced the door on its hinges. Someone climbed barefoot over the bales of straw. As though in a dream I recognized that it was Mrs. Szube. She crawled around the roof of our pit spreading straw. Then she camouflaged the opening and left.

We wrung our hands. "There must be a German emplacement in the yard!" We died inside. "It's all over!" We were up to our necks in water. We'll either drown or be captured.

Ephraim said that his feet were dead. He could feel his blood, and his limbs and organs, congealing. Esther gasped for air: "I can't see! Help! Open up! I want to go out!"

I said: "We'll give ourselves up!" Just to have at least one more breath of fresh air!

I'm about to pass out. I'm drenched in sweat. I can't see in front of me. Froiman and Itche are gasping for air. Zippora's head leans against me. She's shaking.

I'll open up. I reach for the pit cover. But, no! I won't do it.

Again I heard someone walking barefoot in the granary. It was Mrs. Szube again. She removed a bale of straw and tapped on the cover. She asked us to open a bit. With trembling hands I lifted the cover. She whispered:

"Hide yourselves well! The yard is full of Russkies! Shut yourselves in tight!"

I trembled. "What Russians? Which Russians?" I could feel myself falling. A gust of wind hit my face.

"Children!" I shouted into the dugout, "the Russians!" I felt I was going to pass out. "What kind of uniforms do they have?" I ask.

"Russian uniforms," Mrs. Szube says, "with red stars on their caps."

I flung the cover aside and ran like the devil, naked except for my torn underwear. I went to the granary door and looked out:

What a dazzling sight, like a wild dream.

The yard was filled with Red Army soldiers! I flung open the door, marched into the yard with my arms outstretched like a sleepwalker, and shouted in Russian:

"*Tovarishchi!*—Comrades!"

* * *

Guns pointed at me from every direction. I raised my hands high, ran right into a gun barrel, and fell into the arms of a soldier, crying: "*Tovarishch!*—Comrade!" and burst into tears:

"*Tovarishchi*, we're Jews! We've been waiting for you underground for years! *Tovarishchi!*"

They surrounded me. I shouted and laughed and cried hysterically. I dragged them into the granary and led them to the dugout. "My people, come out! quickly! The Russians are here! The soldiers of the Red Army!" The troops and officers stood and gaped.

Pale shadows climbed out of the ground, soaked, ragged, filthy. They looked around fearfully.

"Children, we're free! The soldiers of the Red Army have liberated us!"

They forced some grim smiles, and fell into the arms of the soldiers; but they couldn't speak.

"Come," I said, "let's go out to the yard!"

They couldn't walk. The soldiers crowded around us. An officer ordered the men to support us and take us out to the yard.

The sun was shining outside. Near the granary door lay Morwa in her rich brown fur. She seemed to be asleep at her post; only a splotch of blood spreading from her open mouth to her head was already congealing.

I summed it all up very quickly in my mind:

I did what I had to do and now I'm free!

* * *

Yes, Morwa did her job, and we were free! We sat in the sun-drenched yard, with the Red Army men crowding around us. We still hadn't grasped what was happening. We were dreaming! Everything, the past few years, this minute, it was all unreal, a nightmare! The soldiers, filthy and worn from the battle, looked to us like gentle children from a tale of the Garden of Eden. We kept staring and opening our eyes wide to make sure that we were really free.

"You are free," an officer whispered to us. The others just stood there looking at us. The officer kept searching for the right words. "You're free! You're free!" he repeated.

Suddenly we caught sight of Szube. He approached us, and his weary face broke into a smile. We all ran over and kissed him. He embraced us with his brawny laborer's hands, and didn't know what to do next. His gray eyes were shining. He pressed us to him and stammered something. Some soldiers wiped their eyes. Someone slapped Szube on the back and called out: "Good fellow! Good fellow!"

We began to diffuse the dream and return to reality. The brilliant sun outdoors shone at us: such an expanse of light! So much air to breathe! Were they telling us the truth? We asked the officers if there were any Jews in their units: we wanted to see them. They told us that the Jewish soldiers were in the trenches, behind the trees with their machine guns.

Mrs. Szube came running out of the cottage, kissed us, and told us about this morning's miracles. The German soldiers were here a few hours. They were the last of the German troops. The remainder of the army had fled last night, all the troops, toward Dobre. They went wild in the dark. They dragged out Kowalczyk's moron daughter and raped her. By dawn they had all gone. Just a few scoundrels remained in our yard to fix up an observation post on the granary roof; they surveyed Russian movements through binoculars. They stayed for a few hours and telephoned reports back to the retreating army. They didn't want to be discovered, so they shot Morwa when she began to bark. Ten minutes before they left, at ten o'clock this morning, they fired at the first Russian soldiers.

"You've got to leave this place," the commander said. "It's very dangerous here. This is the front line. They'll be shooting again soon. Go now, you'll meet other Jews on the way!"

We kissed the Szubes once more. Suddenly we heard a bleating sound. The soldiers laughed. On the threshold of Szube's cottage stood two fleecy white lambs. Szube took them inside.

We set out for Kaluszyn. Everywhere peasants came out and gazed after us. We could hardly drag our sore, swollen feet. A tempest seemed to carry us along. We passed an endless stream of Russian soldiers, and happily saw many Jewish faces. We stared at each other. They were hurrying to the front. We couldn't stop them. We hurried along as if on strange feet. We raised our hands, and greeted the army.

"Zdrastvuitie!—Hello!" the soldiers shouted. Their voices carried far into the distance.

The Jewish soldiers glanced at us, waved, and even turned around to give us a smile of greeting. We couldn't believe what we were seeing.

Half an hour later a car drove up behind us carrying several soldiers and an officer. He was a colonel, the commander of this sector. The car stopped and he told us to get in; he took us near the outskirts of Kaluszyn. As we got out of the car, he said to us: "Remember, it was Soviet Marshal Rokossovsky's army that liberated you!"

* * *

Then we met the first Jewish soldier. Captain Doctor Nahum Golger, a man in his early thirties, brown-haired, in a striped uniform with golden braid. He was galloping along on horseback, and nearly fell off at the sight of us. He leaped off the horse and embraced us. We couldn't speak.

"Dear brothers and sisters," he said, "I've been looking for you all the way from Kharkov! I haven't seen a single Jew until now!" He wept with joy. He told us he was from Odessa. He had lost his entire family. He showed us photographs: his father, a Jew with a long, white beard. Nahum Golger wouldn't let go of us. We sat on the grass together for a few hours. His very presence warmed our hearts.

It was late, and he had to continue to the front line. Golger mounted his horse, and waited. "Good luck! Others are waiting for you!" I said. We shook hands and he rode off.

We walked aimlessly, not knowing where to go. The world was wide open to us, but it was barren and empty. Our eyes looked east, far across the sea. We walked in a vacuum, staring straight ahead.

After a while, we turned around. Not far from us, Golger sat on his horse, a sad expression on his face. We waved to him. He rode over to us, extended his hand, and said gravely: "You can proceed to Kaluszyn, then to Minsk, and from Minsk to Lublin. From there on the whole world is open to you!"

We walked on. We were exhausted. I felt sick. How we longed for a bed! Though the sun was high in the sky, it was afternoon, it felt like dawn. We had seen God's face and lived. We walked through the green fields toward the town. Behind us was the pitch-dark night. Ahead of us was the unknown. But it was the unknown of life rather than the expectancy of death.

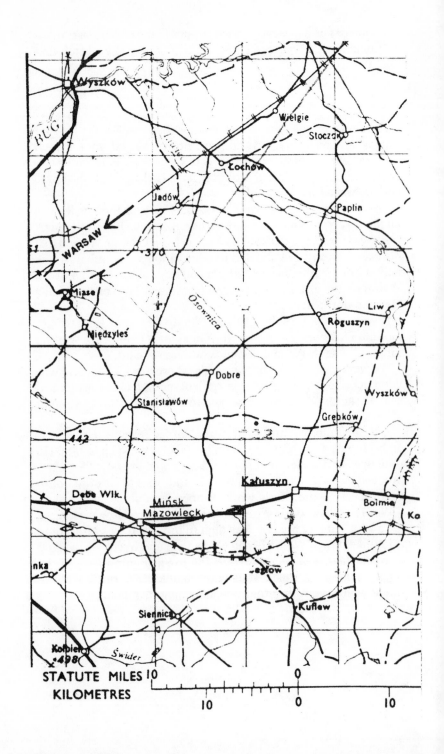

STATUTE MILES 10

KILOMETRES

10   0   0   10

CANCELLED